Black and White

Two Different Perspectives

An Honest Conversation

About Race In America Today

Bob Bohler and Jamie Scott

Black and White

Black and White

ISBN: 978-0-9915389-4-2

Cover Design: JoeSchlosser.net

2021 – First Edition

DEDICATION

To our family and friends, along with all those who have helped make us who we are, especially James' mother, Ellen Palmer, and grandmother, Rosa Bell Echols, and Bob's parents, Robert and Ann Bohler.

"All this is from God, who through Christ reconciled us to himself and gave us the ministry of reconciliation; that is, in Christ God was reconciling the world to himself, not counting their trespasses against them, and entrusting to us the message of reconciliation."

II Corinthians 5:18, 19

ABOUT THE AUTHORS

Bob Bohler is a Presbyterian pastor in the ECO denomination. He grew up in Decatur, Georgia and graduated from Georgia Tech with a degree in Industrial Engineering. After working for several years in engineering, he responded to a call to ministry. He has served churches in Lakeland, Florida; Charlotte, North Carolina; and Athens, Georgia. He and his wife, Kim, have two boys. One recently graduated from the University of Georgia in Mechanical Engineering and is working as an engineer. Their youngest son is a senior at the University of Georgia. Bob has a Doctor of Ministry degree and has served the church for over 35 years as a pastor. In his spare time, he plays tennis, reads theology, travels, and takes his wife to dinner.

Jamie Scott is the Director of the Sparrow's Nest ministry in Athens, Georgia. He grew up in Athens and has two brothers. At the age of 37, he was released from prison for the final time. A commitment to Christ changed the direction of his life, from crime and drug addiction to Christian ministry. Jamie is married and his wife Terri works as a nurse. They raise their granddaughter Chyna. The Sparrow's Nest is an Athens ministry that works with the poor and homeless in the city. It distributes food and clothing, serves regular meals, and teaches life skills to the homeless and newly released prisoners. Jamie recently received a special congressional commendation for outstanding and invaluable service to the Athens community.

CONTENTS

INTRODUCTION | 1

PART 1 – GROWING UP | 5

    Chapter 1 – First Memories | 5
    Chapter 2 – The Neighborhood | 11
    Chapter 3 – Values | 17
    Chapter 4 – Conversation About Growing Up | 23

PART 2 – FAMILY | 31

    Chapter 5 – Parents | 31
    Chapter 6 – Dysfunction | 39
    Chapter 7 – Conversation About Family | 47

PART 3 – EDUCATION | 59

    Chapter 8 – Expectations | 59
    Chapter 9 – Attitudes | 69
    Chapter 10 – Conversation About Education | 79

PART 4 – WORK, POVERTY, AND WELFARE | 97

    Chapter 11 – Perspectives On Work | 97
    Chapter 12 – Acquiring Assets | 105
    Chapter 13 – Conversation About Work, Poverty, & Welfare | 119

PART 4 – RACISM AND PREJUDICE | 131

    Chapter 14 – The Old South | 131
    Chapter 15 – The New South | 137

Chapter 16 – Conversation About Racism and Prejudice | 147

PART 6 – CRIME, POLICE, AND THE CRIMINAL JUSTICE
      SYSTEM | 161

    Chapter 17 – The Police | 161
    Chapter 18 – Crime | 169
    Chapter 19 – Conversation About Crime and the Criminal
        Justice System | 177
    Chapter 20 - Conversation About Policing | 185

PART 7 – AMERICA AND POLITICS | 207

    Chapter 21 – America | 207
    Chapter 22 – Democracy and Capitalism | 215
    Chapter 23 – Conversation About America and Politics | 223

PART 8 – GOD | 231

    Chapter 24 – Finding God | 231
    Chapter 25 – What is Christianity? | 241
    Chapter 26 – Conversation About God | 255

PART 9 – WAYS FORWARD | 267

    Chapter 27 – Family, Welfare, and Work | 267
    Chapter 28 – Education and Safe Communities | 283
    Chapter 29 –God and the Problem of Racism | 299

Black and White

INTRODUCTION

I
T WAS AN EARLY FALL DAY in 2020 as the two of us sat at lunch together drinking iced tea and waiting for our meals to arrive, enjoying being outside in the warmth that is typical of Georgia in September. From our two perspectives, one as a Presbyterian pastor and the other as director of one of the leading nonprofit agencies in our town of Athens, we had lots to talk about in terms of ministry connections and ways we might cooperate to make our town a better, safer, and healthier place to live. It was good to get better acquainted, since we had not spent much time with each other, serving only briefly together in leadership at a spiritual renewal retreat some years back. Some people just get along, however, and we had a delightful lunch, talking about life, Christian ministry, family, and our common interests.

2020 had certainly been an eventful year at that point, with the COVID-19 virus virtually shutting down the country, not to mention most of the rest of the world since March. At that point, it was not clear when things would open up again and no one knew it would be another year before that would begin to happen. But the COVID-19 virus was only one of the problems facing the country at that point. Summer and fall of 2020 were filled with riots, first over the death of George Floyd, who died while being arrested in Minneapolis, then in protest against other black deaths at the hands of the police. The cities of Atlanta, Rochester, Minneapolis, Portland, Chicago, Seattle, Kenosha, New York City, and others would experience riots and property destruction, some of the protests lasting more than 100 days. A new season of national racial distress, anger and complaint had erupted in America.

As people involved in Christian ministry, we had been in numerous conversations within our own organizations about the racial problems facing our nation, with viewpoints and opinions ranging across the spectrum. Despite our differences, one as pastor

1

of a mostly white congregation and the other as director of a ministry working with many racial minorities, we both felt our people's frustration at not being able to bring hope to such a challenging problem, especially with so many discordant voices vying for attention, often calling for solutions that differed radically from one another. We both felt frustrated that, in a nation undergirded with many Christian values, we could not treat each other with dignity and find reasonable solutions to our problems. In addition, with passions running so high, it seemed impossible even to have civil conversations with those of differing opinions without things devolving into rancor, anger, and misunderstanding. How can we solve our problems if we can't even talk together about them?

As we were finishing lunch, getting ready to head back to our various responsibilities, an idea began to form. What if we, one of us white and the other black, were to write a book together, telling stories about our life, from our different perspectives? What if we then used those stories to talk about whatever racial issues emerged and try to have honest conversation together? The more we talked about the idea, the more excited we became about the possibilities.

We recognized that we came from different backgrounds, though at the time we did not realize just how different. What was so intriguing about the idea of a book, however, was the opportunity to have *honest* conversation about racial issues. Our differences in experience and perspective might create the opportunity to explore issues of race in a way that would reach below the surface. If we could tell our individual stories, as a white and black person, then talk about them together, we might be able to enter into meaningful conversation without the rancor and emotion that are so often part of these discussions. Our hope was to bring light to the conversation about race, not just heat. We thought that it would be useful for white people to hear a story about the black experience. We also thought that blacks could benefit from understanding the experience and perspective of whites.

We left lunch that day with the germ of an idea that has turned into this book. We recognize that our stories and experiences will not resonate with everyone. One story is about a white person growing up in middle-class America with many advantages. The other is about a black person growing up in the inner-city housing authority projects, with generations of poverty in his family history. One of our stories led through college and into many years of work as a Presbyterian pastor, laboring quietly in local congregations throughout the Southeast. The other story led to incarceration, persistent trouble with the law, and a life that was going nowhere until a Christian conversion turned everything around. What we have discovered, however, is that telling our stories has opened up numerous lines of conversation about race, as you will discover.

This book is designed to be enjoyed by individual readers but also useful in group settings. One of our hopes is to help people engage in honest, respectful conversations that will allow us to come to appreciate one another, encourage one another, and even, as the Bible encourages, love one another. People will probably not agree with everything we say or all the conclusions we reach. We hope, however, to promote meaningful conversation. To that purpose, at the end of each section there is a set of discussion questions to provoke further thought and facilitate group discussion.

One of the challenges in writing a book like this is the realization that we cannot present a comprehensive study of any of the topics we will discuss. Each topic could be the subject of its own book. With that limitation, we simply hope to talk about issues of race together from our own limited experiences and perspectives, realizing that there will always be more that could be said. It seems to us that, in America today, we ought to be able to treat each other with respect, promote each other's welfare, and resolve racial differences. It is to these ends and with this hope that we have written this book.

We have changed some of the names of people involved in our stories. In instances where someone might have been engaged in criminal behavior, we have changed the names of those people. Other than that, however, we have used many names of the real people involved in our lives. We hope they will understand that we appreciate the various roles they have played in making us who we are.

With that brief introduction, we begin by sharing our stories. The format we will use is to take our lives and experiences, one piece at a time. We will talk about our experiences and then pause to reflect on them. It is these conversations together that we hope will offer opportunities to reflect on our racial tensions today as well as other important aspects of life. Thank you for joining us in this adventure. Neither of us knows where it will lead, but it seems an important journey to take. If it adds something useful to our current racial conversation, our endeavor will be the worth the effort.

Bob is currently serving as the pastor of an ECO Presbyterian church in Athens, Georgia, Alps Road Presbyterian Church. Jamie is the director of the Sparrow's Nest, a nonprofit organization that ministers to the poor in downtown Athens. We begin with a discussion of our lives growing up.

Bob Bohler and Jamie Scott

PART 1 – GROWING UP

1

FIRST MEMORIES

Bob

MY FIRST MEMORY COMES FROM age 2 1/2. I was standing in a hallway in my home, looking cautiously around the corner into the living room, a timid child, watching my mother come home from the hospital, with a number of people standing around observing. An ambulance had pulled up in front of our house, quite a happening for a boy my age, certainly out of the realm of my limited experience, and even more alarming since it was my mother who had arrived in the ambulance. I remember the stretcher on which the medical personnel brought her into the house being rolled into the living room, as official-looking people in uniforms tended to her carefully. My father was in the room watching, as well as a number of other people whom I can't recall in my memory, all this momentous for a timid boy of 2 1/2.

As it happened, this was not a major medical crisis; my mother had given birth to my sister. I know I was 2 1/2 because that's how much older I am than she is. My mother and her new baby, my sister, were coming home from the hospital, with the kind of ceremony that accompanied most births in the early 1950s. The strangeness of this event must have made an impression on me, young and tender as I was at that point, since it is my earliest memory.

I date myself with that story. Today, with our medical knowledge, none of this happens when a woman gives birth, but I grew up in the era, the 1950s, when medical knowledge was still very much evolving. New mothers generally stayed in the hospital, and in bed, for a week after giving birth, giving their body time to heal after the trauma of childbirth. Times have certainly changed, as today new mothers are encouraged to get up and walk the very day of giving birth, and are on the way home soon after.

Jamie
My first memory comes from about age 3. I remember opening the refrigerator at my house and looking in for the first time. Up until that point, I had not noticed the refrigerator or wondered what it was. For whatever reason, I noticed it and opened the door. That moment made a mental impression that I have not forgotten. I remember thinking, "Wow! So this is where Mom keeps all the goodies!"

I lived in a small two-bedroom apartment in the projects for most of my life growing up. These were the projects in Athens, Georgia, in the early 1970s. In our apartment, you entered the kitchen through the living room. To the right was an open pantry. I remember that, at one time, my mom dated a guy from Africa, who made beef jerky. He hung it on clothes hangers against the heater furnace that was inside the pantry, so it could dry out. I remember those strips of beef jerky hanging there. Farther down on the left was our refrigerator. My first memory is opening the refrigerator and finding a new and exciting world.

At that time, we ate a lot of USDA [United States Department of Agriculture] food, which my mother got through the government assistance program. It all came in its own identifiable packaging. I remember that we had welfare honey that came in a little quart-sized jug. We had block USDA cheese, and we had big boxes of USDA cereal. We had USDA powdered milk. Sometimes food was scarce, but as long as we had bread and some cereal, we could get by. I remember having cereal without milk at times, only water.

Bob

My parents owned their own home. It was certainly not a large or impressive one. When I think about the house in which I grew up, I remember the closets and marvel at how small they were. Each bedroom, including the one in which my parents slept, had the tiniest of closets, enough for only a small wardrobe of clothes and a few pairs of shoes. I don't remember this ever being a topic of conversation, and my parents always seemed appropriately dressed. So were my sister and I as children, though I do recall that my mother made some of my sister's clothes, which was a source of some anxiety on my sister's part, as it seemed to her that she was the only one in her class wearing clothes that did not come from the department store.

All houses, at least in our neighborhood, were small like ours. The truth is that most people in that era didn't have many clothes, so small closets were not a problem. Today all the closet space in that entire diminutive house would not be sufficient for my wife's clothes, or, to be truthful, mine either. It was a simpler era and one in which most people, at least the ones my family was acquainted with, were of moderate means.

My father had served in the Second World War, being fortunate, in his own words, not to be too close to the "action," then gone to college on the G.I. Bill. The G.I. Bill was a government program that provided benefits to returning soldiers, and more than 7 million veterans attended college or vocational school because of it. My father was one of them.

After graduation, he got a job with Georgia Power, in Atlanta as an electrical engineer, which was his dream job. He had wanted to be an engineer since he was a young teen, having watched his uncle install an electric light in a shed behind the house and thinking it was a very cool thing to be able to do. His engineering department at Georgia Power was filled with people his age, also coming back from the war, having just graduated from college and starting their careers and families. To them it seemed a great time to be alive, and America was the best place in the world to live.

Jamie

Grandmothers are very important in the black community, and that was true for me. Without any disrespect to my mother, I think I loved my grandmother as much as anyone. I feel like she raised me as much as my mother did. My mother would sometimes go to Africa with the guy she was dating. She was very attractive and always had men who wanted to date her. She'd go to Africa for three to six months at a time, and I'd stay with my grandmother. That was OK with me because it was "fun and games" time. I loved my grandmother, in part, because she spoiled me. Whenever I asked for something, she would go out of her way to get it for me. She also wouldn't let my mom whip me when I had messed up on something, if she was around. Of course, when I had done something wrong, she made sure to express her opinion.

I remember that she could make a terrific peanut butter and jelly sandwich. She would pile on the peanut butter and jelly so high that it looked like a Big Mac. It was completely delicious and made an impression on me as a young man who liked to eat.

At one point growing up, I remember praying, "Oh God, don't let my grandmother die before I do. I don't think I could take it." Even when my mom and I were living out of state and I didn't see my grandmother every day, I didn't know how I could deal with losing her. And when I was doing things of which I knew she wouldn't approve, I still worried about my grandmother and how I would deal with life if she weren't there.

My grandmother ended up having a heart attack. One day, in my early 20s, I came into her house and could see that her health was not good. Breakfast was my favorite meal and I often ate it at my grandma's house. On that day, Grandma got up to fix me a breakfast. I had been out using drugs for several days so I wasn't in the best mental condition, but I still remember the awful feeling I

8

had when I realized she was not well. When she came back to sit down, after fixing me a bowl of cereal, there was a crackling in her breathing. A couple of days afterwards she had to go to the hospital.

We went to visit her in the hospital, and I knew she was very sick. She did not recover, and that illness led to her death. I had begun doing some bad things at that point, and my mother put me on the spot in front of my grandmother. She wanted to put as much pressure on me as possible to change my ways. My mom said to Grandma, "Now, you tell Jamie to stop doing that crack cocaine." She knew I listened to my grandmother more than her; she had been fussing at me for my lifestyle for some time, to no avail. My grandmother told me, "Son, don't be doing that," and gave me a lecture that I had heard many times at that point in my life. She said, "Try to live your life the way you know you should and that will make me proud."

I wasn't making her proud at that point, and I was under great conviction about all the bad things I was doing. To make things worse, it happened that, while I was sitting there, a stem through which I smoked crack cocaine dropped out of my pocket onto the floor. My grandmother didn't see it, but my mom saw it and just dropped her head. I knew how deeply disappointed in me were both my mother and grandmother. It broke my heart and was totally embarrassing, but didn't make me stop because, at that point, I was addicted.

2

THE NEIGHBORHOOD

Bob

THE NEIGHBORHOOD IN WHICH I GREW UP was full of children my age and young parents. My mother was 25 when I was born and my father seven years older. My mother has said to me, "We were just kids and we all grew up together." That may have been the case, but from my point of view, my parents knew exactly what they were doing, and I knew who was in charge.

In my early years, I had a friend who lived next door with whom I played regularly. His name was Buster. We had a somewhat testy relationship, as he was more outgoing and aggressive than I was. At one point, probably about kindergarten age he started hitting me while we played together. I obviously didn't like it and came in crying on some days but didn't know what to do. At one point, Buster threw a piece of wood across the fence at me. I must have been a bit slow in both my movement and my mental recognition skills because I didn't get out of the way. The piece of wood hit me in the face. That was bad enough but it also had a nail in it. The nail hit right beside my eye, and I still have a small scar from it today. Had it been a half-inch to the left, I probably would be blind in that eye today. I was very fortunate.

My mother saw what was happening in the backyard when Buster started to hit me. She had grown up with eight brothers, all rowdy and full of mischief, at least as she told us about her childhood years, so she was used to seeing fights and knew what boys were like. She also had a maternal instinct that told her that I needed to take up for myself, rather than have her march into the situation to save the day. Today, I suspect many mothers would be tempted to intervene and make sure the problem was resolved by them. My mother was quite wise, however, as I would observe over many years as I grew up. She determined that it would be to my advantage to deal with things myself rather than be saved by her.

I remember that for several days she coached me on what to do. I needed to ball up my fist and punch Buster back, right in the nose, since that, she assured me, was a very vulnerable target and something he would not appreciate me doing. For the next few days, I tried to get up the courage to do so, only to get punched myself. Finally, I stoked up my courage, balled up my fist, and, in a moment of herculean courage for a 5-year-old, punched Buster square in the nose. To my utter surprise, my tormentor crumbled into a mere mortal and went home crying. He never hit me again, and it was a small victory for a shy kid but a victory that gave me a small degree of confidence that I didn't have before. This instance is illustrative of a childhood in which my parents were present to help me navigate the waters of growing up with advice when I needed it. They were not absentee parents but right beside my sister and me in what we did, not fighting our fights for us but coaching us in them, not doing for us things we could do for ourselves but encouraging us with the practical, commonsense wisdom of that era, not making things easy for us but helping us deal with life as it came along.

Jamie

My neighborhood was "the hood." I grew up in the housing authority projects known as Pauldoe. It went from the Jack R. Wells projects to Pauldoe. It was a very big complex, one of the biggest in Athens. It was even bigger than Nellie B. Some people would say Nellie B was biggest and some would say Pauldoe. In the complex, there were rows of apartments, four in a row, A through D. We stayed in a small two-bedroom apartment, my mother, brother, who was four years older than me and me. There was a pretty decent-sized living room; of course I was small in size in those years so maybe it just seemed big. Our closets were extremely small. We had a fair-sized kitchen and a very small bathroom. The bathroom was

12

no more than an 8-by-8 room, very compact for three people. My brother and I shared a room.

In our neighborhood, no one knew anybody's real name. In an inner-city neighborhood, you don't know people's real names. You get a name by something you've done or what you look like. For example, I grew up with someone we called "Boo Shay." He had a sister named Shay Boo, and his mom's name was Venus. The only way I knew Boo Shay's real name was when we tried out for the football team together in high school, and they called his real name. There are so many guys I grew up with whose real names I don't know today. We had Shack, Tonk, Deat, Deck, Big Man, and Di Woo. Di Woo got his name because he was very black and had high cheekbones like someone from Africa. I'm not sure what the name Di Woo had to do with Africa, but that was the name he got in the projects.

My first best friend in the projects was named Garfield. I think that might have actually been his real name. Or maybe it was from the cat in the comics. He was a light-complexion person who stayed across the street from us. He and Preston were my first two best friends. We had a lot of wooded area around the housing authority complex, and it stretched all the way to a more upscale suburban neighborhood, named Forest Heights. They had actual houses in their neighborhood. Some of the white kids had built motorcycle trails in the woods near the neighborhood, and we would go in the woods sometimes to watch them ride dirt bikes. We were bummed that they had dirt bikes and we didn't, but we knew that kind of thing was not in the equation for us. At one point, as we were watching, the kids stopped and we chatted. They even invited some of us to get on and try to ride the bikes. That was pretty fun.

One of the things we did was have stick wars. Because our complex was big, there was an uphill section and a downhill section. There was also an around-the-curve section. The downhill section would challenge the uphill section to competitions. It wasn't a gang but just groups of kids being kids. One of the games we played was

13

stick wars. When I was 7 and 8 years old, my job would be to collect the sticks, with my cousin, for the guys who were older than we were. Sometimes I would even throw the sticks myself.

No one was spared in stick wars, and you grew up fast in the projects. Everyone got busted in the chest, smacked in the head, and hit in the face with things, both in the neighborhood and even in your own household. In stick wars, we would play until everyone got tired, or someone got hit in the eye, or someone got to bleeding badly. Then we'd finally disperse. You didn't win until you drew blood. I was in the downhill group, and we pretty much won every time. We had some guys who were a little bit rougher and a little meaner than the guys up the hill. We also outnumbered them.

Bob

One of the things we did in the neighborhood was ride bicycles. I remember how hard it was to learn to ride my bicycle, but once I had mastered the skill, I raced down the street with a group of boys in the neighborhood for many adventures. These were minor adventures, of course, not being allowed to venture too far from home. My limit was about five houses up my street, downhill to the bottom of the street across from us, and about halfway down the street on the other end. There was no hesitation about my being loose in the neighborhood, and my mother didn't feel the need to watch over me. When dinner was ready, my father would call from the front porch, and I would hear and come in for dinner.

I do remember one evening when things went badly. When my father came home from work, I was down the street on my bicycle and decided to race the car to our house. I pumped my bicycle hard and tried to keep up the best I could as the car in which my father was riding came down the street. When my father got out of the car that he had carpooled in to work, he took me inside and spanked me. I never did quite know why and still don't to this day. He must have thought what I did dangerous. I was just being a kid.

14

When we went somewhere, my mother would say, "We are going to the store, and here's what I expect of you." Then she would explain how we were to act. We knew if we did not behave, there would be consequences to pay. While some parents take the approach that if you teach your child to love you, they will come to respect you, my parents took what was the more traditional approach in that day. They made sure we respected them and assumed we would eventually come to love them. They were right about that, as my sister and I grew to both love and respect them deeply.

I got spanked growing up. My father would take off his belt and say, "This hurts me more than it does you." I hated that comment and couldn't imagine how it could possibly be true. He then administered what felt, on my bottom, like a very efficient and effective spanking that left me in tears. I had to go to my room and think things over. Then my father would come in and make sure I knew what I had done wrong and why I had been punished. After he left, I could come out when I was ready. The good thing was, when I came out, it was all over.

I have heard my parents use the phrase, "Spare the rod and spoil the child." They took that to heart as it was how they were raised. My parents, however, never disciplined my sister or me in anger; it was always done for a greater purpose, which was to teach us to behave and do the right things. It was also how most parents disciplined their children in that simple time before there were so many parenting experts on television, radio, and the internet.

Jamie
I got my first tattoo at age 5. My brother Dexter was 4 years older than me, and he was getting one. He was 9. It was obviously a homemade tattoo. There was an older boy in the neighborhood who was giving them to any kid who wanted one. The way it was done was that he took Indian ink and scratched it into your arm with a needle. I was watching my brother get one, and I said, "I want one

too." The guy giving my brother his said to him, "I'm not going to do it unless you give the OK." My brother told him it was okay with him, so after his was finished, I got a "J" for Jamie tattooed on my right bicep. I was small then, so it was very small. I had to get it redone several times as I grew because it faded. Now it's a large "J" on my bicep.

My mom was furious with my brother and me, but there was nothing she could do at that point; the damage was done. It's just another illustration of how fast I grew up in the 'hood.

3

VALUES

Bob

I GOT A LESSON IN HONESTY ONE DAY, when I was 11. I came home late one afternoon with a box of nails from the woods behind our house. We had moved to a new subdivision at that point, into a larger house, and there was a stretch of woods that ran along behind our street. The boys in the neighborhood would play in the woods and explore, although we would not get too far from our homes. One day, however, we wandered into a section of the woods that was unfamiliar. We came across a fort that someone, probably the older kids up the street, had been building. Nearby was a box of nails. My father was always building something and, for some reason, I thought he might like having a box of nails. When I came out of the woods, he was in the backyard. Holding out the box of nails, I announced, "Look what I found."

If I had expected appreciation, it was not the reaction I received. He immediately began to ask me where I got them and to whom they belonged. When I had no answer, he began to explain to me that those were not my nails. They obviously belonged to someone else, and I had no right to take them. What was I thinking in doing so? My father was honest, to a fault. I remember that one day at a McDonald's drive-through, the cashier gave him too much change. He looked at it and noticed the overage. He told her what she had done and gave the excess back. As a young boy, my father's honesty made an impression on me.

The result of the conversation about the box of nails that early evening was that I needed to take them back and put them where I found them. Because it was dusk and the light was fading, my father said, "I don't care if you do it tomorrow." But what I had done was weighing heavy on my conscience at that point, and I didn't want to

17

have to worry about it all night, so I headed into the woods with the light growing dim and a box of nails under my arm. The only problem was that, when I got into the woods, I couldn't find the spot I had taken them from, and the woods were getting darker and scarier by the moment. I kept looking for the spot, thinking it was just behind the next set of pine trees, but discovering that it was not. Finally, I got as close the spot as I could and just dropped the nails, racing back to my house, hoping not to trip in the darkness and trying not to see scary things leaping unexpectedly out at me. I was glad to have discharged my duty that evening, even though I had not done it exactly the way I was supposed to. It was a lesson in being honest that I would not forget.

As I think about my life growing up, it was one of the best possible situations in which a young boy could grow up. My parents loved me and loved one another. I had a sense of security but also boundaries. I knew what I was not supposed to do, and that helped me build my own inner compass. I was taught lessons about honesty that helped form my character.

If this sounds like the formula for a wonderful childhood, it was. It was stable, safe, and secure. My neighborhood was full of children my age. In every other house was someone with whom my sister and I could play. Though we were very middle class, I did not want for much. We had warm family times, and I felt loved and affirmed. My family was the gyroscope for the trajectory of my little world, keeping everything stable in whatever turbulent conditions I might encounter. I did not have to think about drama or turmoil at home. I could worry about being a child, and that is what I did.

Jamie

There were values, some good and some bad, that I learned as a child. Some of those values were: You don't talk back to grown people, you don't get into grown people's business, you respect your elders, and you don't pick on the handicapped. I was taught those from an early age, both from my mom and grandmother, and within the community. These were values that were highly held among the people with whom I grew up.

When an adult came into our home and I was in the living room, I had to get up and go to my room. I knew better than to stay in the room or to sit with an adult and try to have conversation with them. You would get backhanded quickly for that and sent to your room for a long time. You would also get the tongue-lashing of your mom telling you, "I'll deal with you later," which she would.

Those were values I learned from my mom. I also learned some values from my friends, but they weren't particularly good ones. A friend of mine had stolen some Copenhagen chewing tobacco. I saw him with it in his lip and thought it looked pretty cool. I said, "Where'd you get that from?" He said, "I got it from the store." I knew he had stolen it because he wasn't old enough to buy it. He said, "Try some." I did and got sick as a dog! It was not a happy childhood moment.

I remember a great birthday party my family and friends threw me one time. My mom gave some money to my cousin, whose name was Pearl. Mom told her to go to the store and buy some things for a birthday party for me. I don't know whether she used the money or not because most of what came back from the Woolworth's store was stolen. My mother probably knew that is what would happen. But we had a great birthday party.

Crime was something that was a part of my community and not considered particularly immoral, so honesty was not a value I was taught. In fact, my cousin Pearl helped me commit my first crime. One day she asked me if I wanted some bubble gum. Of course I did, and she proceeded to tell me how we were going to get it. When we went into the store, I was to act like I had a stomachache. A friend would then distract the employee while they loaded my pockets with gum and other things. I would then go to the restroom where they would unload the merchandise, throwing it out the restroom window. My first attempt was successful, and we repeated the process again for what turned out to be a decent haul of stolen items. I had committed my first crime. It would not be my last.

Bob

One of the things I experienced growing up is grace. My mother had a sweet tooth, and every once in a while she would encourage my father to take us to Art's Mart, the local convenience store, for some candy. We would get a little bag from Art, and our father would let my sister and me pick out any candy bars we wanted. We kept picking out candy bars until we had filled up the entire bag. This probably did not cost very much money but seemed a great extravagance to us.

When we got home, we would eat candy to our heart's content. Anything left over, we'd finish the next day. I remember doing this five or six times growing up. I didn't spend much time reflecting on this as a child but have since. These moments picking out candy at Art's Mart were moments of sheer grace. Caution was thrown to the wind; money was no object. My parents weren't disciplinarians in that moment. We were just a family having a good time together.

What these moments did for me was give me a sense of grace. Life wasn't always difficult. Someone wasn't always watching me to make sure I stayed between the lines. There were moments of joy, laughter, and fun that were just as important in life as doing our duty, being responsible, and doing the right thing. These moments served to give balance to what was a strict home in other regards. They were rays of sunshine breaking through on a cloudy day, bringing warmth, light, and hope. It was another way my parents let my sister and me know that we were loved and that life, on the whole, was very good.

I recognize how fortunate I was in my upbringing, though how I was raised was not very different from most of my friends, in that era.

Jamie

Violence was part of the community in which I lived, and I witnessed many instances of it myself. There was a man who stayed two apartments down from us, to the left of my grandmother, in another row of apartments. He lived with his mother. His name was Ray Ray, Ray Ray Chester. One day he got into a gun battle with a man named Dabo. When I was about 4 or 5 years old, I heard gunshots one day. I ran out on the porch to see what was going on. There were two cars parked facing each other, by my grandmother's row. Ray Ray Chester was in one car with the driver's side car door open. Dabo, who was a cousin on my dad's side, was in the other. He had the passenger door of his car open, and they were hiding behind the doors and shooting at each other. One would shoot and then duck behind the door. Then the other one would come up and shoot then duck behind his door. I suppose car doors had more steel in them in those days because neither of them got killed.

I heard someone from inside my apartment say, "Where's Jamie at?" They ran out and brought me inside and started to scold me. "Look here boy, bullets don't have any names on them. You'd better sit your bad ass down before you catch a stray bullet." The gunfight ended when someone yelled that they were calling the police. They had emptied their guns and reloaded, but no one died that day. I know that Ray Ray was in two more shootouts in the neighborhood and would eventually end up in prison. Dabo got a job with the city driving a bus.

My next encounter with violence was shortly after this and more deadly. My uncle had an apartment in our same projects. He had a girlfriend with whom he had several children. I never did know if he married her or not, but they stayed together. He was always very well dressed and a handsome guy. That's why the ladies liked him.

One day I walked up and saw them both standing there, with another cousin holding a stick and standing nearby. My uncle had done something that had upset his girlfriend, whose name was

Belle. I remember hearing my uncle say, "Belle, don't shoot me anymore." I can't remember if she shot him again, or not. My cousin, who was standing there, said, "Shoot him again, if you want to." However many times she shot him, the wound was fatal.

He fell down face first in the dirt. I saw his face, and it was turned to the side. I saw him close his eyes for the last time and die. It was my first experience with death and especially watching someone die. The strange thing about the place that he fell was that years afterwards, when it would rain, there was a quarter-sized circle in the dirt, where he took his last breath. In the housing projects there isn't much grass, just dirt. Years later, we would be walking by that place and see the spot where my uncle took his last breath.

When he died, my uncle's girlfriend walked back into the apartment they shared. She would say that the reason she shot him was that she had told him not to leave her children alone in the apartment by themselves. He was a ladies' man, and she knew he was up at his brother's house, which was a bootlegger house, drinking and flirting with other women. He had left the children at home to go carouse. I guess she had had enough. Strangely, she didn't do any prison time for the murder. She would claim that it was because she went and talked to the Root Doctor. I'll say more about that in an upcoming chapter.

Violence was simply part of life in the projects and I grew up around it. It wasn't uncommon to hear gunshots at night and sometimes even in the daytime. People had guns and used them in their criminal activities, which often spilled over into the apartment complex. I grew up on the "mean streets," and if things had not changed for me, I might have died in them, like so many people I knew.

4

CONVERSATION ABOUT GROWING UP

Bob

AS WE BEGIN, let's talk about the language we are going to use. As a white person, it's sometimes hard to know exactly what terms to use when talking about race, so let's start there. Would you rather me use the term "black" or "African American?" I'll be happy to use the term with which you are more comfortable.

Jamie

In regard to the terms to use to describe my race, I don't get hung up on this, one way or the other. It doesn't really matter to me and, to be honest, I'd rather use the term "black." It seems to me that some people overthink this issue, and it does not need to be so complicated. I called myself "black" until I was in my 30s and started to hear the term "African American." I understand what people mean by that and why some people prefer it. But in the 'hood, no one really uses that term. They don't say, "See that African American guy standing over there." They say, "See that black guy over there." So black is the term I grew up with. Let's use that."

Bob

That sounds good to me. I'm comfortable with you using the term "whites" or "white people." I hope people will understand, if they would prefer other terms, that we mean no disrespect by using the terms we use. But we have to use some terms, and we have agreed together to use the terms "black" and "white." No offense is meant in any way, especially toward those who prefer other terms.

In terms of how this book is organized, we have agreed to focus on particular parts of our own story and experience in each chapter. Various chapters will focus on particular areas, such as family, education, policing, racism, etc. We will try to keep our discussion, for the most part, confined to things pertinent to each chapter. In the end, we want to get to a number of major points of contention between our communities today, but we will do so one topic at a time, even though there is certainly going to be some overlap.

In starting this conversation, I have also realized that we come from slightly different generations. I am a "baby boomer," and you are from the generation that is called, "Generation X." There is going to be some difference in our experience in that regard, but our goal is to get to conversations about issues of race today. I hope that the difference in our generations won't hinder that too much. I also realize that many who read this will be younger than we are, but I hope this can still be a resource for people to have authentic conversations with one another.

Here, then, is a question to get us started. After having written your story of growing up, what are your reflections on it?

Jamie

One has to do with discipline. You talked about how you were disciplined by your parents. I was pretty much allowed to run the streets, and my mother only disciplined me in extreme cases. She tried when I got to be a teenager, but it was too late by that time.

Most parents in the projects didn't have a clue about effective discipline. For that reason, there were some bizarre things done. There was a kid in the apartments whose name was Shaggy. His mom's name was Daisy. He wouldn't get a spanking or whipping; he'd get a beating. She would take extension cords and beat him with them. She even put the children in the freezer at times, when they had done something really bad. I remember some extreme forms of discipline like that. I don't know what made her do those things; perhaps she had a lot of pain and hurt in her own life. Or maybe she was disciplined that way growing up herself, and it was all she knew.

Let me ask you the same question. What reflections do you have on your experience?

Bob

One thing I realize is how sheltered I was. As I hear your story, you grew up a lot faster than I did. I had a sheltered childhood, and I was very naïve about many things. From my parents' point of view, this was intentional; they wanted it this way. I didn't have a lot of trauma in my experience growing up. There might have been bad things in the world, but, for the most part, I didn't know about them. My wife and I have tried to raise our boys with a similar degree of naiveté, but with the advent of the internet, this has certainly become harder.

Here's a question I want to ask you: What kinds of conversations do you hear in the black community? What sorts of things do they talk about, in terms of racial issues today?

Jamie

There is a sense among black people that racism exists in many places. I know a young woman who is a nurse. After working about six months as a nurse, she noticed that the white and black patients were treated differently. When the nurses were having difficulties with a white patient, they would be very deferential. "How can we help?" they would ask. But when black patients gave them trouble, the person was being disruptive and was potentially dangerous. They were more likely to call Security on a black patient than a white one. After seeing this, she asked for a meeting of the nurses and called them out. Her sense was that they made a show of remorse, but nothing really changed.

A black person feels a lot of pressure to declare all white people racist. If I am honest about things, however, I think everybody has a little bit of racism in them. It's only natural.

25

Everyone has been offended by the other race in some way or the other, so everyone feels like they have a grievance. If I put myself in a white person's shoes, I can understand it. They may think, "My father was in the armed forces; he fought for this country and helped build this land. We discovered this country and built it. It's ours!"

Black people suspect that whites don't want to lose power. They have always been in power, and now they are afraid of losing it. People of color are starting to get into positions of power, and it scares them.

There is something I notice, however, that has changed in the last 20 years. It is that more black and white people interact than ever before. There are more mixed communities and more kids in school with different races. I used to hear white people called "Crackers," which was a derogatory term for racist white people. I don't hear that term anymore.

Let me ask you the same question. What kinds of conversations do you hear about race in the white community?

Bob

As I listen in the white community, I hear a couple of kinds of conversations taking place. One reveals a kind of vague guilt. We hear so many people talk about systemic racism and prejudice today that it's hard for white people not to wonder if there is some truth in those statements. Some white people are sure there is. Most people with good hearts are willing to self-reflect. Lots of white people hear these terms and ask themselves if they might be prejudiced or racist without knowing it. They may not think they are or feel like they are, but they wonder if there is something they are missing. They wonder if they are guilty in spite of the fact that they don't think they are.

The question of systemic racism can certainly be complicated. Are there ways in which society favors one race over another? Is the black community disadvantaged in some way? I hear a great deal of empathy and concern in the white community, particularly in the white Christian community, for those who, for whatever reason, can't find a path toward a better life.

Most white people would acknowledge that there have been many bad laws in our nation's history that discriminated against black people and plenty of atrocities. Slavery was not a good thing, and it is hard to believe that our country allowed it for so many years. It is certainly a blight on our national history.

The problem is that many white people aren't convinced that today the system is rigged against black people. They think other problems are at work and that black people could make more of their lives if they fixed some of their own cultural problems. Most white people realize that these issues are complex and not simple. They are open to thinking about them and working to fix things that need to be corrected but don't think the entire burden falls on the white community.

This leads to another thing that I hear among the white community, which is resentment. They resent being called racist when they don't think they are. In fact, they tune out or simply ignore people who are always crying "Racism!" As an example, we are going to talk about education in an upcoming chapter, but a person who graduated from college resents being told that another person who dropped out of high school lives at a lower standard of living because of racism. The person with the college degree thinks the problem lies elsewhere, such as in the disparity in the level of education, and it isn't a racial disparity but an educational one. Again, we are going to look at education in a future chapter, and the issue is more complicated than I have indicated, but it is just to say that there is deep resentment among many whites for being called racist when they don't think they are. Nor do they honestly think that racism is the most pressing problem in the black community or that it is the primary factor that creates our social inequities.

DISCUSSION QUESTIONS
PART 1 – GROWING UP

1. If you are white, how similar to Bob's experience was your experience growing up? Dissimilar?

2. If you are black, how similar to Jamie's experience was your experience growing up? Dissimilar?

3. How do you think life has changed for whites since the 1950s when Bob grew up? For blacks since Jamie grew up in the 1970s?

4. What was your life like growing up? What good values were you taught? What do you wish you had been taught?

5. What privileges do you feel like you had growing up? What disadvantages?

6. How have you (or did you or will you) tried to give your children a similar experience to yours growing up? A different experience? In what ways have you been successful and unsuccessful?

7. In terms of the advantages and disadvantages you had growing up, which were things in your control (such as your willingness to work hard, having good values, etc.) versus not in your control (such as the country in which you were born, your parents, your health, your intellectual abilities, etc.). Do you tend to view aspects of your life that were not in your control as achievements you have "earned"?

8. What kinds of conversations go on about race in your community? What things are said openly? What things are said privately? Are there any things that your community feels afraid to say openly?

9. Do you think blacks and whites interact in meaningful ways in today's culture? Where is the most interaction? The least? Where do you interact the most with people of another race? The least?

10. What things do you think hinder honest conversation about race today? What might help?

PART 2 – FAMILY

5

PARENTS

Bob

MY PARENTS MET ON A BLIND DATE, or what was supposed to be a blind date; it did not turn out as expected. My mother worked for the telephone company in Atlanta, Southern Bell, as it was called at the time. She was a switchboard operator, one of an array of young women who sat at the switchboard, moving actual connections from one place to another to connect calls. She was 19 years old and glad to be away from her home in Tennessee. More about that in a moment.

My father was getting ready to ship overseas in the Second World War. He had gone through basic training and been stationed in the United States for several years. In 1944, he received orders to get on a boat for the long overseas trip to the war in Europe. My father was young and handsome, with a full head of curly black hair, at least before his army haircut. What occasioned the meeting of my father and mother was my father's aunt, who worked at Southern Bell and was anxious to introduce the two of them.

My mother was very attractive; she had been considered, since she was young, as particularly pretty. There is some fine line between having nice features, having a pleasant appearance, and that elusive quality that makes a face actually pretty. Whatever that thing is, my mother had it; when you looked at her, you immediately thought how pretty she was. She was also bright and engaging, a people-person by temperament; for those reasons, she had caught the attention of my father's aunt, who began to plot to introduce my father to her.

The problem was that my father was on the verge of being shipped overseas, his orders already in hand for the ship he was to board. For that reason, my aunt had to work fast. She arranged that my father would come to the office to take my mother out for lunch, a sandwich together at one of the small sandwich shops nearby in downtown Atlanta. Everything was arranged, and my father came to the building, but something went amiss. I do not know the exact details of the story, but my mother was not able to get off for her lunch break. Something came up where she had to stay at her post. The only thing my aunt was able to do was bring my father up to where my mother worked and introduce them.

That meeting made an impression on my father. I don't know if he was immediately smitten, but I suspect he was. He wanted to make a good impression, and he did something he hoped my mother would remember. He went to one of the sandwich shops for a sandwich and had half his sandwich sent up to my mother with a note that said, "Sorry we could not have lunch, but I thought I'd share half my sandwich. Robert." That meeting would begin a correspondence between them, my father a lonely soldier overseas, trying to stay alive, and my mother a single working girl in Atlanta. My father would write her almost every day, and my mother would write back. I'm sure my aunt assured her that he was a young man of fine character, which he was. When he came back from the war, they would begin dating and marry not long afterward.

Jamie

Like so many black children, then and today, I did not have a father in my home. This did not seem particularly unusual to me, since no one I knew had a father. In the closet of my room, I used to see some "jump boots." I knew they didn't fit me or my brother. There wasn't a guy in the apartment. I asked my mother one day, "Now whose shoes are these?" She would brush me off and say, "You quit asking questions about those boots." But I kept asking her, and finally she said, "Those are your Daddy boots." I thought, "Daddy? What's that?"

No father had ever been in my life. She had been hiding the identity of my father because of the crimes he had committed. As it turned out, my father went to prison when I was 6 months old for armed robbery and a double homicide. He spent 41 straight years there.

One day I stumbled across a small wallet-size black-and-white picture, but it wasn't a happy family picture with my mother and our family. It wasn't a picture of my father holding me as you might expect a proud father to do with a newborn son. It was my dad's mug shot from his arrest. There was my father holding numbers across his chest showing that he was incarcerated and under arrest.

I don't know how my mother and father met. In fact, I rarely heard her mention him, only about four or five times. One of the words I have heard used to describe my father was "gangster." In the view of many, he was a bad man, meaning someone you didn't want to mess with, a gangster. One illustration of how my mother thought of him was when he finally got out of prison, after serving his time. I remember her saying to all our family, "Don't tell him where I live. Don't anyone tell him where he can find me. I don't want that man to come looking for me." So, I don't know anything about how my parents met. I do know they were married.

At one point, my mother took me to see my father in prison. She had a purpose in doing so; she wanted me to know where I was going to end up if I didn't change my ways. I didn't want to go see him because he hadn't been in my life. To me, he didn't feel like my daddy. He hadn't been there for me, to tell me how to do things, like use a wrench or change a flat tire. But my mother took me anyway. I was 17 years old at that point. She could get me in because I was his son, though I remember she had to bring my birth certificate, just to show I really was his son.

We went down to the Central State Prison in Macon, Georgia. I didn't know what to expect. But I went in and said to myself, "I guess I'm going to see my dad for the first time. Whatever." I took a lunch bag with me, and it was full of change. This was to use in the vending machines that were in the large visitation room where the prisoners met with visitors. They let me into the room, and I started looking around. I didn't even know what he looked like, so I had to ask the officer.

There were lots of tables in the room, where people could sit down with their family members. You can have a Coke together and a bag of potato chips or a candy bar. There are guards there, standing near the doors, just to make sure nothing happened that shouldn't and that no one got out of hand. The guard pointed my father out to me; he was sitting at a table. The guard said, as far as he knew, my father had not had a visitor in the 15 years he had been there. So this was new for both of us.

When I sat down, I said, "Hey. how're you doing?" He didn't say anything; he just looked at me. I said, "Do you want something from the vending machines?" He said, "Yeah," and told me some things to get. I got him some chips and candy and a soda. He said, "Now, who are you?" I said, "I'm your son." He replied, "Oh, Dexter." Dexter is my older brother. I said, "No, I'm James." Again, he said, "Dexter?" I replied, "No, I'm James."

He said, "How's your mom doing?" I told him that she was fine. Then he began to ask about some of the relatives, and he'd smile when he heard about them. At this point, I realized that he kept talking about things that happened a long time ago, in the 1960s and even the 1950s. I was born in 1970, so they were before me. It also dawned on me that maybe my father's mind wasn't all there. We talked for about an hour.

I did see my father another time; it was when I was in prison too. I was on a disciplinary transfer for messing a guy up at a level-5 prison where I was incarcerated. Level 5 is the worst kind of prison. I was being booked at my new prison assignment when the man at the desk said, "There's already a Mr. James Carter Scott here." I knew from doing time that they don't let family, especially immediate family, into the same prison because it can potentially cause a disturbance. I also knew that my dad was there, and I was looking forward to seeing him again. But I said that I didn't know anyone by that name. I lied because I wanted to see my dad. At that point I was 27 years old.

From there I headed to my dormitory with my net bag, which had in it all my clothes and hygiene products from my previous prison. I walked down the steps to go to the dormitory, and I saw this guy standing at the bottom of the steps. I didn't know who he was; I didn't recognize him as my dad. Someone figured it out later and said to me, "I think that's your dad." He ate in the chow hall right after my group, but one day I lingered until his group came in. When he sat down, we had the chance to talk.

He still called me Dexter and could only remember events from a very long time ago. I realized his mind was getting worse. I felt sorry for him and asked him how he was doing and if he needed anything. I tried to get money sent into his account. He seemed to always be hungry. He sat next to the place people bring their trays when they are finished eating. If anyone didn't eat everything, they'd scrape it onto his plate.

So that's my experience of my father. He went to prison when I was 6 months old for a double murder. They gave him a concealed life sentence. That means there is no possibility of parole. He ended up doing 41 years behind bars.

Bob

Both of my parents grew up poor, my father in almost abject poverty. My father grew up, in his teenage years, with his grandmother, "Big Mama," and various aunts and uncles because both his parents died when he was young. His mother died in childbirth, giving birth to his sister. My father was the oldest of four children, three boys and one girl. Medical understanding was not what it is now in the 1920s, and a mother's death at childbirth was not uncommon. Today about 15 women die for every 100,000 live childbirths.[1] A century ago, the number was 600 per 100,000. My grandmother was one of those. One of the reasons was that most women gave birth at home, where emergency procedures were not possible. The story that I have heard is that, as my grandmother knew things were not going well for her and that death might be upon her, she sang a verse of "Jesus, Lover Of My Soul," and expired. It is a sweet story and the only one I have about her; it does give me a small glimpse of her as a woman of faith.

The death of my grandfather was different. My father's father died at his own hands. My father was born in 1919, so when he was an elementary child, the Great Depression hit America. When that happened, the economy went into shutdown mode, and the depression reached into every corner of the country. There was no work anywhere, from Wall Street to the south Georgia town of Butler, where my father's family lived. My grandfather apparently tried his hand at a number of occupations, being at one point a salesman, but none of them enabled him even to eke out a meager living. My grandfather's uncle ran a peach orchard, and when he died my grandfather got the job. It proved too big for him and, for whatever reason, he couldn't do the work and lost the job.

When he lost that job, his world crashed in on him, and so did a deep darkness of despair. He had lost his wife some years earlier, and there were no job prospects open to him. One day, he decided that his life had no future and was not worth living. He instructed one of his sons, not my father, to go to the well and bring him a ladle of water. As I have considered this, it seems a particularly cruel thing to do to one of your children, ask them to assist in your own suicide, but this is what he did. I hope it was more thoughtless than intentional cruelty. When the water came, he put strychnine, rat poison, in it and drank it. Strychnine is the basic ingredient in Warfarin, which is a blood thinner. In small doses it can help people avoid strokes and has saved many lives. But in high doses, which is what my grandfather took, it causes massive internal bleeding. Once the internal bleeding began, it took about 15 minutes for my grandfather to die, and there was no reversing its effects. As I heard the story, one observation of those there was that he did not realize what a horrible way to die it would be. At age 12, my father was an orphan.

In those days, extended family often lived in the same community, and my father's family rallied around the four orphaned children – my father, his two brothers, and their sister. They were farmed out to live with various relatives, my father living with his grandmother for a while and several aunts. This was a particular burden on the extended family, since no one had any resources, but they did their best, out of good hearts, and pity for these four poor children. When he got old enough, they sent my father to boarding school at Berry, in Rome, Georgia, which was established as a school where the poor could work in exchange for an education. It was both a way for my father to get some education and a way to take the burden of feeding him away from the already tight situation of the extended family. He worked all summer at the school to pay for the next year's tuition. It was one of the reasons he was extremely handy and could build almost anything.

My father's attendance at Berry did not suddenly raise him out of poverty; his poverty went with him. Some years he would arrive at school either without a pair of shoes, or with a pair that was falling apart. Every child was supposed to bring a nickel to school with them to pay for the pair of overalls, for the boys, that they would wear every day during the upcoming school year. It does not sound like much, but for my father's family even that was a difficult sum to raise.

I have heard my father tell the story about one year when he lost his nickel. He was walking with it in his mouth and accidentally swallowed it. He had it in his mouth because he was young, and kids do all sorts of things without thinking. I cannot remember what caused it, but he swallowed it before he got to the school. When he

37

arrived, there was a great commotion about the nickel. Had he lost it or stolen it, or did he not bring one at all? I do not remember whether they tried to retrieve it after it passed through his body or not, only that it created quite a stir, at least in my father's memory.

My father attended high school and one year of college at Berry, with little change in his standard of living. What would end up pulling my father out of poverty, at least in part, was the Second World War. He was drafted into the Army, along with millions of other young men. That would be the event that would pull America out of the Great Depression, and a great many people, such as my father, out of poverty.

6

DYSFUNCTION

Jamie

IN THE PROJECTS WHERE I GREW UP, most of the young people were like me; they didn't have role models of a family with both a father and mother. There were not many men living in the projects, and there was a reason for that. It was much easier for women with children to get into the projects. It was hard for a man to get authorized for an apartment. The housing authority felt like men could go out and get a job; then they could live in another place. So it was easier for a woman, especially one with children, to get authorized for public assistance housing. There were some men in the complex, but most of them lived with their moms. For example, there was a 50-year-old man who lived near us, but he was only there because he stayed with his mother.

The outcome of this was that most men didn't really consider themselves fathers, even if they had children. In fact, the term that got used more than father was "baby daddy." They weren't fathers, just baby daddies. This is because they may have gotten a girl pregnant, but they had no intention of being a father to the child. In fact, as soon as someone knew they had gotten a girl pregnant, they split. This was supposedly because they thought the girl was going to try to get child support from them. But that wasn't really possible because the guys generally didn't have jobs and therefore didn't have any money. Some of them had welfare checks, so they worried that the girl might get their welfare check. They were also running from the responsibility. They didn't want the responsibility of raising a child.

One of the things that would happen was that guys would come in to try to hook up with a new girl in the complex. A new girl would come into the complex, and all the guys would show up.

They weren't only trying to get in good with the girl but trying to find a place to live. Since the girl had an apartment, it was an opportunity for some guy to move in with her.

As I think about why marriage wasn't valued in the projects where I grew up, I realize that it wasn't modeled for me and those like me. In fact, I had actually never seen a wedding until my own. My mother got married at one point to a man who was in the service and stationed overseas. I didn't go to that wedding because I was young, and they got married in Japan. So the very first wedding I went to was my own. I got there and had to ask the person doing the wedding what I was supposed to do. He had to explain my own wedding to me.

One of the problems in the 'hood is girls getting pregnant very early. This was just a part of growing up there. There was this game we played, called "Hide and Get." The girls would hide, and the guys would go looking for them. This wasn't "Hide and Seek." It wasn't about seeking but getting. When you found the girl, you got to have sex with her. It was a culture in which most people became sexually active at an early age.

You can see that young girls doing this without birth control is a problem. But no one was on birth control because they would have had to tell their moms, which would not have gone over well. There was a lot of sneaking out, guys crawling up on roofs, sneaking up on roofs to get into girls' apartments. Guys had access to birth control means but didn't really use them.

So young girls got pregnant and had children. The fathers were not in the homes, so the mothers got welfare checks. This ended up making people dependent on the government because all the money they had was from those welfare checks. In a sense, the government became like a little god, who provided what people needed and on whom they relied. It also became the husband that girls didn't have and the father that children didn't have.

When I grew up, young boys like me found their heroes in other places besides their father. Sports stars become heroes. One of

40

mine was O.J. Simpson. This was before he got into trouble, when he was a great football player for the Buffalo Bills. Today kids look up to sports stars and rappers. Having heroes gives kids dreams. They don't dream of growing up and getting married and raising their own kids. They dream of being professional athletes and rappers. But these dreams don't come true for most. The sad thing is that the dream of a great family life is one that kids in the 'hood just don't have, even today.

Bob

My mother grew up poor like my father but for different reasons. Her family's problems were because her father was an alcoholic and gambler. When he was home and sober, he made a good living. When he was absent, which, on occasion, he would be for six months at a time, the family struggled to make ends meet.

My mother was the seventh of 11 children, eight boys and three girls, my mother being in the middle of the three girls. They grew up in a small town in Tennessee, where in the 1920s and '30s most everyone knew each other, she being born in 1925. Because she had a number of older brothers, generally athletic and handsome, she was someone of note, being the younger sister of such a brood of strapping young men. As I said earlier, she was also pretty, being voted the prettiest girl in school from the 10th grade through her senior year in high school.

My mother's father was quite a personality. He was engaging and had the gift of gab. When he was sober, he was a master salesman and made a very good living when he worked. His profession was being a horse trader. Today that seems a profession that is deceitful by its nature, but in the early 20th century it was not. Like a car dealership today, people traded their means of transportation before the automobile became widespread, and horses were a main means of getting around. My grandfather bought and traded horses.

The only experiences I had of actually seeing my grandfather were on two occasions. My grandmother had divorced him by the time I came along. When we were at a family reunion in Tennessee, I met him on two occasions. One was when we were at a restaurant owned by several of my mother's older brothers. He was sitting at one of the tables, and my mother introduced my sister and me to him. The only other time I saw him was once when my mother thought we ought to have some acquaintance with him, if only a slight one. He had an apartment over the restaurant owned by her brothers, and we went to his small room one day to see him. I remember him as a rather shriveled old man; he must have been in his 70s or 80s at that point. There must have not been much to talk about because I remember that he showed us his gun, which was a small revolver pistol. That he thought this something he ought to proudly show his grandchildren tells you something about the kind of person he was. The reason my sister and I saw him only twice in our lives is that my mother despised him.

When my grandfather was first married to my grandmother, as the stories are told, they were deeply in love. There is a picture of her sitting on his lap in the early years of their married life, happy and blissful in their relationship. I don't know what happened, but something did along the way. He became an alcoholic and a mean drunk. Some people are quiet drunks, others get talkative, and some want to take a nap. My grandfather, whose temperament was boisterous by nature, became more bombastic and viciously mean. He would terrify the family and send them scattering to their rooms when he came home inebriated. The older boys felt his wrath most acutely. When he took one of the older boys into the barn and beat him badly one day, that son left home and never came back. While some of the boys respected and admired his abilities with others and his ability to make a deal, my mother hated him.

My mother always had good sense about her. She had the ability to see through things, and she saw through her father clearly. He was a mean drunk whose bad behavior was creating havoc in the family. When he worked, they lived in a nice house and had plenty of food on the table. One night however, in an early morning poker game, he ran out of money and bet the deed to the house. He lost, and the next day the family packed up and left their home. On one occasion, they all got into a truck and drove to Arizona, where the family would live until things cooled off back home. Whatever her father had done, it had made some people mad enough that the entire family had to leave town.

There were many adventures in a family with eight brothers and two sisters, and I remember sitting at the dinner table growing up, listening to my mother tell stories from her childhood. She also had the gift of gab and was an engaging storyteller. She mostly left out the stories about the bad times and focused on all the fun things she did with her brothers and sisters. The truth is, however, that she could not wait to get away from the havoc her father created in their home. When she was 18 years old, she got the chance to come to Atlanta with her sister and a friend to work for Southern Bell. She bid her family a sorrowful goodbye and her father good riddance and left home, ready to start a different life. She was determined about one thing very clearly. Whoever she married would not be like her own father. The man she would meet, my father, would be in almost every way a perfect opposite.

Jamie

I somehow recognized from an early age that I had limited opportunities. It was the feeling I got from the community in which I lived. We all knew we were not going anywhere; our life was going to be lived in the projects. I did have the chance for some adventures, however, when my mother married a man in the armed services. He was stationed in Japan, and we went over to live with him. He was in the Navy, and she met him in Athens. His next assignment, after Athens, was in Yokohama, Japan. I remember how much I enjoyed the adventure of that, taking my first airplane ride and across the ocean at that. Up to that point, I had hardly been out of my community except to go to Six Flags in Atlanta one time. I was pretty proud and thought, "How many black boys are in an airplane on their way to Japan?"

We lived in Japan for a few years. His next assignment was in New Jersey, so we lived there for a while after Japan. The place we lived was a rather middle-class neighborhood. There were a few more black kids there than when we lived in Japan. This was my first experience of having a father in the home, a stepfather. He provided for us, but he also didn't know much about being a father; maybe he didn't have one either. I do remember being spanked by him one time, when I was about 9 or 10. He "set me on fire," figuratively, and I can still remember it. But my mother eventually got divorced from him, and when that happened, that part of our life was over. I came back to the projects in Athens with my mother.

All in all, I felt like I had a happy childhood. Kids adjust to whatever their situation is, and I did. I certainly got some life coaching from my mom. I called her by her first name, Ellen, most of the time. Lots of kids in the projects called their moms by their first names. Only when she got married did I start calling her "Mother." That is one of the things I learned from my stepfather. He told me to call her "Mother" instead of by her first name.

My mother used to tell me what to do if I got into a fight. She said that if I didn't think I could beat the person, then I needed to pick up a stick or whatever I could and "bust him in the damn head." This was how you were taught in the projects. She didn't realize that she was raising a gangster, but that's the way it was going to turn out.

My mother didn't want us to embarrass her in front of other people. This was part of how children were expected to behave, even in the projects. When my brother and I went to the grocery store with her, she would tell us beforehand, "I don't want you acting up or putting candy bars in the cart when I'm not looking. Don't embarrass me in front of other people. If you do, I'm going to tear you up." Tear us up is what she had to do to my brother and me on a couple of occasions. Right there in the middle of the store, she would wear us out in front of everyone. When we got out, we'd say, "Why'd you do that?" She'd say, "I told you I meant what I said." What she would do is hold us by one of our arms and spank us on the bottom or wherever, right there. And if you threw a tantrum and just fell out on the floor, she would get really mad, "I'm going to give you something to really cry about," she would say. I learned not to throw a tantrum.

Bob

When my father came back from the Second World War, he and my mother started dating and married in a reasonably short period afterwards. That is what people were doing in those days, coming back from the war and getting married. From all accounts my mother and father were genuinely in love, and each met the other's basic requirements. My mother was pretty and was considered an outstanding "catch" for my father. My father, from my mother's point of view, was stable, decent, and hardworking, everything her father was not. They found each other, fell in love, and got married.

My father had wanted to be an engineer from age 12, and the G.I. Bill provided him the opportunity to have his education paid for, in honor of his service to the country. He applied to Georgia Tech in Atlanta and was accepted. He had a year of college at Berry College under his belt and with a couple of years of education was not far from being able to make a decent living for himself and his new bride. They lived in various apartments and spare rooms while he was in school, my mother's job at Southern Bell providing a living for them. When my father graduated from college with his degree in electrical engineering, they purchased their first home, a very small one, with his salary from working at Georgia Power Company, in Atlanta.

As I reflect on my family life, it was stable. There was very little disagreement or arguing in our house. My parents generally got along, and if they had major disagreements, they kept them behind closed doors. I heard my mother say, on several occasions, that the only thing they argued about was exactly how to raise us, as children. Whatever disagreements about parenting they may have had, from my point of view they presented a united front, and when discipline was administered, it was with the wholehearted endorsement of both.

In the neighborhoods where I lived and even through high school, I hardly knew any families that were divorced. In the 1950s and '60s, divorce was a rare phenomenon. That seems surprising today when divorce strikes so many families, but it was not so in the era in which I grew up. What the difference was, I am not sure, but couples generally stayed together. As I think about the families up and down the street on which I grew up, they generally got along with one another. If they didn't, it was not public knowledge. Whatever difficulties they had, they worked them out, and most of the marriages seemed happy.

What the stability of my family did was give me a solid foundation from which to grow up. I didn't worry about trauma or tension at home, only the various problems I was facing at school, such as being liked, keeping up my grades, and doing well in my athletic endeavors. Those were difficult enough for me, and I had enough struggles there to keep my mind occupied. I realize how fortunate I was in my family situation, but it was not an aberration. My situation was how, at least from my parents' perspective, every child ought to grow up. It was both my parents' faith and their good moral values that motivated them to create, nurture, and maintain a good family environment. They had grown up poor and in families that were in disarray. They were determined to create a different life for themselves and their children. A healthy family was also, they thought, the best way for them to be happy, find fulfillment, and raise children who would be good members of their community and the nation. This was the American dream, and in the 1950s and '60s, they were part of a generation of people seeking their piece of it.

7

CONVERSATION ABOUT FAMILY

Bob

YOU HAVE MENTIONED GRANDMOTHERS and how important yours was to you. It sounds like she was a wonderful woman. I haven't heard you talk about grandfathers. Did you know your grandfathers?

Jamie

I didn't know either of my biological grandfathers. I never met them and hardly ever heard them talked about. In the inner-city black community, there aren't many grandfathers, just like there aren't many fathers. My grandmother actually had a boyfriend whose name was Johnny and who lived in Atlanta. I suppose he was the closest thing I had to a grandfather. He worked at Macy's downtown and had been in the military. They never did marry, and I'm not sure why because they were together for almost 40 years. I think that maybe my grandmother had really loved her first husband, who was my grandfather, but he got burned up in a house fire. I've often wondered if she just didn't want to marry anyone else after he died. And of course marriage wasn't a huge value in our community either. I think Johnny would have liked to marry my grandmother because sometimes he'd say to me, "You know, "Rhobell won't marry me." Her name was Rosa Bell, and he called her Rhobell. There's a lot of broken English in the inner city.

Bob

One of the real differences in when I grew up and today is that the 1950s and early 1960s were a very different social environment, even for the white community. One major difference is the prevalence of divorce today. Most families who were married in the

1950s didn't get divorced. In the first two neighborhoods I lived in, through high school, I hardly remember any families who were divorced. It wasn't that people stayed together just because they had to; most couples seemed happy. I knew the parents of all my friends, and all the families in the neighborhood socialized. I can't think of any set of parents who seemed to be mismatched or unhappy. I was a child, of course, so there were probably lots of arguments behind the scenes that I didn't know about. But families seemed happy, and they made their marriages work. The result was that for everyone I knew, there was both a mother and a father in the home.

Jamie
I know that divorces have increased dramatically in all racial groups, but particularly the white community. Isn't that true?

Bob
It is. I did some research on divorce statistics and found that the divorce rate has dramatically risen in the United States in the past 50 years. It began to rise significantly in the 1970's and peaked in America about 1980 at around 50%. Since then it has gone down but is still significantly high, hovering around 40%. The decline, though, isn't entirely good news. In part, the divorce rate has gone down because more and more people are living together instead of getting married. They may be living with someone but don't feel the need to get married. Because of the high rate of divorce, some don't want to take the chance. Some men also hesitate to commit because of the negative financial consequences a divorce can bring them and the greater willingness of women to abandon their marriage in the midst of difficulties. A study done in 2010 found that only 51% of the people in America were married, as compared to 72% in 1960.[2]

All of this is a huge change in the family since I grew up. In the 1950s, most people got married and only 20% of marriages ended in divorce. Now marriages are becoming less common, and divorce rates are 2 to 2 1/2 times what they were when I was young. I was interested to discover that though there are fewer marriages in the black community, divorce is also a problem in it, and black marriages experience divorce at twice the rate of whites.

One thing that has certainly affected the number of divorces in America is the introduction of no-fault divorce laws. The first no-fault divorce law was passed in California in 1969 and went into effect in 1970. This introduced a type of law, soon enacted in most states, in which a judge could grant a divorce in response to the request of only one party, without that party having to show that their spouse had broken the marriage covenant in some way. Up until then, the spouse who wanted the divorce had to show some inappropriate behavior by their partner. This sometimes led to false or exaggerated claims and ones that were difficult for judges to assess. No-fault divorce solved this problem but made it easier for people to get a divorce for any reason. It became much more common for people to simply cite incompatibility or irreconcilable differences. These may be good laws in many respects, but they are also ones that had the unintended consequence of making divorce much easier.

Jamie

One of the things I know is that it is hard to know what a good marriage ought to look like if you have never seen one. Most inner-city blacks have not seen many healthy marriages. You tend to practice what you see modeled, and the example from which you learn most is your own home. If there isn't a healthy marriage in your home, you don't really know what one looks like.

Bob

It's clear that the family today is facing a number of challenges. From my perspective, there seem to be a thousand reasons people get divorced in white America. Changing roles for husbands and wives have certainly placed stress on the institution of marriage.

49

Careers for both spouses, varied schedules, child-rearing responsibilities, opportunity and mobility, along with an onslaught of media promoting personal fulfillment have brought new challenges that make it difficult for couples trying to build their marriages. The sociological and religious acceptance of divorce as a norm adds to the tendency for couples to consider divorce as a viable option more readily than in former generations.

No one wants to bind people to marriages that are harmful, detrimental, or dangerous, but the children almost always suffer when there is a divorce, although it may, at times, seem the lesser of two evils. My generation's parents had different norms than we do, and there is a much less well-defined norm for people today concerning marriage. Most people I know who have gone through a divorce have found it an excruciating experience. They feel a sense of shame, loss, and deep guilt. It is a failure in one of the most important areas of life. But when faced with an unhappy life situation, as painful as it may be, it sometimes seems better to cut their losses, start over, and try again. When it is their spouse who makes that decision, people are left with wounds of betrayal, hurt, and sadness that take a long time to heal.

Jamie
The reality is that marriage is hard. Two people molding their lives together is not an easy task. There are many challenges, even in the best of circumstances.

Bob
That's really true, isn't it? The differences that intrigue while dating, irritate in marriage. When dating, we are each other's biggest fans; in marriage, we become each other's biggest critics. It takes two mature people to make a healthy marriage. You have to be adults and not act like children. If you are petty, jealous, and manipulative, it makes for a bad relationship. You have to learn to forgive, let go of little things, be kind, and affirm your spouse. When you love

your spouse, they flourish and blossom. If you are always harping at them, they get angry, discouraged, and much less fun to live with. It is a fine balance that has to be achieved and a gift from God when a marriage flourishes.

Jamie

The great crisis in black culture relating to the family is the absence of fathers in the home. Not only is marriage not valued but mothers are abandoned by the men who father their children. Oddly, this doesn't get talked about much. I don't really know why. Maybe we have just gotten used to the problem. Maybe no one knows how to solve it. Maybe it brings up too many underlying issues. Perhaps it's too sensitive. I do know that it is very discouraging for women. The guy who fathered their child now doesn't want to have anything to do with her or the child. Perhaps the girl thought he loved her, but suddenly he's gone. It's very demeaning.

Bob

The makeup of the family has changed dramatically in America over the last 70 years. In 1950, the rate of births to unwed mothers among the white population was 2%. Today it's about 29%. That is a huge increase. So the absence of fathers isn't just an issue in the black community but a significant one in the white community. Among Hispanics, the problem is even worse. In 1950, the rate of births to unwed mothers was about 4%. Today it's just over 50%.

This is where the black community has seen a particularly dramatic increase. In 1950, the rate of births to unwed mothers in the black community was 18%; today it's over 70%. In black households, 7 out of 10 children are born to unwed mothers. This does not necessarily mean that there is no father in the home, but in the vast majority of the cases, they are not. What do you think about these statistics, from your point of view? Do these seem right?[3]

Jamie

I'm not at all surprised at them. They sound about right. I know the black community hasn't always been this way. It seems to me that the welfare system as it is currently structured has to carry some of the blame for this significant dysfunction in the black family.

Bob

I recently read an article that asserted, with accompanying statistics, that the change in the black family structure really began in 1964 with U.S. President Lyndon Johnson's War on Poverty.[4] What government welfare programs did was support single mothers who had dropped out of high school by providing them a number of sources of income, such as food stamps, child nutrition programs, Medicaid, public housing, and other social services. This inadvertently reduced the need for marriage, however, and enabled unwed mothers not only to survive but have a livable wage, although one that kept them poor. These mothers became "married" to the welfare state, rather than the fathers of their children. What was intended to have positive consequences by taking care of those who lived in poverty had the unintended consequence of fostering fewer marriages, which in turn created more poverty and the need for more government assistance.

Welfare rules disincentivize marriage by penalizing low-income couples who do marry. In practical terms, a mother who marries a working father will find her benefits reduced significantly. This is another unintended consequence that encourages unwed mothers who have boyfriends not to allow them to become husbands. Does this sound accurate to you?[5]

Jamie

I see this all the time. When the government came in with the offer of money, especially in inner-city neighborhoods, they began to tell women that they could get certain benefits if the father wasn't in the home. Women realized that they could get assistance with food

52

stamps and get a government check, but only if the father wasn't there. That made some women think, "I don't have to go to work. They will put me in a place to live where I'm only paying a small amount. That sounds pretty good." So it seemed a win-win situation, but it has definitely disrupted the black family.

The reality is that there isn't much shame about this in the black community. There should be. It would be better if people were embarrassed to have a child out of wedlock, but that's not the case. There certainly isn't shame about taking government assistance. Mothers with children think they deserve it, since they are raising a child or children all by themselves.

There's a verse in the Bible that says, "He who finds a wife finds a good thing and obtains favor from the Lord" (Proverbs 18:22). There is favor from God in being married. I certainly experience that now that I'm married. But lots of folks in the black community can't see it. It's too bad.

Here where I work, at the Sparrow's Nest, we help mothers get birth certificates for their children. We started to see women come in here who didn't just have 2 or 3 children but 5 and 6. We said, "Why are you doing this? Why are you having so many children without a father in the home?" But the more children they have the more federal assistance they get.

Bob

When government assistance replaces fathers in the home, it's not a good exchange. There is a great deal of research that details the impact on children of not having a father in the home.[6] These studies show that children who grow up in a home without a father are four times more likely to live in poverty. They are more likely to have behavioral problems, go to prison, commit a crime, and abuse alcohol and drugs They are twice as likely to drop out of high school. This is across the board for both whites and blacks. From your experience, as someone growing up in a home without a father, and in a community without many fathers, do these seem accurate?

Jamie

Absolutely. This is it. I've lived these statistics. My dad wasn't in the home. He went to prison when I was 6 months old, and I am living proof of how many difficulties a young boy can have if he doesn't have a father in his life. The statement about behavioral problems? I can check that box. I got kicked out of school in the seventh grade for getting into a fight with a teacher.

Substance abuse? I can check that one too. My uncle had a bootlegger house where people could go get liquor. He obviously didn't have a license, so he was doing it illegally. He'd buy booze and bring it home. Then people could come and get a dollar shot or a two-dollar shot. He'd pour up the liquor, which he'd cut with water and rubbing alcohol, and make money doing it. You could get half a pint or a pint or some beer. You could get other things too if you wanted it. When I would go up there, he'd tell me that if I danced like James Brown and did a split, he'd give me a candy bar or a drink of beer. I was pretty good at doing a James Brown imitation and had my first drink of beer at age 5.

I can also check the box about drug abuse. I got introduced to that early too. Then of course I got into crime. I went to jail for the first time when I was 14. I didn't get out of jail for the last time until I was 37. You do the math; that's a lot of years in trouble with the law. I've been incarcerated 54 times. I've been to level 5 prisons, maximum security, where the very worst offenders go, five times. That's where they keep the killers and guys who have done horrible things.

I also dropped out of high school, like the statistic said, except that I didn't exactly drop out. I was in the 10th grade and was facing two life sentences, so that pretty much took care of my high school career. But school wasn't a priority. I used to hear my cousin say, "You know when you hit 16, you can drop out of school. You don't have to go to school, and they can't lock you up for not going." Among my friends, that was something to look forward to, the time when you were old enough to drop out of school.

The problem with not having a father in the home is that there are just things a mother can't teach a boy. Not only does a guy need a father to teach him how to change a tire and use a wrench, but he needs his father to teach him how to be a man, a decent and responsible man. Boys especially need fathers to teach them how to control their desires in the areas of sex and violent behaviors. Fathers also bring a level of discipline to their sons that a mother by herself cannot.

All this is to say that those statistics are right. Not having a father in the home does make a difference. My story is the sad and perfect example of the negative impact of a home without a father.

DISCUSSION QUESTIONS
PART 2 - FAMILY

1. If you had to make a statement on the state of the family in America today, what would you say? What would you say are the greatest problems, in relation to family, in our culture?

2. How would you describe the state of the family across different segments of American society? Do you think unstable family structures are more related to economic class or race? Or other factors? Explain.

3. What do you think is missing when a father is not in the home? For boys. For girls.

4. Were you surprised at the comment about the absence of grandfathers in the inner-city black community in which Jamie grew up? What do you think are consequences of this? The causes?

5. What do you think are reasons the divorce rate is much higher today than in the middle of the 20th century? Which of the possible reasons for the increase in the number of divorces today seems reasonable to you? Can you think of other reasons that were not mentioned?

6. Were you surprised at any of the statistics about divorce mentioned in this section? Which ones? Explain.

7. Premarital sex seems commonplace today among young people. Do you think the values and behaviors of young people prepare them for healthy, long-term marriages? Why do you think the

idea that sex is something special and reserved for marriage is seen as old-fashioned? What are the consequences?

8. Some people have suggested that no-fault divorce laws, intended to reduce the notoriously bitter legal battles in divorce cases, are one cause of the increased divorce rate. Would you agree or disagree? Can you think of well-intentioned policies and social trends that make it harder for marriages? What should be done about these?

9. Can you think of other cultural trends that impact our view of marriage and the family today?

10. In a 2008 speech on Father's Day, then-Senator Barack Obama said the following. "I know what it means to have an absent father, although my circumstances weren't as tough as they are for many young people today. Even though my father left us when I was 2 years old, and I only knew him from the letters he wrote and the stories that my family told, I was luckier than most. I grew up in Hawaii, and had two wonderful grandparents from Kansas who poured everything they had into helping my mother raise my sister and me..." What people and/or resources might help children overcome not having a father in the home? How successful do you think these can be?[7]

PART 3 – EDUCATION

8

EXPECTATIONS

Bob

THE SCHOOLS I WENT TO, in the 1950s and 1960s, from elementary school through high school, had three levels of classes. There were "3" level classes, "2" level classes, and "1" level classes. The "3" level classes were for the brightest students; the "1" level classes for the least smart, and the "2" level classes for those in the middle. In the third grade, I was in the "2" level class.

I did not know this until some years later, but toward the end of my third-grade year, my mother went to see the principal. She wanted to know why I was in a "2" level class, not the higher-level class? The principal apparently explained to her that my test scores were on the edge for those who were placed in the higher class. He thought I would be best served by being in the level "2" class.

My mother strongly disagreed. She made the case that I ought to be in the higher class and that I would do fine there. My mother was a spitfire when she wanted to be, and I suspect she "raised holy hell" with the principal until he finally relented; the next year I was moved to the "3" level class. I did fine in that class, and it turned out to be a good fit. I wasn't the star student in the school but did fine in the higher-level classes. My mother thought it important that I get the best education possible and that I be pushed academically; she knew that education would be a significant element in my pathway to success.

Education has a high priority in much of middle- and upper-class white America. It may not be true for poorer white communities, but other than those, most white Americans recognize that a good education is the key to a good standard of living in the United States.

I have made this point to my two sons on occasion, as we sat at the dinner table. I have said, "Boys, tonight I am going to tell you how to make a million dollars," which piqued their interest. I said, "Boys, here is the way to make a million dollars. Graduate from college!" After they finished rolling their eyes, I explained that college graduates will generally make at least a million dollars more, in their lifetimes, than those who only have a high school diploma.[8] It was a way of saying to them that we expected them to go to college, apply themselves, and graduate with a degree in which they could get a job. We simply made this a family expectation; we talked about college and implanted in them the value of a good education.

Jamie

When I grew up, the expectations, in terms of education, were very low. The idea that I would finish college was a million light years from any conversation I ever had growing up. That possibility was simply not on the table. In the projects, none of the kids believed that college was a possibility for them. For that reason, it just never came up. I never heard going to college talked about by anyone as a real option for their life.

I was definitely going to school every day, but it wasn't because I needed an education in order to have a better life. My mother never said to me, "Education is your lifeline out of these projects, so you don't end up in my situation or that of your grandmother, uncles, and cousins." Instead, her attitude was, "I need a break from you, and you are getting out of here." One time I told my mother that I wasn't going to school because I was sick. I wasn't really sick but was trying to play her. She replied, "You may not be going to school, but you are getting the hell out of here. I don't care where you go, but I don't want to see you until 3:15." I said, "But I don't have bus fare to get to school." She said, "Here's a token for the bus; now get out of here."

Today young people who are poor might be able to get grants for college, and there is the HOPE Scholarship in Georgia that helps young people go to college, but there was none of that in my day. As far as the financial ability of my family to send me to college, well, we didn't even need to have that conversation, because it wasn't happening. My mom was just trying to survive; there wasn't any money to send me to college.

I got held back in school twice, once in the first grade and again in the fourth grade. So in the fourth grade, I was two years older than everyone else in my class. It wasn't that I was dumb; I just hadn't learned what I needed to learn. I wasn't getting it, and they did the right thing to hold me back. So, I had to do those grades over.

Like so many young black boys, my dreams had nothing to do with education. My biggest dream was to be a football player; that's the dream of a lot of young guys in the 'hood. Lots of kids today want to be football players, or rappers, or something like that. You don't need a good education for those things. But of course, the numbers of people who make their living doing those things is very, very small. But you don't think about that as a kid.

I went to school in some different places. I grew up in Athens, Georgia. When my mother married the man in the service, we went to Japan, and I went to school there. When he got transferred to New Jersey, I went to school there for a while. When they got divorced, we moved back to Athens, then to Atlanta, because my mother had a boyfriend there.

We were always a family package. I said previously that my mother was pretty and lots of guys wanted to date her, but she always told them that we were a package deal. If they dated her, they had to put up with us as well, and there were now three of us kids, my brother Ernest having been born in Japan. So my mother's boyfriend lived in Atlanta, and that is where I went to high school before I got kicked out.

Bob

I started elementary school in 1957 and high school in 1964. This was before integration and my school was very homogenous. I remember a very pretty girl who had black hair and dark eyes who lived on the other side of the neighborhood from me; she seemed quite exotic looking. On reflection, I realize she was Hispanic, one of the few in my circle of acquaintances who weren't white and European in origin.

My elementary school experience was mostly ordinary. I made friends and had many acquaintances. Education was a priority, but so was having fun. At recess, in elementary school, we played softball and kickball. Things weren't always organized on the playground, so groups of kids picked teams. When you got picked early you felt good; when you got picked last, it was a bummer. I experienced some of both.

I got my growth spurt in the fifth grade and started to get some athletic ability. This gave me a degree of self-esteem that I had not had before. I got pretty good at arm wrestling and, in the seventh grade, won first place in the county meet in the pullup event, with 20 pullups. My father had made me a chin-up bar in the back yard, so I could practice.

There is always plenty of drama in schools where you have young people but, in my schools, it wasn't mostly disruptive. In high school there would sometimes be fights after school in the lower parking lot, which was mostly out of sight from the administrative wing. I remember one spring week during my 10th-grade year, when there was a fight every day after school. People would gather around to watch several eighth-grade boys go at it. It seemed great fun until two older boys fought. One was a football player and the other what we called a "hood." The hood happened to be a local Golden Gloves boxing champion, and he bloodied and bruised the face of the football player very badly. It was a disturbing sight and ended the fights for the rest of the year.

There were always people getting into trouble in high school. Cigarettes were not allowed, so kids would secretly smoke in the bathrooms between classes, just to try to get away with it. Occasionally someone would light a cherry bomb, which was the most powerful firework you could buy, and flush it down the toilet. It would explode the pipes underneath the building and put the bathroom out of commission for a few days.

When I was in high school, there were a couple of weeks in which people would skip school and drive along the long front of the building where the classes were held blowing their horn. Someone in the back seat would "moon" the school through the open window. The highlight was a double bouncing moon, front and back seat, that some creative students pulled off. I don't know whether the administration caught them, but it was the highlight of the year's student pranksterism.

I was not part of any of this foolishness. For one thing, I feared the wrath of my parents, whose presence in my world was a governor that inhibited any bad behavior I might have considered. I was in school to grow up, learn something, and not get into trouble. I had heard my parents say that "an idle mind is the devil's workshop," so they were glad when I got involved with sports in high school.

I played most sports in high school and ended up focusing on football and track. In football I played fullback and defensive back; in track I was a pole vaulter. It gave me a place to make friends and find a sense of identity. It also kept me out of trouble because so much of my time was taken up in practice and trying to achieve my athletic goals. I had a moderately good high school sports career and one that gave me something on which to focus my energies.

In the long run, it was my education that would count the most of all my school experiences. I enjoyed athletics and even ran track,

63

as a sprinter, in college. While those pursuits seemed very important at the time, it would be my education that would allow me to move into the vocation in which I have invested the majority of my life.

Jamie

The elementary school I went to in Athens was Oglethorpe Elementary. The racial makeup was about 60-70% black; the other kids were white. Most of the black kids came from the projects; the white kids came from a neighborhood near the school, Forest Heights. We had a few black teachers, but most of them were white. I went to elementary school some in Japan but don't remember much of that.

My problem with school, at that point, was that things just weren't clicking, and I couldn't really read. I could do a little math; I could add, but not much else. The thing that saved me was that a teacher took an interest in me when I went to elementary school in New Jersey. I went to Martin Luther King Elementary School in Burlington, New Jersey, and had a teacher who realized I needed help; she took it on herself to help me. She was a white lady, and she would come by my desk and encourage me. She was a very nice and humble lady who was especially patient with me. This was probably in the fourth grade, the second time through; I can still feel how good it felt when I finally began to acquire the ability to read, and I am appreciative of her to this day.

When I think about why I had a hard time reading, one factor was that no one ever read to me at home. I don't actually remember us having a book in our house. My mother did get my brother and me a Bible one time, with some color pictures, but that was the only book in our home. We didn't have any books and didn't do any reading growing up. It might not be a surprise, therefore, that I wasn't doing well at reading. My mother could read, but it didn't dawn on her that she ought to read books to my brother and me. Again education wasn't stressed, and maybe she couldn't afford to actually buy any books.

Looking back, I am very grateful for the teachers that took an interest in me. When I came to Atlanta, one of my teachers taught me to subtract. I didn't know how to do that, only add. She taught me to subtract; then I learned how to multiply. These teachers will never know how much their extra effort did for me, but I will never forget it or them. During these years, I bounced around a lot, from place to place, so it may be another reason my lessons didn't sink in as well as they might.

Bob

My father had an engineering degree from Georgia Tech. My mother did not go to college because she came to Atlanta at 18 to work for Southern Bell. That the G.I. Bill provided a way for my father to afford college was a gift from God; otherwise he would certainly not have been able to attend Georgia Tech. My mother always wished she had a college degree and felt some sense of insecurity about it. She was extremely bright however and would have a good career as a real estate agent after my sister and I graduated from high school. She was also an amateur artist with natural talent; she painted portraits and had the rare ability to capture a likeness, as evidenced by the various family portraits in the home of my sister and myself today.

My parents expected me to make A's and B's in high school. I did not have to make all A's, but it was expected that I would not make any C's. I remember doing my homework for about an hour every night after football practice. I wasn't the best student, as I was more interested in my athletic career and my social life than my academics. But things generally came easy for me and I made decent grades. From the 10th through the 12th grades, I won the football team academic award for my grade every year. I'm not sure that was a reflection on my abilities as much as the fact that I was in upper-level classes and got extra points added to my grade-point average because of that.

I was better at math and science than other subjects; I was, at least, more interested in them, so it was not surprising that, like my father, I would attend Georgia Tech. It was easier to get into in those days, and I was accepted on my first application. It appeared that I was destined to be an engineer.

The reality is that I studied mostly to pass my classes. I passed two years of calculus at Georgia Tech, but can't say I actually learned the subject. In retrospect, I wish I had been more interested in my various courses, but I had other things on my mind. I wanted to graduate from college, and passing my courses was the way to do so. What I needed to do to pass, I did. For that reason, please don't ask me anything about calculus today because I don't have a clue. What my technical degree did give me however was an acquaintance with the sciences, which has, surprisingly, proven invaluable to me as a pastor.

When I graduated from college, I got a job working as a systems analyst for a company in Atlanta. Systems analyst was a fancy name for computer programmer; the company I worked for developed computer programs for engineering applications for the utility industry. I would spend three years working as an engineer before I went to seminary. It took me that long to figure out that my interests and calling did not lie in engineering.

It was a culture shock to go to seminary from an engineering school. I went to seminary essentially never having written a term paper. Instead of poring over a few dense formulas, trying to figure out what in the world they meant, I was suddenly faced with hundreds of pages of history, philosophy, and theology to read. It was a shock to me when my preaching professor took his red pen and circled words I had misspelled on the draft of my first sermon. It took me a while to adjust to a new environment in which there was lots of material to read and you had to spell words correctly.

I graduated from theological seminary with a four-year Doctor of Ministry degree. Upon graduation, I had assumed I would know all I needed about the Bible, Christian theology, church history, and congregational leadership. What I realized, instead, was that I only had a beginning. Upon graduation, I had the framework to begin a lifetime of study, which is what it would take to be a good pastor and theologian.

9

ATTITUDES

Jamie

IF YOU HAD ASKED ME what my favorite subjects were in middle school, I would have probably said math and social studies. I liked starting to understand math and I liked learning about history. Social studies gave me a sense that the world was a lot bigger than the little world I had been used to. It expanded my horizons, and I found that intriguing.

I did study some. I remember doing my homework at nights; I probably did it 90% of the time and didn't struggle too much with doing it once I got past elementary school. You had to do it because the teacher would call your mom if you didn't, so I knew I had to do it to avoid the hassle of them getting my mother involved. But by that time, I was getting high with drugs and alcohol, so that created other problems.

Early in my life, I got into bad things. By the sixth grade I was smoking marijuana and drinking. I was also starting to commit crimes, like shoplifting. My cousin had given me an early lesson in how to shoplift, and I was continuing to perfect the skill. I was also hustling at school.

By hustling, I mean that I was selling things on the side to make money. Hustling was a way of life in the projects, and it was also fun. It was fun to sell something at a profit, especially if you had shoplifted it and it didn't cost you anything to begin with. That's what all the bootlegger houses were about; it was just people in the 'hood hustling. We were all little businessmen and women trying to make a buck.

I had created a hustle at school selling candy. It was mostly candy I had shoplifted. I had it in my backpack, a big blue Speedo backpack, and I'd sell the candy out of my backpack. About a fourth of the backpack might have candy in it, so I had a lot. In fact, I had an entire grocery store of candy in my backpack. I'd sell it to people I saw in the hallways and in the bathroom and in class.

This got me into trouble, however. I had been selling candy in class, and it was causing a distraction for the teacher. I didn't realize it, I suppose, but I guess I wasn't paying that much attention to the teacher anyway. My teacher said, "Jamie, stop selling that candy. If you keep doing that, I'm going to take your backpack away from you." Well, after a little while, I started selling candy again. So she said, "Jamie, come up here and bring your backpack." I obviously didn't have much respect for her authority at this point, or authority in general. I said, "You can't take my backpack. This is my candy." I said, "My mom bought this candy for me; you can't take it." That was a lie, of course: my mom hadn't bought it for me, but I wanted to make it difficult for my teacher.

That was the first time we got into it. The next time was worse. One day she caught me selling candy in class again, and she came up to my desk. She grabbed my backpack and took it back to her desk. I decided that she wasn't going to take my backpack and went to get it back. She wouldn't give it to me, and we got into a struggle, both of us holding on to the backpack. The class was laughing hilariously at this point. In the end, I got really mad. I picked my teacher up and slammed her down on top of her desk. She was probably in her 30s, so she wasn't an old teacher. But she was wearing a skirt, and I'm sure it was an embarrassing moment for her, on top of everything else. It probably scared the daylights out of her as well. I took my bag and went back to my seat.

She immediately started crying and ran out of the room. I knew where she was going; she was going to the principal's office or to get another teacher. So I had to think quickly. I told the class that when they came back, everyone was to tell them that she had called me a "nigger."

Soon another teacher from the room next door came in. She must have heard the commotion, or maybe my teacher had gone to her first, before going to the principal. She called me over and said, "Why did you do that, James? What's wrong with you?" I told her what had happened. Of course I didn't really tell her what happened, but I told the story I had made up. I said, "Miss G, she called me a 'nigger." She said, "What?" Everything got real quiet then, and I could tell that she believed me, because, after they sent me back to my seat, she brought in another teacher. I could see them whispering together, and they were upset. I could tell from their faces that they had bought my lie.

The next thing I knew the assistant principal was in the class, and I got called to the school office. I held to my story, and the class backed me up. They suspended my teacher. She would eventually come back to our class, and I had to deal with her as my teacher for the rest of the year.

By a strange twist of fate, I had her as my teacher the next year, in the seventh grade. I was still determined that I was going to sell my candy, even in class. But she had her eye on me and certainly had reason to have a vendetta against me. By this time, I was also into more serious crimes. I was doing more than just stealing candy bars; I was running out of stores with cases of beer. Some friends and I had also started to experiment with stealing cars. In addition, I was getting high pretty regularly and would often come to school smelling of marijuana. I was only in the seventh grade, but my life was beginning to get out of control.

It was inevitable that my teacher and I would get into it again, and it was about me disrupting the class by selling candy, just like the previous times. It got physical and I pushed her. I also made the statement that got me suspended from school. I said, "You know, I don't really care about any of this." I meant that I didn't really care about whatever she might try to do to me. Then I said, "I'll kill everybody on this school wing. I'll come in here and shoot this place up." I didn't really mean it, of course; I was just trying to explain how much I didn't care about anything she had to say to me, but I probably looked like I would do it, with my bloodshot eyes

71

and the smell of marijuana on me. By that time, I was a big kid and two years older than other kids in my class. Obviously the principal didn't want a mass shooting at Bunche Middle School, so they suspended me completely from school.

Bob

In retrospect, I recognize how important teachers are in one's school experience. This was brought home again, when my own children were going through school. Your first-grade teacher is very important and becomes a special person to you. My wife and I were always very grateful for the attention, care, and energy our sons' teachers put into our boys' educational experience.

I don't remember too many of my early teachers. My third-grade teacher knew French and taught us to say some phrases in French; that made an impression on me. Several of my seventh-grade teachers made a significant impression on me – Mrs. Chandler, who was very bright but also gracious; she was the mother of one of my good friends. Mr. Walker was our physical education teacher and the first person I knew who worked out with weights. He was extremely cool, had big muscles, and was a hero to many of us aspiring seventh-grade athletes.

In high school, my coaches became important people. This is not to say they were always friendly; in fact they demanded a respect that bordered on fear. But, in retrospect, this was healthy and pushed me to try my hardest, even when there was some difficulty or pain involved, such as the "Oklahoma" drills in football. The football coaches made a big deal about the first one to get bloodied at practice, and it was a sign of appropriate effort on your part when that happened. I learned grit, discipline, and the value of hard work in my athletic endeavors. I also learned that you don't get everything you want. There wasn't much demand for only moderately coordinated 5-foot-10-inch guards on the basketball team and my basketball career ended in the 11th grade.

I mostly missed the era of integration and the drug era in both high school and college. My high school began to integrate my junior year with a few black students. There were six black students in my class my senior year. In college, the student body was mostly white and predominantly male, with a few black athletes and a number of Asian students. Georgia Tech would eventually become much more mixed, both racially and in terms of gender, but that was after my time.

Jamie

Our family was living in southwest Atlanta when I was in the seventh grade. We weren't exactly in the projects but a large set of apartments along Campbellton Road. The school I was in was predominantly black, about 95%. There may have been a couple of white teachers in the entire school, the teacher with whom I got into the fight being one of them. When you got kicked out of school in southwest Atlanta in those days, you got referred to the South Metro Psychoeducational Center. That sounds menacing, and in some ways, it was. They made my mother go to the school to hear about what I had done and why they had suspended me from school.

To get to the middle school, I had been taking a bus then getting on the commuter train. I rode a bus, then got onto MARTA, the Metro Atlanta Rapid Transit System, then another bus to get to school each day. The Psychoeducational school was on the other side of town however, so I had to ride a bus, but it took me all the way there. When I got suspended, my mother said, "They're going to come by and pick you up on a bus for your new school, so be ready when the bus comes."

The next morning, I was up waiting for the bus. I may have been having a little beer or a joint while I waited. I had been looking out the patio window daydreaming when suddenly I heard a loud honking, like a taxi cab. My mom came out of the back room. I heard the horn but wasn't really paying attention. I didn't want to get on any bus to go to any new school. She said, "Get up and get out there. That's your bus." I looked out, and there was a short bus. I said, "What? I don't want to get on that bus." She said, "Get out there. That's your way to school."

I went out the door and looked around quickly to see if any of my friends were watching. I didn't want them to see me getting on that strange bus. The woman driving was a stout black woman. When I got on, she told me her name and told me to sit down. She said, "Don't stand up on my bus. If you stay seated, everything will be all right. If you stand up, we're gonna have some problems."

The very first person I saw on the bus was a white boy wearing a football helmet. I said to myself, "This might be OK. Maybe this is a place where they play sports." I didn't know what to expect. There was a little girl there too who didn't look quite right. When the bus started off, I realized fast why the little white kid was wearing a helmet. As soon as the bus started up, he began to bang his head against the seat. About 15 minutes into the ride, the driver had to stop the bus and strap him into his seat. The little girl rocked back and forth the entire way. At that point, I said, "Am I tripping on weed or what? This is too weird. Where am I headed?"

At that point, I was already on probation from juvenile court. Some friends and I had broken into our elementary school. We thought there might be some money there from various fundraisers they had been doing and the candy sales at lunch. They must have taken the money to the bank because we didn't find any. All we came out with was a couple of rotary phones. We got caught and locked up. What I discovered is that I fit right in with a lot of the kids at the Psycho school who had also been in trouble with the police.

The school had two sections, one for the kids with mental disorders like the boy and girl on the bus, and the other for behavioral disorders. That was me. When I arrived, I had to report to the office of the assistant principal. He said, "We know what your record is and that you are on probation. So, welcome to South Metro Psychoeducational Center. We have lots of guys like you here who have been diagnosed with behavioral disorders." I didn't know that's what I had, but that's what he said. I knew that what he said about other guys from the 'hood being there was true, because I had already seen some guys I knew from hustling downtown or from the juvenile lockup. They had also been kicked out of the Atlanta public school system.

The assistant principal told me what was at stake for me. He said, "You have one last shot at getting an education. If you mess up here, you don't have anywhere to go. If you mess up here, no school system anywhere in the state will take you. We are the last ones who will give you a chance." If I had been smart, I would have realized that I needed to get it together, but I didn't. All I could think about was that before long I would reach an age where I didn't have to go to school. Then I'd be done with it.

I didn't like my friends seeing that I was going to the Psycho school, though they all knew it. For some reason, I didn't want them to see me getting on that little bus. So every morning, I'd pull my hoodie over my head and run out to the bus. Sometimes, they'd see me and all gather around the bus. I'd lay down in the seat to try to hide so they couldn't see me. They'd get around the bus and say, "Jamie, are you in there? We see you. You can't hide from us." They'd say, "I see him hiding. That's his coat." Then they'd bust out laughing. Though it was early morning, they were probably already high from smoking marijuana, just like I was. When I told my mom I wasn't riding that bus anymore, she gave me tokens so I could take MARTA to school.

I did eventually get back into the public school system, going to Carver High School in Atlanta. I'm not sure how, but I did actually learn some things while I was there. My math skills got better. I especially remember one teacher who took an interest in me. She must have been Muslim because I remember she always had her head wrapped; I also had a crush on her.

I made it through the 10th grade. It didn't take me long at Carver to get into trouble. What ended my school career, however, is that I got incarcerated for murder and armed robbery. At that point, even though I was only in the 10th grade, I was 17 years old, since I had been held back twice. This meant I was no longer eligible for juvenile court but had to go into the adult system. That is where things get very serious. I was 17 years old, facing two life sentences and things did not look good for my future.

Bob

I graduated from Georgia Tech with a degree in Industrial Engineering. After working for three years in Atlanta, writing computer programs for engineering applications and trying to figure out what I was supposed to do with my life, I discerned that I was being called into the ministry. With great excitement about the adventure of it all, I left my engineering job to attend a Presbyterian seminary.

I got a number of good things from my seminary education. One was obviously my biblical and theological training. The courses in Bible, theology, church history, and pastoral care have been invaluable to me as a pastor. I also made great friends, some of whom have been close friends and ministry companions for many years.

The other thing I acquired at seminary was curiosity. I had a roommate who graduated from Duke University in biomedical engineering. What was different about him was that he had actually learned his subjects in college. He had been interested in them and learned them, mostly for the sake of knowledge, irrespective of whether he would use them or not. This was a revelation and curiosity to me but a quality I admired.

He also had a dictionary and looked up words he didn't know. I'd say, "Morton, what does loquacious mean?" He'd reply, "That's an interesting word. Let's look it up in the dictionary." I'd reply, "Can't you just tell me what it means?" He wouldn't, and I'd have to listen to him read the dictionary definition, including the various origins of the word. That turned out to be quite a useful practice, and I would start doing the same thing myself. At one point I had a number of pages of difficult and unusual words for which I had written down the definitions. It increased my vocabulary and instilled in me a love of learning. I don't use "loquacious" in a sentence often, but if someone does, I know what it means.

Curiosity is a great gift and one that often lies dormant in us. Once we become curious, however, the sky is the limit because there is so much to learn. Life is incredibly interesting and, especially today, it is easy to learn about almost any subject. If there is one gift from which every child and young person would benefit, it is curiosity. This is a gift that education tries to impart to young people, though it does not always succeed.

10

CONVERSATION ABOUT EDUCATION

Jamie

I WANT TO START US OFF. This is a great topic to be having conversation about because we come from very different backgrounds, in terms of both our education and our culture's emphasis on it. I really enjoyed reading what you said to your sons on one occasion, telling them how to make a million dollars. Everybody wants to know how to get rich, and I loved the way you used that desire to implant in your sons the importance of a college education. The way to make a million dollars, over one's lifetime, is to graduate from college. I thought that was very sly of you.

Bob

I did some research to make sure I was right in what I said. It turns out that my fatherly joke was correct. Those with college degrees will, on average, earn a million dollars more during their working career. This is, in part, because there is an average yearly wage gap of at least $20,000 between those with college degrees and those without them.[9] To do the math, someone who works from age 25 until 65 will work 40 years. That extra $20,000 times 40 is $800,000. If you or the company you work for puts just $2,000 a year into a retirement fund and even it if only earns 6% interest over that time, the amount will be over $300,000. So that comes to $1.1 million total. Many college graduates will have the resources to purchase homes that will appreciate in value, which is an additional amount. So $1 million may actually be a low figure. The chances are that a college degree will earn you at least $1 million above what you would make without it. That turns out to be a lot of money that people leave on the table when they don't get a college degree.

It is also true that, in today's world, many of the newer jobs require college degrees, while those that do not require a college degree are declining. According to studies, people with only a high school degree are twice as likely to be unemployed as those with a college degree and three times as likely if you are a millennial (born between 1982 and 2000).[10] Especially during times of recession and economic difficulty, unemployment is higher for those without a college degree. Their jobs are also slower to return than those requiring higher education.

Jamie

These are all things I certainly didn't understand, growing up in the 'hood. I wanted to make a lot of money, but I didn't think education was the way to do so.

Bob

Here are some more statistics I find interesting. Those with a college degree are more likely to have health coverage. For that reason, they have a longer life expectancy. College graduates are more likely to be happy in their job and get a sense of satisfaction from their occupation. They are more likely to be homeowners, with 75% of home purchasers being college graduates as compared to only 11% who only have a high school education. They are also 10 times more likely to have a bank account as compared to those with only a high school degree. College graduates make good members of their communities, with 40% volunteering in their communities, as opposed to only 17% of those with only a high school education. In addition, they give three times as much money to charity.

I think it needs to be said that everyone may not wish to go to college or may not need to. My mother did not go to college and ended up having a very good career in real estate. The option of going to a trade school or technical college is also a good one that suits the preferences of some young people; no one should be ashamed of taking this route if they prefer or if it best suites their interests. There are lots of good jobs that require just a technical school degree that are good options for those who don't want to go the full college route, can't afford it, or just don't think they are suited for it.

You said that you had some teachers in New Jersey who were really helpful, giving you the individual attention you needed at that time. One of the things educators have learned is that there is a crucial window for learning to read; it is the third grade. The third grade is when students need to start to master reading because it's then that they have to begin to learn material. In this grade you go from "learning to read" to "reading to learn." If students get behind in the third grade, they have a hard time catching up because they are not able to master the material they need to learn. I also recently heard someone say that between the third and fifth grades is a crucial window for both reading and math. Children who are behind in reading and math after the fifth grade are much more likely to drop out of high school. For that reason, it is crucial to help children succeed in those areas during these critical years.

Jamie

That is really interesting information. I wonder how many parents realize this. If more of them did, they could help their children, especially at these ages. They could read to them and work with them to be sure they can read well by the end of the third grade. They could make sure they understand math, which I certainly could not do very well during those years.

Bob

This also highlights one of the major problems in some segments of society; it is that family systems are dysfunctional. In some of these situations, there aren't parents at home who encourage learning. Whether it is homes without fathers or homes where there is drug abuse or other issues, children don't have home lives that help them succeed. They don't have parents who are willing to work with them to help them do well in school. I know that it is also true that some parents, because of their own lack of education, don't really have the skills to help their kids with their studies.

Our church tutors at a nearby elementary school and one of the tutors was telling me how far behind was the girl with whom she worked. She was in the third grade but could only identify 11 words on sight. She should have had over 200 sight-words by that point. The problem was that she lived with her grandmother, who didn't have the educational background to help her. Our tutor didn't really know where to start.

Disdain for education also perpetuates itself in some instances. I had a teacher tell me that sometimes families discourage their children from higher education. A teacher might say to a student from a poor background, "You're really bright. You should think about going to college. We can get you grants to help you do so." When the student brings that message home, however, they don't get encouragement, in fact, just the opposite. Because the parent doesn't want to feel shamed about their own lack of education, they might reply, "So, what we have here is not good enough for you?"

Jamie

Like we said in the last chapter, so much of this comes back to the family. All families need fathers in the homes. It is a great crisis that there aren't more of them in homes in the black community. With the disarray in many black families, you can understand how a lack of educational motivation becomes generational.

Bob

You have a bright young black lady working here at the Sparrow's Nest who has just graduated from college. I have met her a few times and am very impressed with her. How is it that she went to college? Do you know her story and what motivated her?

Jamie

She had parents who both stressed education to her. The strange thing is that they are not black Americans; her family moved here from Ethiopia. Even over there they understood the value of education. That's why they came here, so they and their children could get good educations. She says that her mom loved school growing up and always stressed it. Her dad had an associate's degree. Her mom went to college in Ethiopia, and when she came to America, she went to Georgia State, in Atlanta.

So this young lady's heritage is not black America but black Africa. She truly is African American. What is odd is that she got her educational values not from black America, but black Africa.

Bob

That is odd, isn't it. America, of all places, should be a place that promotes and values education. It is rather convicting that someone in another country understands this better than we do.

Jamie

She is on her way to another degree after college. Her parents made it clear in their family that college was not optional. It was a mandatory expectation. I wish that had been the expectation in my household, but it was not voiced, not even once. It was never even spoken about.

My wife and I now have our 15-year-old granddaughter living with us. I have been pushing the importance of education to her. One of the great things these days is that you can get online and see your kids' grades. We can track her grades and her attendance. If she is late for school one day, we know it immediately and can address it. We've also put up guardrails to help her stay within certain boundaries. If she messes up, she doesn't get her allowance. If she gets good grades, we reward her. We've also discovered that taking her electronic device from her is great motivation. Since we pay for her phone, we feel comfortable taking it away if she does not apply herself. I've even got an app where I can shut off her access to the internet using my parental controls. I love that! We want to give her a shot at having a productive life. If she can get an education and keep God in her life, she will have that shot.

Many young black people don't realize how much money it will take to live. They think they can drop out of high school, get a job at McDonald's, and make a living wage. This isn't true. You can't have a decent standard of living that way. I heard about one young person who wasn't worried about finishing high school because his mom only paid $14 a month for her government housing. He assumed this is all it cost to rent an apartment. When his teacher told him what an ordinary apartment would actually cost, he was stunned.

In America, education is a great equalizer. For one thing, if you get a good education, you have the capacity to be mobile. It's one of the wonderful aspects of our country; you can move around. You can change cities, you can change neighborhoods, you can get a different job, and you can rise out of poverty. The great vehicle for movement in America is education. Sadly, not everyone in the black culture understands this. In fact, there seems to be a bias in some parts of my culture against academic achievement.

Bob

I suppose that some people might think of the lives of my two sons as privileged, and perhaps they are. One has graduated from college, and the other will do so shortly. But the reality is that, if they had chosen not to go to college, or dropped out of high school, their futures would be very different. I'm not saying that it might not be easier for a white high school dropout than a black one, but I am saying that it is my children's education more than their privilege that is going to make the difference.

My wife was a tremendous help in this. She understood, really more than I did, that we had to stay on them and make them do their homework every night. This wasn't always easy, especially when

84

they were young. They didn't want to do homework. They didn't like her checking their assignments and making them complete them when they would rather have watched TV. But she did, and it paid dividends. They eventually learned to study and realized they had to do so. When they got older, she made sure they took advanced classes to help with their college application process. When they were not doing their best, she made sure they knew that was totally unacceptable. We are all lazy, and our sons were no exception. They had to be trained, coached, and sometimes made to study. Today they would say that they are glad we did.

There is also something we did that I thought important. I tried to affirm their hard work. When they made a good grade, I would say, "You made a good grade because you studied hard. I'm proud of you for doing the work to get a good grade." I tried to commend their hard work because I knew good grades would result if they applied themselves.

We've also talked a lot about the importance of education in our family. There will be some people reading this who did not get a good education and for whom it might seem too late. The window of opportunity for most people is between 18 and 25. If they don't graduate from high school and complete college, or some technical college, by that time, it gets much harder. They have families and must spend their time working to make ends meet, so going to college or completing it becomes much harder.

I've thought about what people might do in those circumstances. It seems like, for those who can't fix the problem for themselves, they need to try to fix it for their children and their grandchildren. I may not have a great education, but I can make sure my kids don't make my same mistake. I can do everything within my power to impart to them the wisdom of a good education and give them the family stability and resources to achieve that goal. That, it seems to me, would be a very worthy goal toward which to strive.

Jamie

It is really hard to break generational cycles. I see it all the time. When I came to my senses in prison, I decided I didn't want to live out my life in the projects. That is what I had seen so many of my relatives do. I even remember at one point that my mother and uncle tried to get out. They had a trailer, and they wanted my grandmother to come with them to live in the trailer. My grandma wouldn't, though. She hadn't known anything but the projects and couldn't see herself leaving.

I decided, though, that I wasn't going to die in the projects like my grandma. My Auntie got killed in the projects. I watched my uncle get shot and killed in the projects when I was 5. As I thought about that, I prayed to God that he would help me. It was like making a vow to God that if he would help me, I would promise not to go back to the projects and that life. I knew if I did, I too might lose my life there. I didn't think that was what God wanted from me. I also knew I had to have a change of heart, and I was determined to do so.

Bob

Did you get your high school diploma?

Jamie

I did. I got it in prison. When I got out, I went to Georgia Technical College and got a business certification. You might say I made a complete turnaround. I didn't get a four-year college degree, but I did go to school beyond high school.

I'm afraid that one of our problems in the black community is that, especially for young black guys, it's not cool to be smart. In fact it's looked down on, like a person is an Oreo, black on the outside but white on the inside. The old joke is that if you want to hide something from a black person, put it in a book. President Obama acknowledged this problem in his 2004 Democratic Convention speech. He said, "Go into any inner-city neighborhood, and folks will tell you that government alone can't teach our kids to learn – they know that parents have to teach, that children can't achieve unless we raise the expectations and turn off the television sets and eradicate the slander that says a black youth with a book is acting white."[11] I'm afraid many young blacks still think that being smart and getting an education is "acting white."

Bob

Just one more thought on education: It is that education helps you think for yourself. When we learn things, it helps us form our own opinions, and that is important. If we can't think for ourselves, then someone else thinks for us; in a sense, someone else controls us. Knowledge helps us think as individuals. It seems to me that if we can't think for ourselves, then we either let our passions control us or, if we are not careful, someone else.

DISCUSSION QUESTIONS
PART 3 – EDUCATION

1. What were the educational expectations in your home growing up? How influential were those toward how you viewed education? Do you feel like you received encouragements or suffered disadvantages? What educational expectations did you have for yourself growing up?

2. Do you think there are educational advantages in middle- and upper-class schools that others do not have? What educational disadvantages do you think children from poorer communities experience? Explain.

3. Were you familiar with statistics, such as those mentioned in this chapter, about the wage and wealth disparity between those with college degrees and those without them? What seems important about this? Beyond the economic value of higher education beyond high school, what other benefits, such as personal growth, do you think might be important?

4. Jamie recounted the physical altercation he had with one of his teachers. Were discipline issues a significant factor in the schools you attended? What effect do you think these have on the learning environment? Are you aware of discipline issues in the schools in your community?

5. What is the best thing you gained from your education? Are there things you wish you had gotten but did not? What would you do differently if you had the opportunity?

6. Do you think that black young people are treated differently in the school system than white children and youth? If so, why do

you think this is? Do you think white teachers work as effectively with black students as black teachers? Why or why not?

7. Do you think that both white and black young people can achieve in today's educational system? What hinders white students? What hinders black students?

8. Were you aware of the importance of the shift, in the third grade, from "learning to read" to "reading to learn"? Also, of the importance of the third through fifth grade window in terms of reading and math skills? Why do you think students who are behind at the end of the fifth grade are more likely to drop out of school than those functioning at grade level?

9. Do you agree with the statement that education is "a great equalizer" in America today? Why or why not?

10. Do you agree with the statement that education helps people think for themselves? Why or why not? What is problematic about not "thinking for yourself"?

Left: Jamie as a young boy. Below: Jamie with his mother and his younger brother, Ernest.

The Bohler family standing outside the first family home on Oldfield Road in Decatur, Georgia. His father worked as an electrical engineer for Georgia Power Company. Below: Bob, his mother, and sister, Vicki in the backyard of the Oldfield Road house.

Jamie's grandmother with whom he was very close.

Jamie's grandmother's 2002 obituary. It was mentioned that she was one of the early residents of the Jack R. Wells homes on Pauldoe Street and was known for the beautiful flowers in her yard. Also mentioned are her deceased son, William Jewell, whom Jamie saw killed when Jamie was 5 and daughter Lucille, who was allegedly poisoned.

AROUND TOWN

MRS. ROSA BELL ECHOLS, gone but not forgotten was the first tenant to occupy Unit 465C Pauldoe Street, of the Jack R. Wells Homes. She moved into this unit in April 1967 and remained there for thirty-one years before transferring to a downsized unit at 190A Pauldoe Circle, where she remained until her passing in March 2002; a thirty-five year icon. She won the best yard of the month in 1968 at the 465C unit. Known for her plants, some which she had owned for forty years at the time of her death, Mrs. Echols was the mother of five children of whom two preceded her in death during their residency at Pauldoe: Mr. William Jewell Echols, 1975 and Miss Lucille Echols, 1980; the late Mr. John R. Echols in 2008, Mr. Leroy Echols in 2013 and surviving child Mrs. Ellen Echols Palmer of, Marietta, GA.

Top: Bob's father sitting in the swing with Bob and his sister, Vicki. Below: Bob with his mother and sister sitting on the steps of the first family home on Oldfield Road.

Jamie at age 9 with his mother and brother at Thanksgiving dinner.
Everyone is having wine with the meal. Below: The house in
Pauldoe where Jamie grew up. It is the one story apartment on the
left. Jamie at 14, which was the age at which he began stealing cars.

Bob standing on the back porch at the family's second home on
Hammett Drive in Decatur. His father built the patio. They are in
their Boy Scout uniforms. Bob's father was the scoutmaster. Below:
Bob in his little league uniform at age 10 and receiving his God and
Country Award in scouting with two others at age 14.

PART 4 – WORK, POVERTY, AND WELFARE

11

PERSPECTIVES ON WORK

Bob

MY FIRST WORK EXPERIENCE was during the summer after my 10th grade year. The county hired high school boys during the summers to work on road crews. It was cheap labor and gave the county the chance to finish projects that were backlogged. Usually they put all the "schoolboys," as they called them, together in crews by themselves. For whatever reason, my application came in late, and I was assigned to work with a regular crew. It was an odd assortment of characters and an early education into a world I had not experienced.

My father got the job for me. He had heard that the county hired young people for the summer. He told me I had a job, and my mother dropped me off at the county work department for my first day of work. I was making the entry wage for employment at that time, which was $1.50 an hour. That seemed fair to me, and I was glad to have some income. My crew's job was to go around the county and patch potholes with asphalt.

The crew was run by a foreman, Mr. Pratt. It typically had about seven people on it. One of the guys on our crew was Jim, who was in his 60s and on the verge of retirement. He didn't do any of the hard work; he was the "pick man." When we came to a pothole, you had to remove the pieces of asphalt that were cracked. Jim would take his pick and loosen them up before someone else shoveled them into the back of the pickup truck. There was some apparent arrangement between Mr. Pratt and Jim that he would be the pick man, and others who were younger and more fit would do the more demanding jobs.

Another member of the crew was named Shorty. Shorty was short in height and walked with a limp. He had a stiff leg; I never did hear why. As a schoolboy on the crew, you didn't ask a question like that of a regular. Shorty was the "tar man." When the pothole was cleaned out, someone took a bucket of warm tar and put it around the edges of the hole. This helped keep the asphalt in the hole. As the tar man, Shorty drizzled the tar around the edges of the hole when it was cleaned out. It wasn't difficult and, again as by agreement, this was Shorty's job on the crew.

I had the sense that Shorty and Mr. Pratt were particularly close. They had a lot of inside jokes between them, and Mr. Pratt did his best to watch out for Shorty. I assumed he, like Jim, was a longtime member of the road crew. The notable thing about Shorty was that he rarely came to work on Mondays. Everyone got paid on Fridays, and he apparently spent the weekend drunk. It took him until Tuesday to get back to work.

The county road crew was my job for two summers, following my sophomore and junior years in high school. There were several middle-aged guys on the crew who all had a bit of an edge to them; I didn't generally interact with them. There was a young guy about my age one summer who had dropped out of high school. He did not seem to have college aspirations. In general, it was an assortment of strange characters who gave me an education about a side of life I had not experienced. I mostly spoke when spoken to, worked hard, and did my job.

My father thought I ought to work some construction in my life, and this job fit that category. His goal was for me to experience hard work, partly for its own value and partly as an incentive to graduate from college, where I would be more likely to spend my life not having to do manual labor. The job served those purposes as well as giving me a broader education about people.

As a schoolboy, you did all the hard work and, quite frankly, I didn't mind. I shoveled the loose pieces of asphalt from the pothole into the dump truck that followed us. You had to heave it over the 6-foot side of the truck, so it was hard work. When the hole was cleaned out and tarred, the asphalt truck would back up and open its gate. We'd shovel steaming asphalt into the pothole until it was filled. Then the younger members of the crew and I would use a hand tamp to tamp down the asphalt until it was flat and hard. We'd then load up to travel to the next pothole.

Mr. Pratt had a favorite saying. When we came to a pothole and got out of the truck, you grabbed a shovel. As various people were doing their parts, you would inevitably end up standing around with your shovel. When it was time for you to do something, Mr. Pratt would say, "While you're standing there holding up that shovel, why don't you get that loose asphalt into the dump truck." The entire experience was a good lesson in the value of hard work. It also taught me the lesson my father wanted me to learn; I needed to get an education so I didn't have to do manual labor all my life.

Jamie

In the projects where I grew up, there were different levels of poverty. You could be poor or really, really poor. For example, there was a family in our neighborhood that had five kids. They were very poor. They didn't have decent clothes because everything they wore had been passed down from child to child so many times. Other kids in the neighborhood picked on them because they were so badly dressed.

This family was poor because they had a father who shot dice. He gambled, and I guess he wasn't very successful at it because that's where the little money they had went. I also heard that he and my father got into it at one point. I think he had cheated my father, or my father cheated him. Whatever happened, my father shot him.

They say he shot him five or six times, and one of the bullets actually ended up staying in his chest. He didn't die, however, which was a miracle. There was another family in the projects that had three or four children and was very poor. Their mother was an alcoholic, and they had it real bad.

In the projects, I didn't know many people who worked. At one point, my grandma had picked cotton. I used to hear her tell stories about it. I actually think my great grandmother was a slave or maybe my great, great, grandmother. I heard little conversations about it a couple of times, but it was a shameful secret no one wanted to discuss.

I had a cousin who worked until he got sick. My uncle worked in a bar from time to time. My grandmother also helped someone clean and would do work for her, maybe once a month and on holidays, like before Christmas. The lady who employed her would sometimes come over and bring us food and things, which was very nice. Really, though, the goal for most people wasn't working but figuring out a way to get a government check, because then you didn't ever have to work anymore for the rest of your life.

This is not to say that people didn't have their own hustles going on. My uncle had a bootlegger house. His name was Leroy, and they called him "Hawk." I think Hawk was short for Hawkeye, because he always knew what was going on. In his bootlegger house, he sold illegal alcohol, and he was open for business 24 hours a day, seven days a week. He was also a sharp dresser. Anytime you wanted something, you could go to his house, and he'd set you up. Alcohol, even some weed; you just knock on the door. So I guess you'd say he was a little entrepreneur. He also got disability.

I knew two people who got disability because they cut off their fingers; my uncle was one of them. That was one way you could get disability, cut off one of your fingers. I had a great uncle named Jimmy Lou who cut off his pointer finger. The way you did this was with an axe. You just chopped it off. He had a nub just below the knuckle. I didn't see him do it, but it was whispered that this is what happened.

My Uncle Leroy was actually missing two fingers. He may have lost one in some sort of accident, but the other he cut off himself to be able to get a disability check. Or he may have cut them both off; I'm not sure. I remember one time, when the family was all together and everyone was drinking. People got to laughing at him about how he cut off his own finger. He got boiling mad about it and didn't like people making fun of him.

There were a lot of nubs in the 'hood where I grew up. I don't know if they had all been cut off, only that I saw a lot of them. There was another man in the projects with several nubs. He was a "gangster" and wore a big diamond ring on one of his nubs. People called him, "Pretty Finger." He drove a "deuce and a quarter," a big canary yellow '67 Chevy. When the liquor stores closed, his bootlegger house opened up. You could go there and get a drink at 3 o'clock in the morning. Sometimes he'd sleep in the living room so he was available if anyone knocked on the door in the middle of the night.

At one point, when I was doing lots of bad things, I went to his house for a drink. He was a big man and had trouble breathing. He wheezed when he talked. I remember him saying to me, in his raspy voice, "Let me tell you something, boy. If you ever come up here and try me, I'm going to shoot the hell out of you." I didn't mess with Pretty Finger.

In the projects, the goal was never to get a job and work. It was to get a disability check. Everyone also understood that doing so was a process. You didn't get it the first time you applied; you had to know how to work the system. When you first applied, they turned you down. That's just how the system worked. Then you applied again. Usually you got turned down a second time. The third time you applied, however, you usually got approved. This is what everyone understood in the 'hood. You had to have a doctor's statement, of course, but if you were patient, you could generally get your check. And, of course, you had to have some disability like having lost a finger in an "accident."

Bob

My father was a hard worker. This was a value that had been taught to him growing up. When he attended Berry High School and College, he had to work for his room and board, and they gave every young person serious chores and assignments. My father remembered spending many days working on what now is a beautiful stone chapel located on the Berry campus.

My father had some sayings that he heard growing up and thought important to pass along to me. One was, "Any job worth doing is worth doing right." He meant that I shouldn't do things halfway but do them well and the way they should be done. I remember one day after I had finished cutting the grass in the backyard, my father made me redo it. Something about how I'd done it was sloppy and he fussed at me for cutting corners. I recut the back yard.

Another of my father's sayings was, "An honest day's work for an honest day's pay." I've said before that my father was honest to a fault, and he thought this particularly applied to employment. If you were being paid to do something, don't cheat your employer. If he hires you to work, do you best and make sure he gets his money's worth. That was a good lesson and one that I continue to hear in my head from time to time.

About the time I was in the eighth grade, my father served as an elder in our church, Memorial Drive Presbyterian Church in Stone Mountain, Georgia. He was chairman of the property committee. The church had a large front lawn that needed regular maintenance in the summer, and he hired an older boy and me to help him with lawn maintenance. Each Saturday morning, we'd go to the church. The older boy would ride the lawnmower and cut the grass. My father was often frustrated that the older boy didn't go around and pick up paper before he began to cut. If you ran over a piece of paper with the lawnmower, the chopped-up pieces went everywhere. The simple solution was to walk around and pick up pieces of paper before you cut. That the older boy often ran over the pieces of paper irritated my father who wanted the grass to look perfect on Sunday mornings, which it usually did.

My job was to do other things that needed doing. I would often edge the very long driveway coming into the church and leading out the other side. The grass at the church sent out runners that would grow over the curbs. All I had was a pair of clippers with which to bend over and cut loose the runners. It was backbreaking work, and I remember many Saturday mornings spent clipping runners off the curbs at church. My father paid me $1.50 an hour and the older boy a bit more. He prided himself in how good the church looked in those years, and I must admit that it had never looked better.

Jamie

In the 'hood, people learn how to get welfare. I knew someone who got it when he was assigned to the Psychoeducational school. When you go to the Psychoeducational school, the first thing that happens is that you see the counselor. This young man's mother went with him to the appointment. When they got home, his mother explained to him what he needed to do. She told him they were going to send him to the state psychologist for a psychological evaluation. She said to him, "Here is your chance, boy. I'm going to tell you what to do, and you'd better do it. When you go see the psychologist, you'd better act like you're crazy. That's the only way for us to get a check." She knew he could get a disability check if he was either physically or mentally disabled.

What she told him he had to do was convince the psychologist that he had a problem. It couldn't be just a behavioral problem; you couldn't get a check for that. It had to be a physical or mental problem; something had to really be wrong with you. It was all a process, but the first step was that you had to impress the state psychologist with your disability. She said, "You want to go shopping downtown and be able to go places and do things? Then you had better get this right!"

So when he went to see the psychologist, he had 20 bows on one arm, all the way up to the elbow. These were hair bows like go in a child's hair to make pigtails. He had a Kermit the Frog hair bow and little ones that were pink and green. He also had a tie around his neck that was not tied right. His eyebrows also had mustard or something like that on them.

She told him, "If they give you wooden blocks to stack, or letters of the alphabet with colors on them to put in order, don't do it. Just push them off onto the floor. Or better yet, throw every damn one of them. Then start talking to your imaginary friend." He had decided to have an imaginary friend that he talked to when he went in there. He gave him the name Kabuki, which was the name of the wrestler on TV who used to spit poisonous mist on his opponents. She also said, "They're going to give you a puzzle to solve where you have to put the horse with the horse picture and the pig with the pig picture. When they do that, you had better not put that damn pig where it's supposed to go. Put it on top of the horse or the frog. Or better yet just throw it."

Apparently he convinced the counselor that he had serious problems. That only starts the process, however. It takes a number of years to get officially approved. A few years later, after he had served time in prison, he discovered that he had been approved for disability. What happens is that they begin your payments from your initial diagnosis. So he had a few years of disability accrued, and when the first check came it was for $21,000. This was a family check that his mom used for the family. Later on, there would be another large check that was about $13,000. That's how you get welfare in the inner city, and that's how people work the system. When people don't have fathers to help provide for them, the government becomes the one who does.

12

ACCUMULATING ASSETS

Jamie

I GOT MY FIRST REAL JOB AT AGE 37 when I finally got out of prison. Up until that time, I had hustled on the streets but hadn't actually had a real job. At that point, however, I had new goals. I decided that I wanted to get married and maybe even have a house. I wanted a car to drive and other things. So one day, sitting in jail, I ran the numbers to see if my government checks would be enough for my new goals. What I realized was that the little amount I was going to be getting from the government wasn't nearly enough for the things I wanted to do. If I was going to make any kind of serious money, I was going to have to work.

When I got out of prison, my mother had me all set up. She said, "Listen Jamie, we've got you a trailer set up on a piece of property. The water and electricity are turned on so you can have TV. It's fully furnished. Go down to the Social Security office and get your disability check reinstated. Now that you've got God in your life you can stay out of crime. You're set; we've got it all worked out." I said to her, "No, mother, I'm going to get a job." She crinkled her face, looked at me with a funny expression then laughed. She said, "What? What you mean? Where you gonna get a job? Who's going to hire you"?

I had not had many jobs up to that point in my life. I had occasionally raked leaves and cut a few lawns. I worked at University of Georgia football games on occasion selling Coca-Cola's or programs. Of course, they never got the money for any of those because I kept it all. Needless to say an ex-felon with no experience can't get a job just anywhere. But I knew I wanted to change my life. I had read where the Bible said, "Let the one who stole, steal no longer" (Ephesians 4:28). I had also read, "If anyone will not work, let him not eat" (II Thessalonians 3:10). I knew I had to get my first job.

I ended up getting a job at the only place that would hire an ex-con; I went to work in a chicken plant. Most of us eat a lot of chicken, but we don't think about where it comes from. It all has to be processed, and that happens in chicken plants. There was one outside of Athens, and I got a job there. In the chicken plant, they don't care what your background is, and there isn't any racism when it comes to hiring. If you are willing to work, they will hire you, because it's hard work and it's dirty. They need people, and if you are willing to process chickens, you can get a job. So I got a job there.

The first position I got was in sanitation, cleaning up. There's a lot of mess in a chicken plant that has to be cleaned up, and that's what I did. I had hoses where I washed things down and some hoses with chemicals in them. It was hard, and sometimes you had to get down on your knees to get things clean.

I almost lost the job right after I got it; I think I'd been there less than a week. I was using one of the hoses that had chemicals in it; bleach, I think. It had pressure on it and got away from me; some of it sprayed in my eyes. Even with rinsing my eyes out with water, they were still stinging bad. So I went to the supervisor and said, "I think I need to go to the doctor." My eyes were bloodshot and red at that point.

He said to me, "Were you wearing the goggles you are supposed to be wearing?" I said, "No sir." He said, "Okay, give me your ID badge, because you're fired. You are supposed to wear your goggles when you use the hoses." At that point, I had just gotten married and needed to keep the job. I said, "No, that's OK. I'm good," and walked away. He didn't say anything, and I kept my job.

I went from that job to being a USDA trimmer in the plant, trimming chickens coming down the assembly line. That's an awful job, but someone has to do it. The plant processed 300,000 chickens a day, and they came down the assembly line very fast. You can't run 300,000 chickens if you don't move them fast. As a trimmer, you have a sharp butcher knife, and you're looking for anything on the chickens that isn't supposed to be there, like parts of the gall bladder. You see something green, and it's gall bladder, so you cut it off. Also anything that's yellow has to go.

You've also got a USDA inspector standing there pointing out things. There is a table with three people at it; one of them is the inspector, and he's pointing out things as the chickens come whizzing by. You've got to catch them, cut off the bad parts, and throw those away. And you've got to work fast.

Like I said, it's dirty work. You can sometimes catch the smell of the plant when you are driving up and it's awful. On the inside they keep the air moving, so it's not too bad. But most people wouldn't enjoy their chicken as much if they knew what it took to get it to them. At that point, however, it was the best job I could get. I started off at $10.25 and then went to $10.50 after 30 days. I also had health insurance which was a big deal to me at that point.

I eventually moved up to being a quality control person. That was a much better job; you got to walk around with a clipboard and check things out. You also got to stay clean.

I had never filed an income tax form at this point; I'd never had enough income, at least official income. Someone said that if I filed an income tax form, I could get some money back. I thought that was great and filed my first income tax form. When I got my tax refund, I thought it was terrific, until I understood a little better how all that worked. In the 'hood, I didn't know anyone who filed tax returns, although I suppose some people did. When I filed my first income tax return, I knew I had moved into a larger world.

Bob

At one point in my parents' lives, it dawned on them that they had the opportunity to accumulate assets. As I have said, they both grew up in significant poverty, my father in particular. When they married and he graduated from college, they began their careers and started a family. My mother worked until I was born and was a housewife until about the time my sister and I graduated from high school. My father worked as an engineer and would spend his entire career with the same company, rising in the ranks to just below the level of a vice president.

The first years of my parents' lives were focused on survival and starting a family. My mother, however, was ambitious and always looking for ways to better our situation. At one point, she saw the opportunity for us to move into a larger home and encouraged my father to take the risk. In the summer after my second grade year, we moved to a new neighborhood that was being built with much nicer "split-level" homes. I remember that the house payment was at the upper edge of what my parents could afford, which I remember as being $121 per month, but they thought it worth the risk. It would turn out to be a perfect neighborhood for our family and situated us securely in the middle class of that era.

My parents accumulated assets slowly, over their entire lifetimes. The company for which my father worked had a "profit-sharing" plan, which meant that, for each year he worked, the company gave him a certain number of shares of stock. This was a perk of working at the company, and it got tax breaks for doing so. Over an almost 40-year career, he would accumulate a significant amount of stock.

When my mother got into real estate, she discovered she had a gift for working with people. Her family was full of great salespeople, and she had inherited both that ability and gift. Her family had a gift for making money; had my mother not spent most of her life as a wife and mother, she would have been very successful in that regard. As it was, she made good commissions that helped pay for college for my sister and me. She made enough to have some left over to put into other real estate investments.

In the process of selling homes, my mother realized the value of letting someone else pay off a house through rent. My parents began purchasing homes as rental properties. My mother would find a good deal, and my father would make the needed repairs. My mother would interview renters and hold their feet to the fire in terms of their monthly payments. To be a landlord required some effort, but my mother knew that to make money required labor; there was no free money. For them that meant keeping the houses in good shape and managing their tenants.

At one point, my mother wanted to purchase a house every year. She saw this as a way to accumulate significant wealth in our family. Her plan was to purchase a rental house every year for 10 years, ending up with 10 rental properties. My father said, "Absolutely not!" At that point, he was tired of fixing up houses and keeping them in working order, getting calls at odd hours about a toilet that didn't work. He would later say that it was a mistake not to follow her plan, but he was simply too tired at the time. In all, they would purchase four rental houses. They did not own them long enough to get any of them completely paid for, but it did allow them to accumulate some equity. They would often sell a rental house and use the proceeds to buy a better rental house or a new house in which to live.

They would own and live in five homes throughout their lives, each one an upgrade from the previous one, in terms of price and square footage. For one of them they had the resources to pay cash for it. At the time of their deaths, they owned two homes outright, a duplex outright, and a large home that still had a mortgage. There was money in their bank account and their stock portfolio. All in all, they had done quite well for people who came from nothing but good values, Christian beliefs, and a willingness to work hard. The best investment they made turned out to be a lake house, in which my father did most of the construction, putting in the wiring and electrical systems, etc. in the framed-in shell. It would accumulate in value over 10 times its original cost. My mother had an instinct that it would be a good investment, and she was right.

My mother always had a big heart and did good in a variety of ways. Whenever our church got a new pastor or associate pastor, she always helped them purchase a house. As part of her generosity, she always gave them her commission, which helped save them some money. It was something she could do and she thought it right not to take money away from one of her pastors, even if she had earned it through her hard work finding them a house.

Another good thing she did was encourage one of my best friends to purchase rental property. He had grown up very poor and always said that one of his life's goals was to "get rich." He caught the vision of purchasing a rental house that someone else would pay off. Over his career as a teacher, he would purchase five rental homes that others would pay off for him with their rent. He ended up being quite successful and acquiring significant wealth; he always gave my mother credit and said that if it had not been for her, he never would have been able to do what he did.

Jamie
One of the ways people survive in the projects is by getting federal assistance through programs like SNAP (the Supplemental Nutritional Assistance Program). Most people still call this food stamps, but now they are accessed through EBT (Electronic Benefit Transfer) cards. These are debit cards that can be used for food, and cash in some states, at certain retail and grocery stores. The EBT cards are an attempt to reduce fraud, but it still happens.

In the inner city, things get sold on the black market for half price. Since most EBT cards do not have a picture ID and most stores don't check the names on the cards, you can sell them or let someone else use them, by giving them the PIN number. A mother who gets $400 put onto her EBT card each month can sell part of it to someone else for cash. She may sell $150 worth and get $75 in cash. That's $75 in cash she gets because she has so many children. Or she may buy food with other money and sell an even greater portion of her monthly allowance. She can then use the money to get her hair and nails done or go to a club or buy something she wants. She doesn't need to save any of it because more money will be put onto her card the next month. It's never a problem doing this, even though it's illegal, because it's such a good deal. And people sometimes sell their actual cards then say they lost them and apply for a replacement. You can see that we are not talking big money here, but for people living in poverty it is a way to survive. People learn to work the system.

When I was growing up, I didn't want to go to work; I thought I'd miss something that was going on. I wanted to be in the streets, so I could be where the action was. I think more black people are working today than when I was growing up. I think more black people are realizing that if you want to have things like a car and a home, you've got to work to get them.

Where I grew up, if you were a black person, you didn't really think about owning a home; that was not really in the cards for you. But you could have a cool car and maybe jazz it up. And you could wear some bling. Even in the projects today you'll see nice cars, a Mercedes-Benz and others. These belong to the guys who are hustling in the streets, selling drugs or whatever else. My uncle who had the bootlegger house always drove a big Cadillac. He had a nice big car and dressed sharp. But he lived in a little apartment. One time he bought some land and put a trailer on it, but he ended up not liking it out there; it was too far out of town. That was the trailer I lived in for a while after I got out of prison.

Of course, if you didn't have a legal business, you had to pay cash for a car, and that's what people did in the 'hood. I don't know where they kept all their cash; I suspect they didn't have bank accounts. I do remember that my uncle always had big rolls of cash on him.

If you are going to buy a house, however, you've got to have a real job and some credit. You can't just walk up and pay cash for a house; that looks too suspicious, and no one has that kind of money. But I think more blacks are beginning to change their attitudes.

They don't want to live in the projects anymore. They want their own homes. It's one of the things I'm very proud of, owning a home.

I do think black people get a little discouraged about working. They think there is a "glass ceiling" they can't break through, and they are not going to get as far as a white person. There was this guy at the chicken plant, a black guy named Jay. He'd been at the plant for 30 years and knew everything about it. He had a good position; he was the third-shift supervisor, and he made decent money.

One day he was telling me, however, that he was always having to train white guys that they hired over him. Maybe they had a better education or something that gave them a leg up on him, but he never got put into one of the top positions. He actually had a college degree himself. He came from California and I think graduated from UCLA.

But he never got the manager positions when they came open; it always went to a white person that he would have to train. He told me, "You may think the sky's the limit, but you are only going to be able to go so high. There's always a glass ceiling for a black man."

Bob

No one in my family ever imagined living on welfare or using food stamps. It was not only a foreign world to us but would have been a source of terrible shame. After graduating from college, I worked for three years as an engineer and then left for seminary to pursue my calling as a pastor. People have asked me if it was hard to leave what would have been a more lucrative career in engineering to become a pastor. My answer is always "no"; in fact, there was nothing that could have stopped me from changing careers once my call to ministry became clear. It was a compelling call that I felt I must answer and that almost nothing could have kept me from pursuing.

It did help, however, that I was 25 years old and single, so starting over seemed a great adventure. If I had a family that would

112

have been uprooted for the endeavor, it probably would have been more difficult, but that was not my situation.

I entered the Presbyterian Church at a time in which the church was taking thought for the salaries of their pastors. The old paradigm was that the pastor barely survived; for that reason, there were retirement communities for former pastors and especially retired missionaries. I heard someone in a former church put it this way: "Our prayer is, 'God, you keep our pastor humble; we'll keep him poor.'" I came up in an era in which that general sentiment was changing.

One way it changed was to move from a parsonage model to allowing pastors to own their own homes. In former generations, pastors could never accumulate enough wealth to purchase a home; instead, churches provided them a house, often on the same piece of property as the church. This enabled the pastor and his family to enjoy a nice home but also kept him close at hand in case of emergencies. In the 1980s, there was a push in the Presbyterian Church to encourage churches to sell their manses and provide housing allowances, so pastors could purchase homes and build equity. The goal was often stated that by their retirement, a pastor would be able to own a home. That way, they would have a place to live, and the denomination would not have to provide extra assistance for them.

For most of my life as a pastor, until just recently when my parents died and I inherited money from them, my family has lived modestly and finances have been tight, without a great deal of cushion in the budget. This is not to say that we lived in poverty, far from it, but rather solidly in the middle class. The philosophy of the church, in the past few decades, has moved in the direction of paying pastors at a level that is somewhat in line with the congregation's general membership. The Bible says that the laborer is worthy of his wages, and I have appreciated being able to live modestly but comfortably. You don't go into the ministry to get rich financially but to be rich in other ways. In the example of my parents, however, my wife and I did find ways to save toward retirement, accumulate some assets, and not live so close to the edge that we didn't have enough left over to tithe to the church and give to others in need. We have also been able to live in such a way that we were not in danger of losing our home if an emergency arose.

Jamie

There is an underground network in the inner city, and it reaches into all sorts of lower-class communities. For instance, during breaks at the chicken plant, you could get access to all sorts of contraband goods. People had all sorts of hustles they were running. You could find someone who had hot merchandise, like pocketbooks and purses. They might be knockoffs, or they might be the real thing. If you went out into the parking lot, you could pick up a flat-screen TV, hot off the shelf, from out of a person's trunk. There were even people who could get you washing machines, dryers, and all kinds of clothes. You could get women too, if that's what you wanted, and it all ran through the dope trap.

The black market is a product of street life, and it's all fueled, in some way, by drugs. At the heart of it is people buying and selling drugs. Of course, the drug trade has changed. It used to be that people had to stand on the street corner and wait for customers. Today everyone has a cell phone. If you want some drugs, you call someone up. That keeps them out of sight of the police. The drug dealer says, "Just hit me up on my cell phone, and I'll come down with what you need or tell you where to meet me."

There are all sorts of levels in the drug trade. You got some guys in supervision and management, just like in a business. You got the people who work at the beginning of the chain and say, "OK, give me some kilos" of heroin or cocaine. You don't usually see those guys. Of course, you've got the "coyotes" who sneak it in from the cartels in Mexico. Then you got the lower-level employees. These are the guys on the streets hustling it to actual users, and these are the guys you see. A white person living in the suburbs doesn't really see any of this, but everyone living in the 'hood knows who these people are. It's why it's so easy to get drugs and why so many people end up having drug problems.

Back when I was doing drugs, my mom took out an insurance policy on me, payable on death. This meant that if I died, she would get a lump sum of cash. I didn't know how I felt about that, but at that point my chances at long-term survival didn't seem very good, so I suppose it was a good investment on her part.

One of the problems with people not working is that they never contribute to Social Security. This is a safety net the government has set up. It helps you have something to live on in retirement. But if you never work, you don't contribute anything to it and can't draw from it. The importance of this finally dawned on me. If I would work, I could contribute to Social Security; that way, when I got to be 65, I could retire and have an income and one that would be a lot better than a small government disability check. I try to tell people this; if you want to get a Social Security check, you've got to get out and work. Everyone's going to get old, and if you are not careful, you won't have anything. I wish someone had explained this to me a lot earlier.

The problem with government assistance is that it does not go very far. I remember one time when I got my disability check at the first of the month. In four hours, I had spent it all and was broke. I had spent it all on crack cocaine and some alcohol. I said to myself, "Man, this is bad; I've got to wait another 30 days for my next check!"

The appeal of a government check is enticing, however. I had a young woman tell me one time that she only paid $14 a month for her housing. The government took care of the rest, including her utility bill. She also got food stamps on top of that.

That sounds like a great deal, but it ends up sentencing you to poverty for your entire life. If, on top of things, you have a drug habit, then you really hit the skids. If you are trying to buy crack or heroin or meth with that little bit of money, it runs out real fast.

Then if you have a couple of children, it's awful for them. They don't even have food to eat because it's all going for your drug habit.

What happens is that the children end up raising themselves because their mom is on drugs. It turns out to be the street that raises the children, and we know how that turns out. The street raises hoodlums, which is why there are so many in inner-city communities.

Kids love their moms however, and a lot of kids on the streets want to help them. They say, "One day, I'm going to do something nice for my mom. Maybe I will buy her a nice house one day." You hope to be a big football player and make lots of money so you can buy your mom a house.

You can see why selling drugs is a big draw; it's the only way people in the 'hood think they will have things. They see the drug dealer, and he's got a shiny car. Maybe he's got some gold teeth, and he dresses real nice. So young guys start to idolize him and think they can better their situation, like he did, through selling drugs. They don't have fathers to look up to, so they idolize the drug dealers. But it never works out. You never acquire any real wealth, and most drug dealers eventually end up in prison.

One of the problems for the black community, particularly in the inner city, is acquiring assets. Without jobs, it is hard to acquire any wealth. This means that children don't inherit wealth from their parents. I do know some people in the inner-city community that have gotten money through lawsuits. They have taken advantage of opportunities to sue stores, individuals, and corporations. Just let a grocery store leave some water standing on the floor, and they see an opportunity. For some, it has seemed the only way to acquire any wealth, and they have pursued it, often successfully.

As I have said, I am very excited that I now own a home. Recently, I refinanced it with a 15-year loan. That means that about the time I get ready to retire, I'll own the home free and clear. That seemed like a good goal, and I am excited to be able to have it.

Whatever people might say, this is still a great country and, in some small way, I feel like I'm living the American dream.

13

CONVERSATION ABOUT WORK, POVERTY, AND WELFARE

Bob

LET ME START OFF THIS CONVERSATION. One of the phrases that has traditionally been part of American culture is the expression "Protestant work ethic." This refers to a set of attitudes, particularly toward work, that came to be characteristic of Christianity, particularly Protestantism, and also characteristic of the American mindset. The idea originated from the earliest chapters in the Bible and their perspective on work. When you read the second chapter of Genesis, you see that God gave Adam work to do; he put him in the Garden to "work it and keep it." (Genesis 2:15).

Christianity has noted that this is before Adam's fall from grace. What this means is that work is not a result of sin or a product of God's displeasure toward humans; rather, it is God's good gift to humankind for fulfilling his purposes. Work allows us to use our gifts, contribute to the good of society, and exercise our particular "calling" from God. The Protestant work ethic says that everyone can serve God, and one way we do so is through our vocations. We serve God by doing well whatever God has given us to do. The New Testament encourages us to do our work with all our hearts and energies, as if we are serving God, not simply working to please others or make a living.

This is an idea that, for many centuries, has permeated white culture. It came to America from Western European culture and is a part of the ethos that was widespread at our nation's founding. The idea is simple: Work has value in itself. For that reason, we ought to find meaningful work to do, do it to the best of our abilities, and consider it part of our service to God. I have been wondering if this perspective is present in the black culture. I gather that it was not when you grew up. I wonder about now?

Jamie

I think many in the black culture have lost the spirit of wanting to work hard and believing they can achieve if they do. I've heard people say that they are not going to work because they will just be "working for the white man." They mean that they are going to be making whites wealthier without sharing in much of that success themselves. This may be part of the reason some blacks shy away from working today.

One of the things that has frustrated the black community for many years is that they don't feel like they have the same job opportunities as white people. They just don't see themselves as having the same prospects of rising to the highest levels that white people have. For example, how many large corporations have black people in their highest positions, such as presidents or CEOs? Or who are the top professors in prestigious universities? Those positions are held by white people.

There are some subtle perspectives at work here. A black person on welfare may say to himself, "White people owe me this. They kept my people in slavery for several hundred years. I never got my 40 acres and a mule. I ought to get something from them for free. It's certainly a lot better than working for the white man, which I will ultimately be doing if I get into their system. I helped them build this country for their benefit, and I'm not doing it anymore."

Bob

I can see how working in what seems like a white world might be discouraging for a black person. It probably feels like they are competing in a system where white people know all the rules and know how the game is played, because they've made the rules and rigged them in their favor.

120

In the white world, certainly the so-called "white-collar" world, where most of the high-income jobs are, there are expectations. It is a world of education, manners, effort, initiative, and where standard English is spoken. Those jobs value ingenuity, creativity, determination, and good people skills. Quite frankly, this is a world in which the competition can be fierce and in which white people often don't succeed. But they probably understand this world better than many blacks. The white middle class understands these values because they have grown up in that environment. Even when they don't have a theological foundation for their view of work, they innately understand that, if they want to succeed, at some point in their lives, they are going to have to expend significant effort.

Of course, there are "blue-collar" jobs that require these same skills and attitudes. Some people make lots of money doing these kinds of jobs too. Just get a plumber to fix a toilet in your home, and you will realize the truth of this when he hands you his bill!

All this is simply to say that I can see how it might be intimidating for a black person to think about competing in the white world. Middle-class whites probably do have an advantage, both by being white but also growing up middle class. I suspect that blacks who grow up in the middle class also understand this world but still may not feel as comfortable in it as whites.

Jamie

When I was being interviewed for the position as director of the Sparrow's Nest, I was actually underqualified. The job description said they were looking for someone with a four-year college degree. All I had was a GED high school diploma and a certificate from a business school. But the board of directors took a chance on me. They thought I had the right spirit, a useful background, and an authentic faith. I also had shown the ability to work hard, so they gave me a chance. I was pretty sure I was in over my head, but by the grace of God I have been able to grow into the role. Thankfully, a lot of people trusted me and helped me along the way.

121

Getting this position made me nervous, not only because the job was a big one but also because most of the board was white. I hoped I could get along well with a group of white people. As it turned out, they have become some of my best friends and biggest supporters. I did a lot of praying and asking God to help me, though.

Bob

We have been talking a lot about people who live in poverty, both black and white. It seems to me that, for a person living in poverty, the question is not how to become rich. If people ask that question, it's really the wrong one. The right question to ask is, "How do I move from poverty to the middle class." In America today, the poverty line for a family of four is about $27,000.[12] If you make above that, you are technically in the middle class, and there is a large range within the middle class. To move into what is called the upper class, economically, you have to make above $187,000. So quite frankly, most people in America are in the middle class.

What is the answer for moving from the lower economic class into the middle class? It is work. You have to go to work, work hard, be responsible, and contribute to the company for which you work. If you do that, people will generally pay you a wage that will allow you to live in the middle class.

The problem is that people who survive on welfare never even make it to the lower middle class. Government assistance always keeps them in poverty. Here's a sad reality. The quickest way to poverty in America today is to be a young, unemployed, unwed mother. The way to guarantee a life of poverty is to have a child young, not have a husband, and have to stay home to take care of that child. One hundred percent of unemployed single mothers living on welfare are in poverty.[13] This is why the fact that more than 70% of black children are born to unwed mothers is a crisis of great significance in the black community. It's a major cause of poverty among blacks. The fact that 29% of white children are born to unwed mothers is also a great problem for whites.

122

Jamie

I don't know how many young women understand this, particularly in poorer communities. They certainly didn't understand this in the projects where I grew up. But are they teaching this to young girls in schools today? I don't know, but they should be! If you are a parent with a daughter, you ought to be telling her not to get pregnant before she is married because if she does, she may very well be poor for the rest of her life. If you had a group of young girls in a classroom and said to them, "How many of you want to be poor for the rest of your lives," none of them would raise their hands. But obviously lots of them are doing things that are not in their best interests in this regard.

There are some hard realities that come with being poor. I have women who come in here all the time and tell me about their situations. There's an urban community near here called Bethel Midtown Village. It's a housing authority project that people call "B Town." It's typical for a mother to say to me, "Jamie, I've got to get out of there. Two more people got shot over the weekend. We hear gunshots all the time there. They just killed a lady in an apartment opposite me. I can't raise a child in this environment." The problem is that this lady isn't working; she can't because she has children to raise. So she doesn't have enough income to get out of the projects. She is stuck. If you want to know what poverty looks like, this is it. This is the hard reality of poverty, and I don't have any way to help her.

Someone might say that she simply needs to get married, but for a woman in this situation, men aren't that eager to get involved. They may like the woman, but she has a lot of "baggage." It's not like a man is going to quickly come in and marry her in order to take her out of her situation. She's just in a bad situation, and so are her kids. I hope schools are talking about these realities. Young people need to realize what their choices are going to mean.

Bob

I wonder if these things are not being taught to our kids today, as much as they should be, because the nuclear family that has a father and mother in the home is a particularly traditional and Christian value? It seems to me that there is a great undercurrent of disdain for all traditional values in culture today, particularly Christian ones, including marriage, especially if it is between a man and a woman. We want to be able to define the family in any variety of ways. Everyone wants to do as they wish and define life as they please, no matter what the consequences might be for others, particularly children. For that reason, the Christian idea of a family in which there is a father and mother, in which you don't have children until you get married, in which you, as parents, stay together as a matter of principle, doesn't carry enough moral force to resist the contrary social pressures.

Jamie

What happens in the inner city is that girls get caught up in a cycle from which they can't break free. When they get pregnant at 16 or 17, they have to drop out of school. They hope their mom might take care of the baby, but lots of grandmothers won't do it. "You had that baby, now you've got to take care of it." Because of that, a young girl can't finish her education and therefore can't go to work. There you have it; it's the formula for a life of poverty. I had several cousins that did this very thing, and they have never gotten out of the projects.

Bob

I saw an interesting study about some efforts to reverse this trend.[14] During the George W. Bush presidency, the government spent $600 million dollars on programs encouraging marriage and trying to teach young girls that it was better for them not to have children out of wedlock. Years later, they discovered that the program made almost no impact on the numbers of young girls who got pregnant.

124

Interestingly the one thing that did make an impact was a television show created by MTV, called "Teen Mom." It highlighted teen moms and showed how hard it actually was to be a teen mom. This show did make an impact and reduced the number of teen pregnancies by about 5%. It helped young girls think twice about getting pregnant early.

Ultimately, I can't believe that the government can fix these kinds of problems; they just aren't equipped. Government programs, or MTV for that matter, can say "it's not in your best interest to get pregnant," but a focus on self-interest may not be enough. People have been doing things against their self-interest since the beginning of time. Instead, what we need is a voice that says "it's morally wrong to treat women as sex objects, it's morally wrong to have children outside of marriage, and it's morally wrong to create a situation in which your child will be guaranteed to grow up in poverty." There is an organization that has the moral authority to speak these kinds of truths; it is the church. I think the church has got to be the solution. The church has to call people to faith, morality, and good choices. But we, in the church, are obviously not doing what needs to be done in this regard.

Jamie

The problem with being dependent on the government is that it is degrading and ultimately boring. If I don't have work to do, I've got a lot of free time on my hands, which is ultimately dreary. If I'm depending on the government, it lowers my self-esteem. I begin to wonder if maybe I can't compete with others. Maybe I'm not as smart or as gifted or as capable as others. The truth is, however, that everyone can do better. Everyone has gifts from God. Everyone can achieve if they want to. Their circumstances may limit them, and people have to work within their situation, but almost everyone can improve themselves if they commit to working at it.

I found this out working at the poultry plant. When I got there, a lot of Hispanics worked there. I don't know if they were legal or not, and this was a time before companies had to check that issue closely. What I noticed, however, is that they were the ones with the nice pickup trucks in the parking lot. They were also the people wearing the blue hats and white hats, which meant they were in supervisory positions. I knew they were making more money than I was, as supervisors, so I began to look around to see what was going on.

What I saw was that they didn't lay out of work. They came to work every day and on time. If there was overtime to be worked, they volunteered to do it. In fact, you had to run them off the clock: they were all about working. What I saw in my black brothers was that they left every day right at 5 o'clock. When it was time to leave, they were running out of the building.

At that point, I started feeling a little jealous. Here I was, born in America, and these people, some of whom had just recently come to this country, were doing better than I was. And no one was giving them anything; they were earning it. So I decided I'd have a change in attitude. I said to myself, "Jamie, you are going to make a change. You are going to get up early, work hard, and improve your situation." That's what I did. I started being the best employee I could. When I did, I started to move up the promotion ladder as well.

That change in attitude has made all the difference. Now I'm out of the chicken plant. I own a four-bedroom house that I'm very proud of. It has three bathrooms. I'm happily married, and my wife has a good job. I have a car that's paid for and another that is almost paid for. At work I drive a company car. None of this would have happened if I'd just decided to be comfortable and lazy. I might still be cleaning floors at the chicken plant. So this is now my motto: "Get up early, work hard, and strike gold."

Bob
One more thing needs to be said. We have talked a lot about education as if it is the only means to the middle class. It is

126

important, but it also needs to be said that work, creativity, and determination are also great assets. When I went back for my 15-year high school reunion, I was struck by one observation. It wasn't the "A" students who were the most successful. It was the "C" students who had lots of personality. They were the ones who owned the apartment complexes, sanitation plants, and tree farms. They were the ones with the most money.

Everyone has gifts. If we use them, we can make our way. To be successful, you don't need a genius IQ. You just need enough intelligence to be able to think, create, work hard, and not give up. As someone said, the "A" students don't take many risks because they are used to succeeding and don't want to fail. The "C" students take more risks because they don't mind failing; they learn from their mistakes and do better the next time. The old adage is that the "A" students will end up teaching the "B" students who will end up working for the "C" students. As an accomplished black leader noted, "A" students come back to universities to teach. "C" students come back to endow.[15] All of which is to say that hard work makes all the difference. Anyone willing to work will certainly make their way better and be able to provide, not only for themselves and their children, but perhaps have enough to help others as well.

One more comment. The latest census data confirms what we have said in this chapter and the last.[16] One commentator summarized the findings from the 2020 census. "People who graduate from college, get a job, get married and have children generally earn more money than those who do not. People who drop out of high school, do not work and have children out of wedlock generally earn less and are more likely to be in poverty."[17] While some look for complex explanations, the statistics bear out simple realities. Married couples led the wealthiest households in America in 2020. Those with college degrees or higher made significantly more money than those without a degree. People who worked full-time for the entire year made more than those who worked part-time or did not work at all. The highest rate of poverty was for single women with a child under 6 in the home. If one wants to know how to avoid poverty, the answer is clear: build a stable family, get as much education as you can, and go to work.

DISCUSSION QUESTIONS
PART 4 – WORK, POVERTY, AND WELFARE

1. How would you describe your first work experience? What did you learn from it?

2. What perspectives on work did you get from your family and community growing up? How have your views changed since then?

3. Have you known people living in poverty? What was or is the experience like for them? Have you known people living on welfare? What was or is the experience like for them?

4. Have you ever seen a "glass ceiling" for black people in the workplace that is hard to break through? Explain. For women? Explain. White people? Explain. Other minorities?

5. How important is a sense of satisfaction in one's work? What should the goal of working be? Do you agree with the statement that work is good for the spirit and that living without work is ultimately dehumanizing? What does the phrase "Protestant work ethic" mean to you?

6. Who makes up the black socioeconomic middle class today? Who makes up the white socioeconomic lower class?

7. Do you think poverty is more about economics or values? Explain. Are there instances in which poverty is not about deficient values?

8. Christianity has the value of giving special attention to the poor and oppressed. What do you think this should mean in modern America?

9. What should the church be doing to fix the crisis of teenage pregnancies and births to unwed mothers? What should the church be doing to help people break the cycle of poverty? How is this different than what government should be doing? Do you think there is a prejudice against "Christian values" in culture today?

10. In what ways do you think that government programs to aid the poor are helpful? Unhelpful?

PART 5 – RACISM AND PREJUDICE

14

THE OLD SOUTH

Bob

IN DECATUR, GEORGIA WHERE I GREW UP, there was a Woolworth's store. F.W. Woolworth was a pioneer in the retailing business and started what became known as "five and dime" stores. Frank Woolworth had a couple of pioneering ideas that would revolutionize the merchandizing business. One was selling general merchandise at discount prices, usually 5 or 10 cents, which undercut the prices in other stores. He instituted the direct purchasing of goods in order to keep prices down. He also put the merchandise out for customers to see and handle, rather than keeping it behind the counter where the salesperson would have to show it. In the late 1950s, my mother would take my sister and me to the Decatur Woolworth's Five and Dime.

I remember walking the aisles at Woolworth's, looking for things that might interest me as a young boy of 7 and 8. As I think about what they sold, most of the goods there were not expensive; it wasn't Lord & Taylor, but then there was no Lord & Taylor store in Decatur. My mother sewed, and I remember her buying fabric. I also remember seeing lots of combs and hair braids and things like that.

Children are more observant than we might think, and one other thing stuck in my memory about that Woolworth's. It was that there were different water fountains for people to use, one for the white people and another for the "coloreds." It must have been an extra expense for the store to purchase two separate water fountains, but it did. One had a sign over it that said "Whites Only"; the other said "Coloreds Only."

Woolworth's also had a lunch counter, and the three of us would eat a sandwich at the lunch counter on occasion. At that point, the family was on a strict budget, so we didn't eat out much, only a trip to "Lefty's Bar-B-Q" about once a year, where we would get curb service and eat in the car. We also had an occasional lunch at Woolworth's. My mother had a weekly allowance for food, and she tried not to go over it, but on occasion we splurged for a grilled cheese sandwich and a cherry Coke at the Woolworth's lunch counter. I don't know whether I realized it at the time, but the counter was segregated. You could not sit down and have lunch there if you were black.

This led to what would become a famous "sit-in" at the Woolworth's lunch counter in Greensboro, North Carolina, in 1960. Four young black men sat down to have lunch at the Woolworth's counter. That wasn't allowed at the segregated counter, and they were refused service. The incident would set off months of protests and boycotts that would become hallmarks of the civil rights movement in America and eventually lead to the Civil Rights Act of 1964, outlawing racial segregation in facilities used by the public, such as stores and restaurants. That actual lunch counter was moved in 1993 to the Smithsonian Institution in Washington, D.C., to commemorate the fight for equal rights in America. That particular Woolworth's store in Greensboro is still standing and now houses a civil rights museum.

I have always wondered what happened to Woolworth's, which was so popular in its day. It turns out that it was overtaken by retail chains that took the principles pioneered by F.W. Woolworth and practiced them more efficiently, some of those competitors becoming Target, K-Mart, and the ubiquitous Walmart. Woolworth's did not completely go out of business however; it began to focus on a portion of its business that sold athletic apparel and eventually became Foot Locker, whose stores are located throughout the United States and around the world. Foot Locker is a billion-dollar company today and employs more than 30,000 people, many of whom are black.

There are obviously no segregated water fountains in Foot Locker stores today, but it was a hard-fought battle to end segregation, not just in Woolworth stores but around the country. Though segregation has ended, racism and prejudice have not, though quite frankly I think of it as something that others have and not myself. I find myself wondering, however, if that is really true. Do I have racial prejudices of which I am not aware, or am I just comfortable in my mostly white world?

Jamie

I remember the first time I experienced something that I would consider racism. I was probably 13 years old and was getting ready to cross West Broad Street to go down to the Kroger grocery store in the shopping center. To be honest, I think we were going to the Kroger to steal something, and I was probably high at the time. I suspect we were all high that day and had the munchies, so were going to Kroger to steal something to eat.

We had gotten pretty good at stealing. For example, you could grab three or four $20 steaks and make some nice money. If you did that, then you had money to get high, but getting high also gave you the munchies, so you had to go steal some snacks.

The way we stole stuff was just to put it on us. We'd put a steak right in the small of our backs or maybe two. We'd put one in the front and some on either side. Those steaks can be pretty cold, but you aren't worried about that in the moment, just getting out of the store. If the steaks were small, you could double them up and get eight steaks out of the store. Then you'd sell them on the black market.

The way it worked on the black market was that everything went for 50%. If a steak cost $20 in the store, it went for $10. If you had something that was brand new from a store and it cost $100, then it went for $50 on the black market. The same with food stamps; when you sold them, they went for half-price.

That day we were heading down to the store and waiting to cross the street. Just then some guys came down the road in an old beat-up black pickup truck that had a rebel flag flying from the back. I can still see that pickup truck in my mind today. Some of the guys were in the bed of the pickup truck; that was when you could still ride in the back of a pickup truck and no one thought anything about it.

When they saw us, they started hollering, calling us the n-word, and they threw their open beer cans out the back at us, laughing and hollering all the time, with beer splashing everywhere. I was shocked because that kind of thing had not happened to me before. That was the first time I ever got called the n-word by a white person and my first experience of racism. It's one reason I don't like the Confederate flag, to this day.

Bob

Our family employed a black lady named Geneva, who worked for us every other Friday. She worked for a number of families in the neighborhood as a maid. She would work at one house a day or sometimes one in the morning and another in the afternoon. In our neighborhood, we kept her busy most of the week. She worked with us on alternating Fridays, and my mother would drive her home at the end of the afternoon.

We loved Geneva as a family, and my sister and I felt a great deal of fondness for her, even as children. Because she came to our house on Friday afternoons, we always knew the house would smell fresh and clean when we came home from school for the weekend. It was just another reason Fridays were great; school was out for the week, the house was clean, and usually my mother had been to the grocery store, which meant we might have dessert with dinner that evening.

134

Geneva was very dark and very strong. My mother often commented on how strong she was; if there was anything that needed strength, Geneva could do it. She could also scrub the bathroom tub with ferocity. She would do cleaning in our home and some ironing. My mother was amused at how she always organized her schedule to do the ironing when the afternoon "soaps" were on television. She would iron my father's shirts for work and watch the soaps.

I recognized, even as a child, that Geneva came from a different culture than my own. She had several children who were much older than my sister and me; I assume that meant she had them when she was young. Geneva was divorced from her husband, who was still around but with whom she had little contact. I got the idea that she thought he was a bit worthless, and that was why she had divorced him.

Geneva also had some practices that were different. When her children did something wrong, she didn't discipline them immediately; she would "whip them out of bed." I had the mental picture of her children sleeping soundly early in the morning, only to be awakened with a belt or switch pelting their arms and back. It didn't sound pleasant to me, and I wondered what it might be like never knowing when you might be awakened in this way. Her son got a girl pregnant at one point, and she complained to my mother that they "made a baby in my bed." Geneva's children had their problems growing up, but she kept on them to make something of themselves, and they all did.

As Geneva got older, she became less able to clean like she had done when she was younger. My mother kept her on anyway, even when she had to work alongside her to get the cleaning done. We knew Geneva needed the income, and our family was in a position to help her at that point, even when she could not do her job like she had before.

My mother had a big heart, and when she got into real estate saw an opportunity to help Geneva. In real estate, she sometimes came across bargains, where you could get into a house for a small deposit. She started looking for a house for Geneva and eventually found one that fit her needs and budget. My mother got the people in the neighborhood to write letters to the mortgage company, affirming that they employed Geneva and that she had sufficient steady income to be able to pay her mortgage. She gave Geneva her entire sales commission and helped her scrape together the small down payment needed. For the first time in her life, Geneva became a homeowner, something of which she would be enormously proud. She said to my mother, "Look at me, a washwoman, and now I own my own home!" It warmed my mother's heart and was one of many good deeds like this that my mother did without anyone knowing about them.

I don't think my family was racist toward Geneva; in fact, we had great affection toward her. One the other hand, we lived in a completely white community that liked being that way. Had a black family wanted to move into that community in the mid-1960s, they may not have felt very welcomed.

15

THE NEW SOUTH

Jamie

THE SECOND TIME I EXPERIENCED RACISM was when I was locked up in the Clarke County jail and a friend and I set the jail on fire. My friend's name was Haze, and we were in a cell beside each other.

Jails are built very sturdy out of concrete and steel so they can stand the test of time. You can have a hurricane or tornado, and it won't knock the jail down. That's why some jails are so old; they are built to last for generations. The jail isn't going anywhere unless you demolish it.

I was in isolation at the time. At the jail in those days, they had different levels of isolation. You could be in isolation but still have some people with you; it just meant you were isolated from the general population. If you messed up in the first level of isolation, then you went to the next level, which was one-man isolation. They called this next level the side pocket. This is where it was just you and one other person who was in a cell right beside you. You could not see them, but you could talk to them through the bars. If you messed up there, they put you into something called H5. That was the worst.

In all the other cells, you had a bunk and a toilet and a mirror, but once you got into H5, there was not even a bunk. There was also no mirror and not even a toilet. All you had was a grate on the floor. The grate was about a foot long and only about half a foot wide. That's where you used the bathroom. If you did some serious business in it, you'd have to wait for the guard to come by before it got flushed, because it could only be flushed from the outside. They were supposed to come by every hour, but sometimes they skipped a shift and just wrote down that they came by. In that case, it might be two or three hours before you could get things flushed down the grate. It was not a pleasant place to be, but I ended up there on several occasions.

In this instance, I wasn't in H5 but in the side pocket. They called it Door 38. If you went to the side pocket, it was through Door 38. At this point, I knew I wasn't getting back into the general population anytime soon. I was young, in my early 20s. Haze was in the side pocket with me. He and I decided that there wasn't much going on, so we'd create a little excitement.

You could smoke in the jail at that time, and we had plenty of cigarettes and even lighters. We got these from the trustees, who were inmates with special privileges. They had been in the jail for some time and earned privileges because of their good behavior, so they delivered the meals to us. It gave them something to do and got them out of their cells, so it was a good job if you could get it, though I was clearly never going to be a trustee. They would sneak us cigarettes and lighters, when the officer wasn't looking, by putting them on our trays when they brought us our meals. Or one of us might distract the officer while the trustee threw in some contraband.

In the side pocket, there was a pipe chase that ran between our cells. A pipe chase is a plumbing wall that covers pipes that run up to the ceiling. The water pipes ran up through the chase, and it had a door on it so someone could come in and cut off the water for that area if they needed to. There was also a light in the top of it so someone could see if they were working on it.

What we did was broke through the place where the light was, and that gave us access to the ventilation system that ran through the concrete walls. It wasn't big enough for us to get into, but we could reach over into it. So we set our sheets on fire and pushed them over behind the concrete into the ventilation system. We had lighters that we had gotten from the trustees, so we had a way to set our sheets on fire. We knew we weren't in any danger; nothing was going to burn down those concrete walls, but it sent smoke throughout the

138

entire prison so no one could see anything. We had the excitement we were looking for.

Bob

When my wife and I moved to Athens, Georgia, in 1999, our oldest son was 1 year old. We had the daunting task of finding a house to live in only coming down for several Saturdays. Our real estate agent showed us lots of houses. The question we had to answer was not only how much could we afford but where to live – in the city where racial issues still troubled the schools, or the county where "white flight" had taken place.

The process of integration, as people have related it to me, was difficult in the city of Athens. In 1971, the black high school (Burney-Harris High) was merged with Athens High to form Clarke Central High School. The merging of the two schools did not go well, and there were riots in the school and city. It was a process that, for a variety of reasons, neither the white nor black community liked. In the end, everyone had to make serious adjustments to get used to the new situation. One of the things that helped the process was that the Athens High football program was outstanding. There would be a few exceptional black athletes who would play a significant role in the school's football success, though the integration of the sports programs did not go smoothly either.

The integration of the schools in Athens resolved itself in two ways. One was that everyone adjusted and learned to live with the new reality. Things were different, and everyone was going to have to get used to it that way. This took time, but the city regained its equilibrium, and so did the schools. White people sent their children to school and assumed they would still get a good education, which they did.

The other thing that happened was a gradual progression of white flight. This was how many white families resolved the issue for themselves and their children. Integration brought social problems to the schools that had not been there before. Not only was

139

there tension between white and black students, but more students in school came from impoverished backgrounds. They had more academic issues than white students had been accustomed to for a variety of reasons. There was also more disruptive behavior among students. White parents looked for alternatives, and those included both private schools and an exodus into the mostly white county school system.

By the time my wife and I came looking for houses, the county school system was mostly white, with the largest minorities being Asian and Hispanic. Our real estate agent did not try to sway us as to whether we should live in Clarke County, which would send our children to school in Athens, or nearby Oconee County. In the end, we chose to live in Oconee, where our children would go to schools that would be predominantly white and homogenous.

When I started my position as pastor of my church, which was in Athens, I had one person who expressed her disappointment that I did not live in Athens. She had hoped I would move my family into Athens and help be part of the solution, not avoid it by joining the white flight to the county. I certainly understood her concern and had some guilt about it. My responsibility at that point, however, was to protect and care for the future of my own children. Bigger problems would have to find their own solutions.

I remember sitting with a friend watching tryouts for the county recreational league basketball program when my son was in the fourth grade. The kids were sitting on the bench at one end of the gym, waiting their turn to dribble the ball down the court and shoot a basket, hoping to get picked for a good recreational league basketball team. What was striking about the group, though I had not noticed, was that the entire line of children was white. The father next to me commented, "Where in America today will you see a whiter group of kids in any recreational program"?

The white flight into the county created the situation in which housing became both limited and expensive. Though it was not verbalized, I suspect that many in the county liked it that way. You simply had to have a level of education and wealth to afford housing in Oconee County. The school system also stayed largely white because the housing projects were all within the city limits of Athens, and no projects existed in Oconee County. Housing is certainly available to all races but generally out of the price range of those with anything but a solid middle-class income. The result is that Oconee County, even today, is mostly white with only 5% of the population being black, 3% Asian, and a small percentage Hispanic.

Does it make me racist to want my children to go to a school system that will be stable and not full of social problems or disruptive behaviors? I don't think so. My children have grown up with some black friends, often through their involvement in sports programs, and have had good relations with them, but other than that they have grown up in a mostly segregated society. I know parents who have sent their children to school in the Clarke county system, where black youths make up 48 percent of the student population and the majority of students are minorities. They have gotten a quality education, and many of them have excelled academically. I have also known many teachers in the Clarke system who are top quality, highly gifted teachers. From my vantage point, the problem in the Clarke schools is not the teachers or educators but the social problems, particularly within poorer families, that do not support the education of their children or which actively hinder it.

The Oconee County school system, though largely white, is not segregated, in the official sense. All races have the ability to attend the county schools if they live in the area. When my wife and I were looking for houses in the area, we had the financial resources, because of my education, job position, and savings, to purchase a house either in the city or the county. We made the choice to purchase in the county and take advantage of the opportunities it provided.

Jamie

Obviously Haze and I got into trouble for setting the jail on fire. They took all our possessions, stripped us down to our boxer shorts and a T-shirt, and put us in H5 for 30 days. For the first two or three weeks we were shackled to the grate in the floor. This was not a happy place to be; all you had were the concrete walls and the grate. And there was a vent in the ceiling that, in the summer, blew really cold air.

The way they shackled us was to use handcuffs and some chains. They'd put handcuffs around our ankles, then with another pair of handcuffs attach those to the grate. It gave you a little room to move, but not much. They did the same with Haze, so we were right there on top of each other. At first, we were also handcuffed behind our backs. They'd unlock us when it was time to eat, but that was all. It was pretty hard to sleep like that, to say the least.

At that point, there was a lady running the jail. I had never met the chief of the jail, but they called us up for a visit with her after a couple of weeks. They unshackled us and took us up to where she was. I'd never been in that part of the jail before, which was the administrative offices. You don't go there as a prisoner. They said, "You're going up to see the Big Lady." We went into her office one at a time.

She said to me, "Jamie, I've heard all about you, how you've been robbing people on the prison wings and getting into fights. I know you're in and out of jail all the time. But I'm going to tell you something: What makes you think you can set my jail on fire?" I remember that I tried to give some excuse and have some comeback that would let me talk my way out of the situation, but I knew I was in big trouble. You don't see the chief for just some minor offense. You see the officers and lieutenants and even the captains, but you don't see the chief, and there I was sitting in her office. I think I told her that I had learned my lesson and asked if I could go back into the general population. She replied that I wasn't going to see the general population for a very long time.

As it turned out, they created some isolation cells for Haze and me. They put us in there and shackled us. They put a big dog chain around our waists then handcuffed our hands to the chain. Then they ran the chain down to our feet and shackled our feet together. When you see people walking like penguins when they come into court, it is because they are shackled this way.

We had bunks, and they had holes in the metal bed frame, so they also ran a chain through the bed frame and shackled us to that also. We had enough room to go to the toilet, which was about 3 feet from the bed, and that was it. You got unshackled only when you ate. Haze was pretty good at picking locks, so he picked the locks at one point, and we got in trouble again. There was also a chain around the outside of the door.

This is a story about racism, and here is where that comes in. One day some of the older white officers came down to our cells. They had their camera and started taking pictures of us. They said, "Look at these boys. They look just like slaves, don't they? They look like they are just now coming over on one of those slave ships!"

I did hear through the grapevine that some of the black officers were appalled at how we were treated. They said to each other, "They can't treat people like this. You can't chain them up like animals." One of the problems was that it was a fire hazard. If there had been a fire, we could not have gotten out, with the chain across the door. But no one really said anything, even the black officers, because they were afraid to do so. I think they felt like we would not have been treated so badly, even in spite of what we had done, if we had been white.

One night, we got pulled out of our cells about 3 o'clock in the morning and brought to the office of some of the guards. There were two white officers there smoking cigars. They said, "OK, Jamie Scott. You think you're such a bad guy, setting the jail on fire. You're doing this and you're doing that. But let me tell you something: If I can get you down to my jail in Watkinsville where

I'm running the show, we're going to have a good time together."
They burst out laughing. "We'll have some fun with you, boy!" I
didn't think that what he thought of as a good time would have been
much fun for me. Obviously they wouldn't have said "boy" to any
white prisoner, nor any of the other things they said to us.

Bob

I have spent most of my life among white people. My friends are
white, those I work with are white, and the people my children went
to school with were mostly white. In that sense, I am not a model of
racial engagement, and it is one of the reasons I wanted us to write
this book together. It has not been a goal of mine to live primarily
among white people; it is just how things have worked out.

It seems to me that white and black cultures are different, and
this is one of the challenges we face in terms of race relations. As
Jamie and I are realizing, our life experiences are not at all alike.
We certainly have many points of connection now, in part because
we both run organizations of significant complexity, I as a pastor
and Jamie directing the Sparrow's Nest. Both our organizations seek
to do good in our community, so we are working toward similar
goals. We also would like to see healing in our country's relations
between blacks and whites. For those reasons, we are discovering a
number of points of connection in our lives. But I suspect we don't
like the same music, or watch the same movies, or read the same
books. Those are cultural differences, however, not ones that ought
to create racial tensions. It does mean, however, that there are
cultural differences in play in building bridges between our two
communities.

I had a friend tell me that many years ago when he was a boy,
his father explained to him what was a common belief at that time
about the difference between the North and South in terms of racial
views. His father told him that Southerners like blacks as
individuals but dislike them as a race. Northerners liked them as a
race but disliked them as individuals. This was intended to be a

144

compliment to the South by saying that Southern people, genuine, God-fearing, and kind by nature, got along fine with Negroes, to use the old term, when they had interactions with them. In the view of Southern whites, however, many aspects of black culture were in need of improvement, both moral and social. The critique of the North was that they had high ideals but did not live by them.

In my experience, most white people today don't think of themselves as racist and try not to be. Martin Luther King's great quote is relevant. In his "I Have A Dream" speech, he said, "I look to the day when people will not be judged by the color of their skin but by the content of their character." When white people meet people who are black, they get along fine if each one treats the other with respect. Character works in most situations, and people with high moral integrity get along, no matter their race.

16

CONVERSATION ABOUT RACISM AND PREJUDICE

Bob

I T IS INTERESTING TO ME that, growing up in the 1950s and '60s, I was very detached from the issue of racism and segregation. I found the "Coloreds Only" water fountains at Woolworth's a curiosity, but little more. Of course, I was only 8 years old. Even when the 1960s came along with their racial protests, I was focused on other things, such as my own high school education and endeavors. Racial rights were an issue for people at a higher level than myself; that's how I saw it. If I am honest, I suppose that I thought of segregation as something rather benign, that really didn't hurt anyone, and that was probably a good way for the different races to have their own cultural practices and standards. I realize, now, that I was wrong about that.

In reading about the history of segregation, it was clearly a way for the white South to deal with the presence of a large black population in the aftermath of the Civil War.[18] When the slaves were emancipated through the Emancipation Proclamation and the Northern victory in the Civil War, a new era began in the South. Blacks began to go to school, start businesses, and run for political office. They were no longer required to work for their owners and could make their own choices. As they began to rise out of the abject poverty in which they had lived for so many years, this became a threat to the white South, particularly since, in 1910, 90% of the black population of America lived in the South. Many Southern whites resented the rise of the black population, and Southern states began to pass laws that limited their rights.

147

When federal troops were withdrawn from the South in 1877, it gave state legislatures the ability to establish laws that would separate the black population from the whites. There would be some very dark aspects of the South's response to the rise of black people in various aspects of society. Organizations such as the Ku Klux Klan used terror, intimidation, and even murder as a means of keeping "uppity blacks" in their place. It was an attempt by some in the South to maintain a sense of white superiority in spite of the new legal freedoms given to blacks.

The *Plessy v. Ferguson* decision of 1896 is now considered one of the worst decisions ever made by the United States Supreme Court. It affirmed that it was legal to pass racial segregation laws that related to public facilities so long as those segregated facilities were equal, though separated. The 14th Amendment to the United States Constitution had decreed that whites and blacks had legal equality and no state could deny any person the "equal protection of the laws." The Supreme Court decision declared, however, that this did not eliminate all "distinctions based upon color." As long as laws were "reasonable," states could pass their own laws concerning health, safety, and morals.

The result of these "Jim Crow laws," which began in the 1870s, was that blacks regularly received inferior accommodations, services, and facilities. In public schools, new textbooks went to the white schools and used ones to the black schools. Efforts were made to suppress the black vote as well as the vote of poor whites. The result was that only a small percentage of blacks were eligible to vote in many Southern states in the early 1900s. One outcome was that, if you could not vote, you could not run for office. This kept blacks out of public office in the South, which suited many whites just fine.

These laws would also be enacted in the North, particularly as blacks moved from the South to the North. The result of such laws throughout the country would be separate schools, hotels, and eating establishments. Blacks had to swim at their own beaches, ride in their separate sections of trains and buses, and use their own restrooms. Federal workplaces were segregated, beginning in 1913. Marriages between blacks and whites were against the law. Some states required tests for voting, such as literacy and proof of property ownership, which were designed to keep minorities from voting. In some election primaries, for a variety of reasons, only whites were allowed to vote. Blacks could not participate in the sports programs of whites, whether at a college, high school, or recreational level.

Brown v. Board of Education in 1954 reversed *Plessy v. Fergusson* and held that "separate but equal" is inherently unequal, but it would take the Civil Rights Act of 1964 and the Voting Rights Act of 1965 to correct these injustices and ensure that segregation laws could not be established or enforced. These changes would be the result of pushback from the black community and progressive whites who began to work for racial equality in the 1950s, much of the energy for this coming from the black Christian community and its congregations along with some white Christian leaders and churches.

Jamie

I do remember one other instance of racial discrimination. I suppose it has to do with segregation, in a way, or at least the desire of some whites to live in all-white communities. I have mentioned that we moved to Japan when I was 7 or 8, when my mother married the man who was in the Navy. Our home was on the Negishi military base in Yokohama, and we lived in a section of the base called Negishi Heights. My mother was obviously black, and so was my new stepdad.

My mother loved cats, and at one point she came home with a couple of kittens. I didn't like them at all, which my mom thought was a problem. I was actually afraid of them; that may seem strange for someone who would essentially be fearless as an adult, but I was. To help me get over my problem, she locked me in a room

149

with them one day. They apparently didn't like me much, or maybe they could sense my fear; what I remember is huddling in one corner with the cats bowing up their backs and hissing at me from the other. I could hear my mother's voice saying, "Boy, you'd better get used to these cats," but I didn't think that was going to happen. In fact, today, I see a cat and think to myself, "I know some of your relatives; they didn't like me, and I didn't like them, so let's just keep our distance."

Finally my mom put them out on the porch rather than letting them live in the house. One morning we woke up and the kittens were dead on the front lawn. Their necks had been broken, and there was a letter with them. I can't remember exactly what it said, but it was something derogatory about "niggers." I remember it as being written in blood or something menacing like that, but I may be mistaken. My mother and stepfather were extremely upset by this. My mother just went crazy mad about it. She had some choice words for whoever had done this; she was from the 'hood, and all the 'hood came out in her that day, including some very ugly words. She wanted to get her hands on the "crackers" who had done that to her cats.

There wasn't any resolution to that incident. My stepfather didn't make a big deal about it; in fact, he tried to hush it up. I don't know if he was afraid of further retribution or just, as a way of protecting me, didn't want us to get mixed up in a big controversy on the base.

I did have a best friend in Japan who was white; his name was Gregory. He had an older brother whose name was Michael. As I recall, I didn't think too much about our being different colors; we got along well, and that was what mattered.

Bob
I've got an issue I want to ask you about. You said that one of your first experiences of racism was being called the n-word by the rednecks in the pickup truck as it drove by. That has become a very

emotionally charged term, and no white person can use it. I notice, however, that black people use it and it's OK. Rappers use it in songs all the time and get away with it. What's up with that?

Jamie

That's been happening for years. I remember 30 years ago, 2 Live Crew used the word in a song, saying "My nigga." It was obviously not used in disrespect but as a way of saying, "My boy, my homeboy, someone in my tribe, my people." So we can use it in our culture, but you can't use it as a white person. We can talk this way within our culture, but we know not to use it outside of it. It's like someone talking about your mama. I might not like what she does, but no one else had better talk bad about her. Rappers use the n-word all the time, and people all buy their music. It's a bit crazy and certainly a double standard. We can call a white person a "cracker" or "white boy" or redneck and talk about white privilege. But it doesn't work the other way around.

The problem today is that someone can do lots of great things in their life. They may even work to help the black community, but if they ever say the n-word, their careers, reputations, and sometimes livelihoods are destroyed. It's not right. Sometimes it's something they said years ago, and they still get destroyed by people because of it. I don't agree with that.

The problem is that there's no grace today. That's a major problem. Everyone needs grace because no one is perfect, everyone makes mistakes, and everyone says things they regret. The person who wants to "cancel" someone because of some little thing they said or did isn't perfect themselves. If their lives were exposed, they would not come out smelling like a rose either. We would all be better off if we'd forgive people for little things and not be so sensitive about words.

Bob

Here's another thing I want to discuss. I have a white teacher friend who worked in a racially mixed school; the school was mostly black. One of the things the teachers would do on a regular basis is have discussions about racial issues. They'd sit down together to have conversation with one another as a way to be sensitive to each other's perspectives and toward all the students. Inevitably, a white teacher would comment that they didn't think they were racist. According to this teacher, that comment would elicit a unified response from the black teachers; "Yes, you are; you just don't recognize it."

The black teachers would then go on to mention examples such as: "When the black young man comes into class with his pants hanging down, your first impression is that he's trouble"; "When you're at a movie theater and you expect the group of black kids to be quiet during the movie, that's racist, because that's not how they have grown up acting in movie theaters – they like to holler and make some noise"; "When you respond with more sympathy to the problems of white children than you do to those of black kids, that's racist"; or "When you assume black young people can do certain things better than white youth, such as dance and sing, it's being racist."

I must admit that I found myself getting very defensive, hearing that story. My immediate reaction is to reject those comments. I know that some people say that my defensiveness is the evidence that I actually am racist; if I weren't racist, I'd more readily accept that I am.

But here is my problem: Do I have to accept what someone else says about me? As a white person, do I have to accept the label a black person puts on me, such as racist, and let another person define me? It seems to me that this is what we are trying to avoid. Black people don't want to be stereotyped or labeled or automatically categorized by white people. It seems only fair that white people don't have to accept a label from someone else either.

152

We have the right to determine for ourselves who we are. We can choose not to be racist if we wish.

Jamie

I agree that we shouldn't let others define us. Blacks certainly don't want others defining them. I also know that white people react against the term "white privilege." I can certainly understand how a white person might say, "I didn't get everything given to me; I've had to work for everything I have. I have worked hard all my life; the fact that I now have a decent standard of living isn't because of my privilege but because of my hard work." I get how someone can resent being thought of as privileged when they have worked very hard in their life.

Bob

Do I have some advantages because I was born white? The answer is absolutely "yes." For one thing, Caucasian is the majority race in America. It's always an advantage being in the majority; that's just common sense. If your race is the majority voice and power in a culture, things will naturally tend to work well for your race. Interestingly, I hear that this is going to change in the next 30 years. By 2050, there will still be more Caucasians in America than any other race, but those who are not Caucasian will actually be a majority. That's because the white population is expected to decrease in numbers while all other races will increase. The main driving force behind this will be that the Hispanic population is expected to dramatically increase in the next 30 years. In fact, there are already more people of Hispanic heritage in the United States than blacks. It will be interesting to see what changes and problems this creates. All this is to acknowledge that there is certainly some advantage to being in the majority race in a culture.

It also needs to be said that there have been many minority groups in the history of this nation. In America, there have been communities of Jewish, Irish, Asian, Polish, Russian, Italian, and

Japanese descendants who have faced challenges in building their life here. They did not come here as slaves and do not have that blight in their history, but they have certainly faced many disadvantages, discriminations, and prejudices. Yet most of these groups have overcome them. What is it about the black experience that holds them back?

You have certainly had some experiences of racism in your story. In reflecting on those, however, they may have hurt your feelings, but they didn't really impact the trajectory of your life. Tell me if you disagree. None of those kept you from attending a certain school, or choosing a career path, or deciding whom you would marry, or either leading you into crime or dissuading you from it. Some people think that racial "microaggressions" are not as harmless as they appear. It seems to me, however, that those experiences were on the periphery of your life. That would not have been true for those who experienced the institution of slavery, but it is for those who feel some occasional discrimination, rejection, or antipathy, for whatever reason. We all have to handle rejection in a variety of forms and need to learn to deal with it. You can make a big deal of those things or let them roll off your back. Perhaps that is easy for a white person to say, but that is how I feel. Life has not always been a bed of roses for me or for any white person I know.

Jamie

It is certainly true that the direction of my life was not determined by racism but my own poor choices. I also think that it is natural that someone in a minority would have to work a little harder to make their way because of some natural disadvantages that come with being in the minority. We do have to put up with what some people call "microaggressions." I don't like that word because it makes a big deal out of incidents that are sometimes insignificant. It's no way to live always being offended by things that happen to you.

154

You told the story about moving here and having to figure out where you would live. You said that you wondered if it was racist to move to the county where the school system was more homogenous than the city schools. As a father, your first priority was to your own children and their futures. In reflection, it seems like that has worked out pretty well for you, and I don't blame you, as a parent. You now have one child who has graduated from college and is working in engineering. Another is on the verge of graduation, so I'd say that it worked out well for you and your children. I don't fault you; it sounds like you made a good decision for your kids.

It is also true, however, that white flight has decimated many of our urban inner cities. When those who are upwardly mobile move to the suburbs, and those with leadership abilities leave for greener pastures, businesses also gradually relocate. Professionals buy larger homes elsewhere, and real estate values go down. Stable families exercise their right to the American dream, but it leaves others vulnerable. Those who cannot make this transition are the elderly, people in broken families, and those near the poverty line. Houses become rental properties and are not kept up as well. Entire neighborhoods begin to deteriorate with less desirable elements, including those inclined toward crime taking up residence. The result is that many inner-city areas today are terrible places to live and mere shells of their former splendor.[19]

Bob

That phenomenon has certainly been a reality. As I think about the general idea of racism, it seems that everyone can be racist. There are plenty of white racists just as there can be blacks who view everything through the lens of race. Everyone can treat another person with disrespect for a variety of reasons, race being just one of them. But it seems to me that I'm not a racist just because I'm born white. It's not morally wrong to be white. One's skin color doesn't make you guilty of something. What is wrong is to act unjustly or be indifferent to injustice to others, no matter your skin color.

I suppose that being white in a white culture does give me the prerogative to be blind to, or at least casual about, the injustices done to minorities. I'm sure I haven't cared enough about injustice because, being white, it wasn't "my problem." One of the good things about conversations like ours is that it lets people see things they never saw before.

The advent of television and the internet have had a tremendous impact on racial issues and often served to keep tensions stirred up. It is one thing to hear about some instance of racial injustice, but to see it on video often raises animosity to new levels. Watching an incident of racial injustice, whether at the hands of the police or someone else, stirs deep passions and resentments.

I do worry, however, that there are some people and groups who intentionally keep racial tensions stirred up. Pardon me for being cynical, but there is money, power, and influence at stake in our racial problems. Wherever these things are present, there is the opportunity for abuse. There is certainly federal, state, local, and private money that flows into programs aimed at racial issues. If we all suddenly got along, those funds would dry up, and so would the jobs they create. In addition, calling America racist gives people platforms to build influence. No one will admit to doing this, but it seems to me that everyone knows this is the case. It is hard to find workable solutions when people keep stirring the pot.

Jamie

I have heard you say that you didn't grow up around many black people. Likewise, I didn't grow up around many white people. In the projects where I grew up, almost everyone was black. There was one white guy about my age in the projects, and we became friends. At one point, we got high together, and that was most of our relationship.

156

It was really when I became director of the Sparrow's Nest that I began to have more interactions with white people. Many on the board of directors are white, and I've made some great friends among them. It has also given me the opportunity to experience white culture in ways I had not before.

For example, I learned that white people have Christmas parties. We didn't have those in the 'hood. White people have Christmas parties, and everyone brings Christmas cookies and so forth. That was new to me. Of course, if you are on the streets or high on drugs, you don't really celebrate Christmas; you are just surviving. I also observe that white people make big decisions over breakfast and lunch. They go to lunch together and talk things over. Then they decide what to do. This doesn't happen in the 'hood, and it's one of the cultural differences between us.

My wife and I had been going to an all-black church but decided, at one point, to try one of the large churches in town. The first thing we noticed was that we got out of church in an hour. That was new to us. I looked at my wife and said, "Is it over?" When I realized that they could do church in an hour, instead of three, I said, "Man, this is nice. I could get used to this."

After we had been there a while, someone asked me if there was anything the church could do to be more inviting to black people. I said that they needed some black folks in the praise band. I don't think anyone had thought about that. That was something they did, and I think it has helped.

The truth is that many black people don't grow up around whites, other than perhaps their school experience, so they don't understand their culture. They think whites are being racist, when it's just a cultural difference. The same is true for Asians and Hispanics; they have their own cultural practices, and sometimes they are just different, not wrong just different. It is also true that most black people don't really want to live in white neighborhoods. They would rather live with other blacks.

Discussion Questions
PART 5 – RACISM AND PREJUDICE

1. Do you remember any of the signs of segregation, such as segregated water fountains? Do you see any signs of segregation today? If you attend church, has your experience of church been segregated or not?

2. Do you think it is possible for people to be prejudiced without realizing it? Is lack of compassion or involvement a form of prejudice? Explain.

3. Do you think that experiences of racism, such as Jamie experienced are "minor"? Explain. How would you evaluate an experience as minor or major? Do all people experience these kinds of rejections, disparagements, and insults in some form? Are racial insults or indignities more harmful than other kinds of offenses?

4. Do you think it is racist to move into an area with a better, more homogenous school district if you have the financial means to do so?

5. How important is it for you to have friends in a minority group or an ethnic group different than yours? Do you have any? How would you describe those relationships? Should a person actively seek them out? Do you think it is true that blacks would rather live around other blacks?

6. What do you think about the degree of outrage aimed at a white person who uses the n-word? Do you think this justified? What does it mean that rappers can use it with immunity in a song? Why is there so little grace surrounding the use of the term?

7. Some people claim that America is a racist country or that certain institutions are systemically racist. Do you think there are certain kinds of unfairness in modern America that are built into the system? What are they? How would people argue for and against such claims? Why do you think there is sometimes so much emotion generated by this area of discussion?

8. Do you think blacks experience more disadvantages in America than other minorities? Explain.

9. Various types of guilt usually have forms of absolution. Is there such a thing as absolution for "white guilt"? Is there a form of "white penance" that satisfies this type of guilt? What might it be? Who determines what an appropriate measure of penance would be?

10. Do you believe that there are people and groups who keep racial tensions stirred up? Explain.

PART 6 – POLICE, CRIME, AND THE CRIMINAL JUSTICE SYSTEM

17

THE POLICE

Jamie

A S THE DIRECTOR OF THE SPARROW'S NEST, I have the opportunity to interact with a number of community organizations, one of which is the police department. The Athens-Clarke County Police Department has an annual Christmas program called "Shop with a Cop." Officers look for families living in poverty throughout the community, then raise money, through grants, to help out those families during the Christmas season. An officer takes a child to the store to "Shop with a Cop," and they buy them toys and other things they need. It's a great program and one that not only helps people but builds good relations within the community.

The police department had called the Sparrow's Nest to ask if we knew of a needy family they could help. We gave them a name, and the police department allocated funds for this family. When it came time to make the presentation, they invited me to come to police headquarters and to be in a picture with the family.

There were some businessmen and others there with a number of police officers. As I was standing there, waiting for the presentation to begin, I saw a police officer who looked familiar. He walked up to me and said, "Jamie Scott! Do you remember me?" I looked down at his badge and saw his name, "Saulters." I immediately knew who he was and said, "Saulters. Of course I

161

remember you." Officer Saulters, now Deputy Chief Saulters, was a police officer with whom I had a number of encounters when I was selling drugs and involved in crime.

He said to me, "Jamie, do you remember the last time I saw you?" I did remember; it was probably 20 years earlier. I said, "Man, do I remember it!"

I was in downtown in Athens at the corner of Broad Street and Magnolia. I had been up for a couple of days straight, hustling and selling drugs. I was standing on the street corner, looking for a ride back to one of the housing authority projects. I had exhausted my clientele downtown and was looking to get back to a more fruitful area for my drug trafficking. That's what I did, move between one set of projects and the next, looking for people in need of drugs. When things were going slow in one place, I'd move to another where the need might be greater. That day I was looking for a ride to the projects or potentially someone downtown who might want some drugs.

It was about 10:30 in the morning, and I saw a police car go down the street. I wasn't paying much attention because I wasn't bothering anybody. But the officer turned the car around, pulled up beside me, right on the curb, and jumped out of the car. I had some crack cocaine in my hand; we called it a "cookie." When you sold someone cocaine in that form, you just broke off a chunk, depending on how much they wanted. When I saw him coming toward me and realized what was about to go down, I put the entire cookie in my mouth to swallow it. When you deal in drugs, you know a variety of ways to get rid of them in a hurry, and one of them is just swallow them. That might be dangerous, but in that moment it didn't seem as dangerous as going to jail, so that's what I did.

Officer Saulters saw what I did and didn't want me to swallow the drugs, so he came at me, and we began to wrestle. He got me in a headlock and said, "Don't swallow it, Jamie. Don't swallow those drugs. It's dangerous. We'll have to take you to the hospital to pump your stomach." He might have been thinking about my safety, but he also wanted to make an arrest. He was new on the force and had just hit the streets. He kept telling me to spit out the drugs, but it was too late; I had already swallowed them.

He finally realized I had swallowed the drugs and let me go. He said to me, "Jamie, why'd you do that?" I replied, "What? I didn't do anything." He said, "You know what I'm talking about. I saw you throw those drugs in your mouth." I said, "You've got to prove that. Those weren't drugs. I swallowed some Tic Tacs."

At that point, he started searching me, and I didn't have anything on me, so he said, "Put your hands behind your back." He was getting ready to arrest me. I said, "Saulters, you know that the camera on the front of your police car has recorded this whole encounter." I knew that I didn't have any drugs on me at that point. So I said, "Check this out, man. You're going to take me to jail, but I don't have any crack cocaine on me. The thing is, I'm going to have to get an attorney and file some kind of grievance, because you just jumped on me for no reason, and I don't have any dope." Saulters looked at me and thought about it for a minute. Then he just sighed, turned around, and walked away. I hadn't seen Saulters since that incident until I met him again at the police station that day.

Bob

I have only had a few encounters with the police; in general, I would not describe them as "warm and fuzzy." When I moved from Charlotte, North Carolina, to Athens, Georgia, I vaguely knew I needed to register my car in Georgia. Eventually. It seemed a bit of a hassle, however, and I didn't get around to it. My registration sticker ran out, however, and a police officer noticed it one evening, sitting behind me in traffic. I was on my way home from a meeting at church, and he pulled me over.

The officer was all business. I have heard of people talking officers out of tickets, but that has never been my experience. I've

163

never felt like an officer gave me that opening. The officer asked for my license and registration. When he asked if I knew why he had pulled me over, I said, "No, sir." I didn't think I had run any red lights or been speeding. When he mentioned my expired registration, however, I knew I was caught.

He noticed that I had a North Carolina license plate and asked me if I lived in Georgia. When I replied that I did, he asked how long. I replied, "About six months." Then I added, "I've been meaning to get my car registered in Georgia but haven't gotten it done yet." He replied, "I'm going to give you some incentive." He did, in the form of a $150 ticket. I had found the needed motivation to register my car in Georgia.

When I was 18 years old, I got pulled over, along with another car, for running a yellow light. I thought it was yellow; perhaps it was red. The officer didn't give me a ticket on that occasion because the other car had apparently run the light worse than I had. This officer was also all business; it must be something that's taught. I can't remember getting pulled over since then for a traffic violation.

I did have a couple of minor fender benders, neither of which were my fault. In those instances, the police officers were nice and efficient, actually very helpful. At the church, we have had an occasional break-in or some other instance in which we have interacted with the police. On these occasions, they have been cordial, nice, and helpful. Other than that, I have had few encounters with the police and certainly not wanted to have any confrontational ones. It has been a comfort, however, to know that the police are around. I have very much liked the idea that, if I needed a police officer, I could call 911 and expect one to show up.

Jamie
Saulters and I had a previous encounter. As we were standing in the police department that day, he brought it up. He said, "Jamie, we had one encounter that scared the living daylights out of me. Do you

remember that night I caught you coming out of the liquor store with those stolen bottles of champagne?" I did remember.

What happened was that I had gone into the liquor store and stolen several bottles of very expensive liquor. Apparently, the police had been told that someone was coming into the store stealing bottles of Moët and other expensive champagnes, so they were on alert. I walked out of the store with two bottles of expensive champagne in my pants. They had said something to me on the way out of the store, but I had cussed at them, and they didn't do anything, except that they must have called the police. It was very dark, and I was headed to a nearby hotel.

Officer Saulters pulled up and got out of the car. Because it was dark, I didn't see him until he called my name. Here's how Saulters told his side of the story to me that day at the police station. "I came on you in the dark and said your name. You immediately reached into your pants, and I assumed you might be pulling out a gun. So I pulled my gun and said, 'Jamie, stop right there.' Then I heard a loud noise that sounded just like a gunshot. Then I heard another one. I said to myself, 'He's just shot me.' But you hadn't shot me. You'd taken those two bottles and slammed them down on the pavement. When they hit, they exploded, and it sounded like gunshots. That is one of the scariest moments I've had as a police officer. I thought I was going to die."

I hadn't shot him, of course, just destroyed the evidence. He said, "Jamie, I know you stole that liquor from the liquor store." I said, "You gotta prove that, and you don't have any evidence. Look at all that glass on the ground. Are you going to put all that glass back together? And put the alcohol back in the bottles?" He looked at me for a moment and said, "Jamie, don't let me see you for the rest of the night." I walked away, and he did too.

Saulters walked the streets at that point, and we knew we'd see each other again. We could speak and be pleasant when we met, but we knew what the other one was about. He had a job to do, which was arrest criminals. I was committing crimes and trying not to get caught. It would not be Saulters, however, but someone else who would make the arrest that would send me to prison for the last time.

Bob

On Saturday evening, Sept. 16, 2017, at 11:17 p.m., the Georgia Tech campus police received a phone call about a student acting strangely.[20] The original call reported that he had a gun. When campus police arrived, they found a fourth-year student, walking around in a somewhat disoriented fashion, carrying what appeared to be a knife. The officers confronted the student and instructed him to put down the knife. He refused and continued to walk toward the officers. The officers continued to attempt to reason with the student, saying, "Nobody wants to hurt you." In a video that a witness recorded, the student is heard to yell, "Shoot me!" When he continued to walk toward police, refusing to drop the knife, a police officer shot him. He later died at Grady Hospital in Atlanta.[21]

The student was Scout Schultz, a 21-year-old white engineering student with a 3.9 grade point average, whom his mother described as "scary smart." He was an activist on campus and president of Georgia Tech's Pride Alliance. According to reports, he described himself as a nonbinary intersex person who liked being addressed with they/them pronouns. Schultz had gone through counseling in the past and suffered from bouts of depression. An attorney for the Schultz family said that Scout was having an obvious mental breakdown. His father simply asked, "Why did you have to shoot him?"

It turned out that the knife he held was a multipurpose tool that included pliers, a screwdriver, and a very small knife. The incident prompted calls for changes in police procedures and questions about how this situation might not have resulted in the student's death. It turns out that Georgia Tech campus police did not carry less lethal weapons, such as a Taser.

166

When a police officer uses deadly force against a black person, it especially makes the news. On Friday, June 12, 2020, Atlanta police responded to a phone call about a man who had passed out in the drive-through at a Wendy's restaurant.[22] The man's name was Rayshard Brooks, and he was indeed inebriated, failing a field sobriety test at the scene. When officers attempted to arrest Brooks, he got into a physical altercation with police, taking the stun gun of one of the officers in the process. He then began to run from the officers, eventually turning and firing the stun gun at them. When that happened, one of the officers pulled his weapon and returned fire, killing Brooks as he ran away.

Brooks was the father of three daughters and had attended the birthday party of his 8-year-old daughter earlier in the day. He was, however, on criminal probation and would have gone back to prison had he been arrested. For that reason, he resisted arrest vigorously that evening. Following the incident, the officer doing the shooting was fired, and the other officer placed on administrative leave pending an investigation. This incident precipitated several weeks of riots in Atlanta during which the Wendy's was burned to the ground by protesters shouting, "Arrest the cops."[23]

It would always be nice if a police officer did not have to use deadly force. A caller to a radio talk show suggested that we ought to change the directive given to police officers from "law-enforcement officers" to "peace officers." Instead of charging them with a commitment to strict obedience to the law, we ought to encourage them to work to keep the peace, find peaceful solutions, and use lethal force only as a very last resort. I suspect this is already the directive given to police, but it is apparently hard to apply in every situation.

The job of the police is the safety of the public and the prevention of crime. People need to understand that confrontations with the police are not in their favor. Walking toward police officers with a knife and refusing orders to stop will generally not end well. It also won't turn out well if you fight with a police officer, take his stun gun, then turn and fire it toward him. Everyone ought to understand that you place your life in grave danger by such actions.

It seems to me that we ought to continue to look for nonlethal ways to restrain people who are not an imminent danger to police officers or others. How to do so is certainly challenging, but we are a creative and inventive nation. People also need to realize that resisting arrest, especially if you carry a weapon, places your life in jeopardy. There should not be anything hard to understand about that!

18

CRIME

Jamie

IN THE 10th GRADE, I was facing two life sentences. The year was 1987, and I had just turned 17. I had a friend in the projects that I hung with sometimes. We lived in Atlanta at the time, and I went to Carver High School. He had a girlfriend who lived in the lower apartments; I had one who lived at the upper end.

My friend and his family were from New York. He had a brother who worked in the sheriff's department but who had grown up in the 'hood. My friend's brother had access to cocaine that the police had confiscated, and he was supplying us with powder cocaine to sell. In the streets at that time, people were selling powder cocaine to freebase. They cooked it up to get it into rock form, then smoked it. Anyway, we hung together and sold cocaine. We'd spend time together with our girlfriends, and his girlfriend had a younger brother who was a little bit younger than my friend.

One night I was at my girlfriend's apartment when there was a knock on the door. Someone said that the police wanted to talk to me down at the bottom of the complex because my friend was in a lot of trouble. When I got there, the police saw me and said, "We've got your friend locked up (they called his name) because there's a guy that has lost his life. You need to come downtown with us."

When I got downtown, they asked me to tell the story from my point of view. I told them that I didn't know what they were talking about and didn't have a story to tell. As it turned out, my friend had told the police that he and I had been hanging out together when I shot this person because he tried to cheat us in a drug deal. My friend even gave them a gun that he said was used in the murder. I didn't know anything about it but realized my friend was trying to frame me.

The police believed him, and I would spend 8½ months in jail waiting to go to trial. He took a plea deal for 20 years with the stipulation that he would testify against me. Needless to say, I had a lot to think about during those months in jail. One was whether or not to take the plea bargain the prosecutor offered me; it was to confess to the crime and serve life in prison. I knew I hadn't done it, so serving life didn't sound like a bargain to me. I also knew that if I were convicted by a jury I could get the death penalty.

I had a friend from the 'hood who was in prison with me about that time. During the mid-1980s, stealing cars was big business, and he had been caught stealing cars. Everyone had a favorite kind of car they liked to steal; there were the Cadillac boys and the Toyota bandits, etc. I don't know what kind of cars this guy stole, but he had gotten caught.

He said to me, "You need to take that plea deal; at least you won't get the death penalty." I said, "Man, I'm not taking anything." He said, "Look man, if they convict you, you are going to fry; you need to think about that."

One day, when we were all in the yard, another person pointed out an old man standing off by himself. He said, "You need to go talk to that guy. Tell him what you're going through." I did, and he gave me some psalms in the Bible to read. He told me to ask God to help me. Then I needed to fast during the week before my trial and pray for God's help.

That got me to thinking about God, something I obviously hadn't done very much. In fact, I hadn't ever been to church except for the funerals of my uncle, my auntie, and my cousin. I told you that I saw my uncle shot when I was 5. My auntie was messing with another woman's boyfriend, and she poisoned her. That's the story I heard. My cousin got gunned down at a club in Athens, on Pope Street. Other than those funerals, I had never been inside a church.

It was a few months after I read those psalms that I gave my life to the Lord for the first time. I'll tell that story later on. As it turned out, God was with me and didn't let me get convicted. My mother got me a lawyer, one that she paid for herself. As it turned out, they just didn't have enough evidence to pin the murder on me. Several witness said they saw me with my friend at the place the guy was shot, but my lawyer showed that they could not actually see the place from their windows. It was also very dark, so it would have been almost impossible to recognize people from that distance.

I would have had an alibi with my girlfriend, but she left town. So did my friend's girlfriend and her brother. They just vanished, and no one knew where they had gone. So she wasn't there to testify on my behalf. My friend's girlfriend also wasn't there to testify against him. None of them wanted to be involved, and they just disappeared.

In the end, the jury found me not guilty and set me free. I think they arrested several other people, but I don't think they ever convicted anyone for the murder. I don't know if my friend did it or not. I did see my friend, who testified against me, in prison later on, and he apologized to me but also didn't confess to it himself. All I knew was that I was free. I was very grateful to my lawyer and my mom for hiring him and even to God. Even though I had prayed to God to help me, when I got out, I forgot all about the promises I had made.

Bob

I have been a victim of crime. When I moved to Charlotte, North Carolina, to be the pastor of a church there, I moved into the church manse across the street. I moved my furniture and some other items into the house then went back to Atlanta where my folks lived before I started work. When I came back to Charlotte, I discovered the house had been broken into. All they had stolen was the microwave oven, but it was an important part of my kitchen. Someone in the church purchased a new one for me.

Over the next month, I experienced an unexpected reaction; it was the sense of being violated. Someone had been in my house and been looking at my stuff. I didn't know how long they had been in

171

the house or what they had done, but it was an eerie feeling. It was surprising how strong the feeling was and how long it took to subside. For the longest time, when I came home, I wondered if someone, or that same person, had been in my house.

Since then, there have been occasional break-ins in neighborhoods in which I have lived, but I have not personally experienced a break-in. When my parents lived in Atlanta, in the suburbs, my mother heard what sounded like someone opening the door to their house, late one night. She awakened my father, who got up. Someone had indeed opened the side door and come into their home. My parents apparently made enough noise that the person realized someone was at home and left. Had the person decided to come in anyway and potentially confront them or overpower them, they had little defense. It might have turned out badly for my parents. They were shaken but very fortunate.

On another occasion, after they had moved to Athens, they had their house broken into while they were away. They were out of town and got a call from the police. The alarm had gone off at their house. When the police arrived, the front door had been kicked in. The alarm had apparently frightened away the burglars but not before they grabbed what they could. As it turned out, our sons, about 8 and 6 years old at the time, had left their Game Boys, their hand-held miniature gaming devices, on the coffee table. The burglars took them and left.

Luckily, we were able to secure the door and lock the house back up until a full repair of the door could be made. The problem was that we had to explain to our boys what happened to their Game Boys. As we thought about it, we didn't want to make them afraid, at their young ages, to stay at my parents' house, worrying that a burglar might break down the door at any moment. So we decided not to mention the break-in. This left us with the problem of the missing Game Boys. Our approach was simply to look for them, wonder with our boys where we might have misplaced them, and eventually replace them. It was a great mystery in our household for a number of years. When they got to be teens and my parents had moved to a different house, we told them what had actually happened. It brought home the reality of crime, as relatively insignificant as this loss was. Someone who steals takes away from someone else, violates their space, and makes their life more difficult. It isn't pleasant to be the victim of crime.

Jamie

I served four stints in prison. By prison, I don't mean the county jail. Prison is where they ship you off someplace because you've been convicted and have to do time. When you are going to prison, you first have to go to the diagnostic center and get processed. They take blood, check you out from head to toe, and process your paperwork. Then they decide which prison to send you to. If you commit armed robbery, aggravated assault, or murder, you're going to prison. You can sometimes get bonded out of the county jail when you are awaiting trial for lesser crimes. Once you go to prison, however, there's no getting out until your time is done.

Most of my arrests were for shoplifting. I probably got arrested for that 30 times. Ordinarily you don't do serious time for shoplifting, and I had gotten pretty good at it, except, of course, that I got caught a lot. We wouldn't just steal shirts from the department store; we'd steal a whole rack of shirts. Or blue jeans. We called it, "Rayfielding." I don't know where that name came from, but that's what we called it when we just ran out of the store with an armful of clothes. If a security guard tried to stop me as I ran out of the store, I'd show my gun and say, "All you have is a Taser and nightstick. Let it go and live to see another day." I started shoplifting at 13 years old. The thing is that you knew you'd get caught but not do much time, so it seemed worth it.

A friend and I would also go into the convenience store across from the apartments and just walk out with stuff, mostly beer and wine. We knew that by the time the clerk called the police, and they arrived, we'd be safe and sound back in the apartment. They'd see us coming and say, "Don't come into this store," but we'd go in anyway, take what we wanted, and walk out.

The first time I went to prison was when I was 20 years old; that was 1990. I had spent six months in the county jail, and there was a guy there who, according to word on the street, had killed a friend of ours from Athens named "El Mongo." The guy was actually in protective custody because the police officers knew people would hurt him if they got the chance. My friend Spoon was also in the county jail with me, and we decided to try to get the guy alone. We schemed to find him alone and stabbed him with some pens we had sharpened into weapons. I went to prison for that, on a simple assault charge, and served a year, from 1990 until 1991.

I did five years to the door from 1994 until 1999 for the sale of crack cocaine. It was a convicted felony with possession of a firearm, which was why I got five years. The third time I went to prison, it was for auto theft. I had stolen a car from Athens and gone to Atlanta. I started to hit up different neighborhoods, hitting licks as we called it, committing crimes in different neighborhoods.

I got caught with the stolen car when I was visiting a friend, and the stolen car was out front. When I looked out the front door, I saw several police cars pulled up. I knew then that the car was hot, and I'd have to abandon it. But I had some things in it, so I waited until the police left and went to get my things out of the car. But the police had circled around, and they pulled up on me.

They said, "We know you stole this car." I said, "What you mean? I didn't steal this car." I knew that, to convict you of stealing a car they had to find you either stealing it or driving it, so I said, "You can't lock me up." When they asked me my name, I gave them the name of a guy who'd played quarterback for the University of Georgia. I said, "My name is Quincy Carter." The policeman said, "You're not Quincy Carter; who are you?" I said, "Quincy Carter, that's my name." We went around and around for about 15 minutes until finally they arrested me and took me to the Atlanta homicide division where they could run my fingerprints and figure out who I really was. As it turned out, they had video footage of me running out of a store with clothes, Rayfielding, and getting into the stolen car. I did two years for auto theft, from 2000 to 2002.

The last time I went to prison was for theft by taking and simple battery for stealing from an ABC Liquor Store. I got the battery charge because I got into a fight with the store clerks. It turned out that there were a lot of them there at that particular moment, about five of them, and they held me down until the police got there. For that conviction, I served from 2005 to 2007. I also had a gun on me and an 8-ball of cocaine, so it made the charges more serious. I got out of prison for the last time in 2007.

All in all, I was arrested 54 times. In total, I have spent almost 20 years of my life in prison. That's because I started getting arrested at the age of 14. I did four stints in Level 5 prisons, which are where they keep the worst offenders, murderers and so forth. At one point, I was in a really nice, relaxed prison situation, but I messed someone up in a fight and got shipped off to a Level 5. As it turned out, I much preferred the Level 5 prisons where the lifers were, though I had never committed crimes that serious. I liked it better because those guys knew how to do time and made sure they had plenty of weed to smoke and got lots of contraband into the prison to make their time tolerable.

My life could have gone very differently. In fact, I had a chance to avoid much of this trouble after I was acquitted by the jury at age 18, because I had just had a religious conversion. This was when I was facing the possibility of serving life in prison for something I didn't do. Sometimes innocent people get convicted, and I knew it could happen to me. I was in deep trouble and needed help from somewhere, so I prayed to God. I told God I would serve him and accept his Son Jesus. If he gave me the opportunity, I'd take his message around the world. This was a real thing, and I was serious about it.

The jury trial went well, and I was acquitted of the murder. When I got home, the first person I saw, even before I went inside my own apartment, was my good friend T-Bone. He got that name because he was scrappy and bad to the bone. T-Bone was really happy to see me and invited me up to his apartment, where he had a 12-pack of Schlitz Malt Liquor. We had some beers, and then he began to tell me about his latest hustle.

He said, "Jamie, we aren't stealing cars anymore or running out of stores. We're moving on to bigger things. No one wants powder anymore; the latest thing is crack cocaine. I'm hustling for Big Al over in Bankhead Court, and I told him I had a friend. He said he'd like to meet you." At this point, he pulled out a bundle of crack cocaine. A bundle was a gallon bag full of little bags of crack. You could have a $500 bundle or a $1,000 bundle, all the way up to a $2,500 bundle, depending on what you thought you could sell.

Then he said, "And we aren't just smoking weed anymore. Look at this." He pulled out some marijuana and broke open his bundle. He began to show me how to put crack cocaine in a joint and smoke it with the weed. People called these "747s" or "ready ready's," because it was all ready to go; you just had to smoke it. I had never done crack cocaine before, and when I smoked it, I was on cloud nine. But that is the problem with crack cocaine. They say that the first high is the best, and you are always chasing that first high but never have it again.

I had come out of jail that day with the best of intentions. I had a Bible in my hand and some religious literature in my pocket. The allure of the streets was too strong, however, and at that point, it was all I knew. My new life with God was quickly out the door. I was back on the streets and into even more serious crime.

19

CONVERSATION ABOUT CRIME AND THE CRIMINAL JUSTICE SYSTEM

Jamie

ONE OF THE FIRST THINGS I NEED TO SAY is that I have had a lot of repenting to do. Now that I am not in my former life, I have the chance to reflect on some of the things I have done, and I've had plenty of moments of serious regret and repentance. I've asked God to forgive me, and I know he has. It's one of the great things about Christianity, the possibility of forgiveness and a fresh start.

I've also tried to make amends where I could. I told the story of the arrest that led to my last time in prison. It was when several of the liquor store employees wrestled me to the ground and held me down until the police arrived. That arrest led to a two-year prison term. After I got out, I went back to the liquor store and apologized to the owner. I told him I had committed my life to Christ and was sorry and knew I'd done wrong; I said I'd be glad to pay for all the things I had stolen. He was very gracious and told me that it was OK; I'd served my time, and that was enough. He also said that I was the first one ever to come back and apologize for stealing from him.

I also had to apologize to my aunt about that too. She had driven me to the liquor store that night. She didn't know what I was going to do; actually I didn't know what I was going to do, but I got in there, and no one seemed to be looking, so I grabbed some liquor and started to walk out. That's when it went bad, and several of the employees jumped me. When the police cars showed up, they surrounded my auntie's car, assuming she had driven me there for the robbery. I told them that she didn't have anything to do with it, and they let her go, but I know it scared the daylights out of her. When I got out of prison, I went and told her how sorry I was about getting her mixed up in all that.

There have been plenty of people I robbed during those days. When I was working the streets, if you were going to rob someone, you'd stand up close beside them, and say, "OK, break yourself." That meant break the bank, empty your pockets, and give me everything you've got, because you're getting robbed. Sometimes you'd show your gun, and sometimes you didn't need to. I've seen a couple of people I robbed and told them I was sorry and was trying to live a different life.

I also told about when my friend and I stabbed the guy who had killed our friend El Mongo; we stabbed him with pens we had sharpened into weapons. He ended up serving 20 years for killing El Mongo. I sometimes see him now at the Sparrow's Nest. He's been in what we call our "returning citizens" program where we try to help people reintegrate into ordinary life after they've been in prison. He now has a job driving a truck and owns his own truck. He has even donated to the ministry. I hadn't said anything to him, but finally I got up the nerve to apologize. I didn't know whether he'd be open to it or not, but I said, "Hey man, I'm sorry about that time we jumped you in prison. That was my bad. I wasn't doing right in my life at that point. I've felt bad about it and just wanted you to know it." He was cool and said he appreciated me saying that I was sorry.

As we talked, I was interested in hearing him reflect on what he had done killing El Mongo. He had actually killed the wrong person; he meant to kill someone else. But El Mongo had his head down on a table, resting, and he mistook him for the person he was angry with. So to make things worse, he had not only killed someone but the wrong person. When we talked, he said, "It was the worst decision of my life. You should never make a decision out of anger, because you can't undo some decisions. And some actions affect you the rest of your life like that one did me. I now tell my son and daughter all the time to be wise in their decisions. I tell them they need to do good with their lives. People can take life through their actions; we can also give life. That's what I tell them they need to do, give life by doing good to other people."

Bob
There has been lots of conversation lately about racism and whether or not white police are racist. Some people have even suggested that black cops treat black people differently than they do white people. What has been your experience? Do you think that white police, or even all police, are racist?

Jamie
Let me answer that question by starting with my experience in prison. When I had my first stints in prison, the inmates were almost all black, I'd say about 95%. That has started to change. When I served my last prison stint, I looked around and said, "Where'd all these white guys come from?" They were serving time because they had gotten caught up in the methamphetamine epidemic.

Black drug dealers tended to traffic in cocaine - first powder cocaine, then crack. What was interesting was that most white users didn't graduate to crack; powder always seemed to be the drug of choice for white users. It was also true that the penalties were not as stiff for powder cocaine as crack. You could get caught with twice as much powder cocaine as crack but get a lesser sentence. President Obama changed the law to make things more equal. I think he didn't like black criminals being discriminated against.

But when meth came along, lots of white people got involved. They both got addicted and started selling. That's when the white prison population got much larger.

When I first got into the prison system, there was a lot of racism in it, from white guards aimed at the black prison population. Now they have cameras everywhere in prison, but it wasn't that way originally. This meant that guards could get away with more than they do now. This was especially true in the south Georgia prisons. For example, if you hassled one of the female guards, the next day her brothers and cousins, who were also guards, would strap you to a chair in your cell and beat you mercilessly. When the next shift came on duty, another set of cousins would come in and beat you. This would go on for a couple of days around the clock. Then they'd put you in isolation until you healed up. If someone from your family came to see you, they'd just say you got transferred somewhere else. If it took a month for you to heal, that's how long you'd stay in isolation. I always felt like this was "good old white boys" taking out their racial hatred on us black folks.

I've had similar kinds of experiences in prisons and even county jails all over the state. It just happens, or used to. Maybe it doesn't happen as much anymore. To get to your original question however, I don't think any of my arrests were racially motivated. I got arrested because I had committed a crime. At that point, it didn't matter that I was black or white; what mattered what that I had robbed someone, shoplifted, stolen a car, or assaulted someone. I honestly didn't think I was treated badly because I was black; I got in trouble because I broke the law.

This was also true for the people in prison with me. If you ask me how many of them were there because they had committed the crimes for which they were convicted, the answer would be all of them, or almost all of them. Sure, many of them said they were innocent, but they weren't. They were all convicted and sentenced to prison because they were guilty, not because of their skin color. Whether the black criminals got different sentences from white prisoners, I don't know. In my case, I always got what was the average sentence for what I had done. Truth be told, I sometimes got a lesser sentence than I deserved.

Bob

So let's talk about prisons and crime. I looked at the statistics about the makeup of the prison population today. There are clearly a disproportionate number of blacks in prison today. For example, blacks are only 13.4% of the population but make up 37.5% of the prison population. Whites are 76.5% of the U.S. population and make up 58.7% of the prison population, although that statistic for whites includes Hispanics and Latinos.[24] These statistics come from the Federal Bureau of Prisons.

A clearer way to look at it might be to think about the numbers in prison per 100,000 residents in the United States. There are more than 330,000,000 people living in the United States today. Whites are 58%, blacks 13.4%, Hispanics and Latinos 18%, Asians 5.8%, and two or more races 3%.[25] At the end of 2019, there were 1,430,800 people in prison in the United States. That was actually down by about 30,000 from the end of the previous year.[26]

Here is the statistic that jumps out at you. According to the U.S. Justice Department's report at the end of 2019, there were 214 white people in prison per 100,000 residents. There were 525 Hispanics in prison per 100,000 residents. There were 1,096 blacks in prison per 100,000 residents. What that says is, by percentage of population, there are twice as many Hispanics in prison as whites, twice as many blacks as Hispanics, and over four times as many blacks in prison as whites, as a percentage of population.

What does this mean? There is an outcry in some quarters that the criminal justice system is biased against blacks. If that is true, it must be biased against Hispanics also, since they are twice as likely as whites to be incarcerated. This glaring disparity, however, has a more obvious explanation. It's that blacks simply commit more crimes; that's why they are incarcerated at a greater rate.

This is what FBI statistics show. Its most recent yearly report makes this clear. As just a few examples, 46% of the arrests for murder were whites, 51% were blacks. Forty-five percent of arrests for robbery were whites, 53% were blacks. Weapons arrests were 56% whites and 42% blacks. Aggravated assault arrests were 62% white and 33% black.[27] This shows that plenty of white people are arrested for violent crimes, but one thing not included in these statistics is that 19% of the arrests categorized as whites were by Hispanics or Latinos, who were included as whites in the F.B.I. crime report.

What this says is simple. While there is a problem with crime throughout the United States and in all racial groups, it is particularly a problem in the black community. The black community has a problem with criminal activity that is greater than any other racial group, though it is also a significant problem in the Hispanic community. If blacks really are committing crimes at a rate twice that of Hispanics and four times that of whites, it is a tremendous problem that needs to be addressed. It needs to be addressed and fixed, if possible, because it indicates how badly the fabric of some parts of black culture is torn.

Jamie

I'd like to have some good defense to all those statistics, but I don't. I suspect they are accurate; young black men do commit an inordinate number of the crimes in the United States today. I know I did when I was young. I got arrested 54 times, but there were a whole lot of crimes I committed but didn't get arrested for. The ones I got arrested for were only the tip of the iceberg; there were a whole lot of others that no one ever saw. And I started at age 14!

As I've thought about crime and the black culture, it would not be surprising that black men would commit crimes, particularly young black men. They have no fathers in the home to control them. Who is it that has the ability to rein in the bad impulses of a young man? His father! That's the person God has particularly ordained for raising sons. But where are they in the black culture? They're absent. Mine was. For that reason, young black males, full of energy, wanting to make their way, often high school dropouts, gravitate to the quickest and seemingly easiest way to make a living; they get involved in crime, and there aren't any dads there to keep them from doing so.

Bob

I know you want to talk about the death of George Floyd and the conviction of Officer Derek Chauvin. What do you want to say about that?

Jamie

The death of George Floyd caused a great deal of outrage in the black community. I remember the video of Rodney King getting beaten up. He got beaten pretty badly by a group of police officers. The difference was that he lived. George Floyd died while being arrested by the police. From all indications, that should not have happened. That was why there was so much outrage.

I know that some people still believe that George Floyd had a lethal dose of drugs in his system, but usually when a person dies from drugs, it is very quick. You shoot up some bad heroin, and it puts stress on your heart. You don't linger; you go into cardiac arrest pretty fast. If the drugs in George Floyd's system were going to kill him, they would have done so quickly. I think it was the knee on the neck that killed him, and that is what the jury decided.

I also know that George Floyd was into things he should not have been doing. I think he had a counterfeit $20 on him. But he also didn't have a weapon.

Bob

He had also refused to get into the back of the police car like the officers told him. So he was resisting arrest, and he was a big guy who was not easy to handle.

Jamie

I agree. But that's why they have handcuffs, to restrain people. The picture I can't get out of my head is the one of Derek Chauvin's knee on George Floyd's neck. To me it looked like a guy who had just killed big game in Africa, and the officer was striking a pose with his prey.

183

Some people have said that this was a technique that he was taught in training, but that's not what his chief said at the trial. Every officer at the trial said he should never have put his knee on George Floyd's neck. I thought that was striking because officers don't usually turn on their fellow officers.

Now, overall I think the police are good people. There's a bad apple everywhere. In all occupations we see this from time to time. I hope police departments, however, are going to take a serious look at their training to reduce these kinds of incidents.

20

Conversation about Policing

Bob

I HAVE HEARD YOU TALK ABOUT how much the drug trade influences everything in the inner city where you grew up. Can you talk about how this is related to policing? I can imagine that many of the interactions between people and police have to do with drugs.

Jamie

Yeah, drugs are a huge problem. We call it the "dope trap." In inner-city neighborhoods, everything runs through the dope trap. This means that the drug trade is the hub around which the entire community life revolves. It's called the dope trap, because dope traps people. They get trapped in it, get addicted to some substance, and will do anything to get another hit.

This is just the way the dealers want it, of course. They will sell people anything to keep up their addiction because it keeps them coming back. And everything comes through this network, pistols, cars, businesses, business equipment, clothes, women, everything. I've even heard of guys selling their homes just so they can get drugs. It's crazy, and it is a trap. It catches you up in that lifestyle, and it's really hard to break out. Not many people do. For the dealers, it traps them in a life of criminality, dangerous encounters with the police, and prison.

I was a young black man who got caught in the dope trap. I not only started doing drugs at an early age but selling them. I didn't have a father to tell me any differently, so I did what all my friends were doing. Someone told me that the Protestant reformer Martin Luther said, "The devil raises children whose parents don't." This was true for me. I didn't have a father raising me, so the streets did. In terms of crime and drugs, the devil raised me. I followed him all the way into a life of bad things. He loves the drug trade because everything bad that happens runs through it. When I started doing crack cocaine, I got addicted to it and regularly had to feed my habit. I was good at hustling, however, and could not only feed my habit but make money in the process. Plus, I liked the high of hustling, making a deal, and having money. But like so many others I got caught up in the dope trap; only by the grace of God did I find my way out.

Bob

The drug trade is clearly one of those things that brings people into dangerous encounters with the police. These obviously put both the police and suspects into dangerous situations. There have been lots of cases in the news in recent years about blacks killed at the hands of police. These are all tragic, and I wish there were ways to reduce these incidents.

One question that continues to be asked is, are these deaths the result of racist police officers? One interesting note is that white police officers do not kill black suspects at a higher rate than black police officers. Black suspects are killed by both white and black officers.[28] In addition, in these shootings, two-thirds of the suspects were in possession of a gun, and almost all others were armed with some other type of weapon, such as a knife. Men were 95.5% of those killed.[29]

Does this mean, therefore, that all police are racist, including black officers? Some suggest so, but there is another more obvious reason. It is simply that more crime takes place in areas where there is drug trafficking and other felonious activity. And one of the places this is true is in inner-city areas, which are predominantly black. It makes sense to focus police efforts where crime is located. For that reason, police are more active in those areas and are therefore more likely to have dangerous interactions with people of color.

The overall number of people killed by police is small, although every death is certainly a loss. In 2019, 999 people in the United States were killed by the police.[30] In 2020, only 765 people were killed by police.[31] Some sources place the number at just over 1,000.[32] The fact that 28% of them were black has raised people's anger, since blacks are only 13% of the Unites States population. It might be considered remarkable, however, that only about 1,000 people were killed by police when we realize that there are typically 10 million arrests in an average year.[33]

In addition, there are a tremendous number of contacts between police and the public every year. In 2018, approximately 61.5 million people age 16 or older had at least one contact with a police officer.[34] Thirty-five million of these were because a resident called the police for some reason. Nine million were traffic accidents, and 30 million were police-initiated contacts. That means that only 1 in 61,500 contacts between the police and the public results in a death at the hands of the police. Only 1 in 30,000 police-initiated contacts result in a death. In other words, it is statistically very unlikely for a person to die at the hands of the police. This is particularly remarkable since 1 in 3 police-initiated contacts resulted in an arrest. It is also true that almost 90% of black murder victims are not killed by police, but by other blacks.[35]

Police work is dangerous. In 2020, there were 295 officers who lost their lives in the line of duty.[36] That number was a significant jump from 2019, in which the number was 139 and 2018, in which it was 183. Those numbers say that in fatal encounters one police officer will lose his or her life for every three people who do.

Could some deaths at the hands of the police have been avoided? I remember watching an old classic television series called "The Lone Ranger." The Lone Ranger was a former Texas Ranger who worked to keep law and order, supplementing the official authorities as a kind of independent agent. It was a great series, and

I loved it growing up. When the Lone Ranger originally made the decision to work for good using his masked identity, his friend and companion, Tonto, asked him, "How will you do this?" The Lone Ranger replied, "I will shoot to wound, not to kill." It was always great to see the Lone Ranger shoot the pistol out of the criminal's hand without hurting him.

Obviously, no one is that good a shot, and police are trained to shoot at the "center of mass." They try not to shoot, but, if they do, they shoot to stop the suspect from doing whatever they are doing. I think I understand this, from a police point of view. You pull your weapon only if it is a life-and-death situation. For that reason, any use of the firearm assumes that either the officer's or someone else's life is in danger. The police officer's job is to stop whatever dangerous behavior is placing his life or the life of others at risk. One indication that they never intend to kill is that an officer will immediately call for medical assistance if they ever shoot someone.

Real life complicates dangerous police encounters. As boxer Mike Tyson said, "Everyone has a plan until they get punched in the mouth." In a chaotic situation, police do not have the time or ability to "shoot to wound." Police are also warned that stray shots ricochet off pavement and buildings, potentially endangering innocent bystanders. It isn't good practice to send stray bullets flying while trying to be like the Lone Ranger.

Police are human and certainly can make the wrong decision in a moment of stress. When weapons are involved, wrong decisions can lead to fatal consequences. It is understandable that a police officer, in a dangerous situation, might err on the side of not being the one who loses his or her life.

Jamie
My time in crime put me in some dangerous situations. I have been in shootouts where things might have gone badly, and I could have been killed. By the grace of God, I wasn't. Fortunately I never took another person's life either. It is also by the grace of God that I

188

never got into an encounter with the police that cost me my life, though I often carried a gun and on occasion was in a physical engagement with a police officer. Though I was deep into criminal activity, there are people who are in much deeper than I was and who end up being very dangerous to encounter.

Bob

I heard someone comment on the fact that just because a suspect is unarmed does not mean he or she is not dangerous. A female police officer might stand 5 feet, 4 inches and weigh 120 pounds. If she is trying to arrest an inebriated suspect who is 6 feet 4 and 240 pounds, he might easily overpower her, take her gun, and kill her with it. Or use his physical superiority to cause her bodily harm.[37] An unarmed suspect can do a variety of things to put an officer's life in danger. One researcher found that, in 90% of the instances in which an unarmed person was shot by police, the person was "attempting to disarm an officer, drown an officer, throw an officer from a bridge or rooftop, strangle an officer, gesturing as if armed with a real weapon, keeping hands concealed despite commands, and charging toward an officer with apparent intent to assault."[38] So while the person may have been unarmed, it does not mean the shooting was not warranted. It also is true that, of the 999 people shot by police in 2019, only 12 were classified as "unarmed."[39]

There is one element that almost always gets left out in reports on cases of "police brutality." It is that the suspect was involved in criminality and resisted arrest. It is a terrible thing when an encounter with the police leads to a suspect's death, but there is also a common theme. The common element is criminal activity and resisting arrest. When these factors are avoided, deaths at the hands of the police fall to almost zero.

Jamie

Whatever the statistics, black people are suspicious of the police. Perhaps they should not be, but they are. There is a conversation that black parents universally have with their children. It has to do with what to do if you are in your car and get stopped by a police officer. I tell my granddaughter that a white young person will just have to show their license and registration, but, as a black person, she has to be more careful. I tell her to keep her hands visible and on the steering wheel, do exactly what the police officer tells her to do, and be very polite. Otherwise it might cost her her life. Even though they may not do it consciously or intentionally, I think the police are more suspicious of blacks than whites. I wish that weren't the case.

That being said, I'm not a proponent of defunding the police either. I don't like police mistakes and misjudgments any more than anyone else. In spite of problems like these, however, there has to be someone to keep law and order; otherwise it will be like the book of Judges in the Bible. Everyone will do what is right in their own eyes, and our country will be in chaos. There really are some bad guys out there. We recently had a guy in the office here looking for help. I knew him from the projects; we grew up together. He was always considered "OG," original gangster. That means he was a bad and dangerous dude. We said that this guy was double OG – that's how bad he was. The problem is, if there are no police, what are you going to do when someone who is OG, or maybe even double OG, comes to your house with bad intentions? You don't want the police defunded if that happens.

You also don't want to take weapons away from the police. Think about approaching a car as a police officer without a weapon. You don't know what you might find. The person in the car might be in a gang, or running drugs for a cartel, or someone who knows that if they go back to prison they may not ever get out. People don't realize that anyone with a warrant out for their arrest for armed robbery or assault with a weapon is considered armed and dangerous. The police have to approach that kind of person with caution because they are very dangerous. You can't just go skipping and whistling up to their car as if nothing bad is ever going to happen.

One of the problems is that all this talk about defunding the police must be terribly demoralizing to them. I hear that record numbers of police are retiring, and who would blame them? If I had laid my life on the line for 20 or 30 years and my wife was worried every day that I might not come home, I'd be tempted to hang it up. Thank God for officers who are still committed to protecting and serving. Some of the cities that didn't think they needed the police are changing their tunes lately, because they realize how chaotic it can get without them.

People who read my story will know where I have come from, and let me tell you, it is a war zone in some inner-city neighborhoods. In fact it is the people in those neighborhoods who need the police most in order to protect them from their neighbors. Some of those wanting to defund the police haven't seen someone killed in front of them like I have. What are you going to do when someone starts kicking down the door of your house? I know what I'm talking about because I was a career criminal. You don't want some of the people I grew up with coming into your house with bad intentions because you probably won't come out alive. What are you going to do if there aren't any police? Let's do more training if we need to, but let's not defund the police! And to any police officer today, I would say, "Please don't resign. Our communities need you!"

There is one more thing I need to add. For much of my life, from age 14 until 37, I was a career criminal. I made my living breaking the law, and it got me into lots of trouble, 54 arrests and four stints of serious time in prison, 20 years in all by the age of 37. When I decided to turn my life around, I stopped committing crimes. It's then that I stopped having problems with the police. Since I stopped committing crimes, I've stopped having trouble with the police! In fact, since then, I haven't had a bad interaction with a police officer. Oddly enough, I've even found myself, on occasion, thanking them for their service. For many black people, their problems with the police can be resolved in a simple way. Stop engaging in criminal behavior, and your confrontations with the police will disappear.

DISCUSSION QUESTIONS
PART 6 – CRIME, POLICE, AND THE CRIMINAL JUSTICE SYSTEM

1. If you are comfortable sharing, what kinds of encounters have you or someone you know had with the police? Have they been positive or negative? Have you ever feared for your life during a police encounter? Have you ever been the victim of what you consider to have been police profiling or misconduct?

2. Have you ever had to call the police for purposes of the protection of your person or property or in response to a crime? Was that experience positive or negative? Have you ever been the victim of a crime? What was that experience like?

3. As a black person, Jamie felt the need to have "the conversation" with his granddaughter about how to act if stopped by the police. If you are a parent, have you had this conversation with your child? Do you think white parents have a different conversation than black parents?

4. Have you known someone caught in the "dope trap"? What effects did it have on them and their family?

5. If you feel comfortable sharing, have you ever felt like you came into contact with a person who was "dangerous" to your personal safety? What do you think motivated that person? Does their motivation matter?

6. What was your reaction to the statistics that said that crime is a greater problem for blacks than any other racial group in America? Do you agree with Jamie's assessment that the

absence of fathers in black families is a significant contributing factor? Explain.

7. Did you know that police are trained to "run toward trouble" instead of running from it, as an ordinary citizen might do? Does that make you feel different about their role in keeping order in communities? Were you surprised that only about 1,000 people are killed by police officers each year, out of 30 million police-initiated contacts?

8. Why do you think some people resist arrest? How should a police officer respond when that happens?

9. Some statistics show that blacks are more likely to be stopped for traffic violations than whites engaged in identical conduct. They are also more likely to be searched after being stopped. Why do you think this is?

10. Police officers generally have "qualified immunity," which means that they are not liable for a violation of someone's civil rights unless that right has been "clearly established." The law establishes this immunity in an effort to balance the need for police officers to act without having to worry about being sued, versus the right of the public to seek redress for police misconduct. Lately, there has been considerable criticism that the standard gives the police too much leeway and too little accountability. What do you think?

Jamie's uncle Leroy, called "Hawk" who had the bootlegger house. He was always known as a sharp dresser and a player.

Jamie in his prison whites being visited by his mother and grandmother. In this picture, Jamie was doing a five-year prison term for a concealed felony with a firearm and sale of cocaine.

Bob and Kim when they were dating. Below: Shortly after they were married.

Jamie in his prison uniform. Below: Jamie on the left with a group of inmates from Atlanta. They called themselves the "A-town Glocks."

Bob and Kim with their sons, Robert (age 5) and John (age 3).
Below: Bob with the boys on vacation at the beach.

 Hays State Prison Kairos #10
April 29 through May 2, 2004 Inside Team

Jamie, front row center, with the other inmates who were a part of the Kairos prison ministry which was significant in his journey to Christian faith Left: Jamie being baptized at Christian Worship Assembly in Hartwell.

Three generations of Robert Bohlers. Below: Bob's sons with their new Game Boy that they received for Christmas. This was eventually stolen when his parents' home was burglarized.

Jamie holding his certificate of ordination to Christian ministry Below: Receiving a congressional recognition for community service from U.S. Congressman Jody Hice.

Jamie at the Sparrow's Nest with judge and former Georgia football star Kent Lawrence. At one point, Judge Lawrence sent Jamie to prison for a probation violation. He was a strong supporter of Jamie's work at the Sparrow's Nest, after Jamie's Christian conversion and release from prison.

Top left: Bob and family after little league games with the boys.
Bob coached John's team. Top right: At Disney World with the
family. A recent photo of the Bohler family in front of the
Christmas tree at church.

Jamie and his wife, Terri on vacation and at a University of Georgia football game. Below: Jamie, Terri, and their granddaughter Chyna.

Top: Bob leading a video devotional from his study in his home. Below:
Bob preaching in the sanctuary at his church in Athens.

Jamie teaching a life skills class at the Athens-Clarke County jail, which is the same jail that Jamie and a friend set on fire when he was incarcerated there. Below: Standing with Athens-Clarke County Deputy Police Chief Jerry Saulters.

PART 7 – AMERICA AND POLITICS

21

AMERICA

Bob

THE PARTICIPATION OF AMERICA in the institution of slavery is a blight on our nation's history. I don't think anyone disputes that. Slavery did not originate in America, however; it had been around since the beginning of time. In the second millennium B.C., the Code of Hammurabi had prohibitions against helping a slave escape his master. The Old Testament considered slavery an established cultural institution and set up laws to regulate it.

Slavery was practiced in ancient Egypt, as indicated by the fact that the Hebrews were enslaved by them before their exodus under Moses' leadership. Ancient Greece and Rome had large slave populations, many of whom had come from conquered nations. It was a common practice to turn captured populations into slaves in order to provide labor to the nation and servants for the wealthy. The continent of Africa practiced slavery and both enslaved indigenous people and imported slaves. In some African regions one-third of the population consisted of slaves.

Jesus made no specific statement about slavery and many other social issues but focused on teaching people how to enter the kingdom of God. Christianity arose in a cultural environment in which slavery was universally practiced. For that reason, the New Testament encouraged slaves to be obedient to their masters, though the apostle Paul listed people who enslaved others as those who went against "sound doctrine" (I Timothy 1:10). In the third and fourth centuries, Augustine and John Chrysostom, in addition to other Christian leaders, condemned slavery as sinful.[40]

When Christianity became the established religion of Europe, slavery began to decrease dramatically, and during the Middle Ages "there was little slavery in Christian lands."[41] The rise of Islam, for whom slavery was a widespread and important institution, brought the practice back to areas that had formerly been Christian. Islamic raiders brought women back to Muslim territories. They also brought back young Christian boys, who would serve as future civil servants. Only under great pressure from the rest of the civilized nations did the Islamic world reluctantly discontinue the practice of slavery in the 19th century, and Saudi Arabia only in 1962. Islamic slave traders would play a large role in bringing African slaves to the New World.

Christians would be a significant force in the abolition of slavery around the world. Popes in Europe had regularly condemned the practice. William Wilberforce, a Christian minister, would lead the effort to have slavery abolished throughout the British Empire, which would happen in 1833. John Wesley supported abolishing the slave trade, and in America Christian clergy, such as John Woolman, spoke out against slavery.

Christianity's record in America includes a surprising and curious inconsistency, however: The southern Christian church did not recognize the injustice of slavery. There were many reasons for this. Some were economic; the South's economy was built around slavery, and many did not see how it could survive without it. Other reasons were based on stereotypes about blacks being less capable than whites. For that reason, people assumed that freed slaves would starve because they would have no way to feed themselves.

Whether or not the Bible supported slavery became a great theological debate in the decades before the Civil War, with heated and sophisticated arguments on both sides. Some of the renowned theologians of my own Presbyterian denomination, such as James Henley Thornwell and Robert Lewis Dabney, argued that slavery

208

was morally right and authorized by Scripture. Those who argued against the institution did so by saying it was inconsistent with a just and loving God who made all people in his image. Those who argued in favor of slavery noted that the New Testament talked about slaves and encouraged them to be obedient to their masters. In the end, it would not be the theologians who decided the theological argument but Ulysses S. Grant and William Tecumseh Sherman.[42] The Civil War decided our nation's position on slavery, and God's providence allowed it to be decided correctly.

When I was growing up in Decatur, Georgia, my best friend, Billy, and I played tirelessly in my backyard. One of the games we played was Civil War. With our toy wooden rifles, we would run through the woods behind my house, running from the Yankees and shooting any we could find. There was no question in our minds who the good guys were, and no one in our group ever wanted to take the role of a Northern soldier. At 10 years old, this was not a philosophical position about slavery on our parts but lingering Southern pride. Even 100 years after the war, the South held onto its pride and through its Jim Crow laws still tried to keep the Negro population in its place.

The Civil Rights Act of 1964 and the Voting Rights Act of 1965 were milestones in our nation's history. They codified into law what ought to have been understood since the nation's founding, which was that every person, no matter their color, was equal in God's sight and should be treated the same. It was an act of repentance on our nation's part, not only of the sin of slavery but its more recent sins of discrimination.

While slavery and its effects lasted far too long, it is remarkable for America to have changed so quickly, considering that some civilizations do not change over periods of a thousand years. That slavery has been officially abolished for more than 150 years and federal law now prohibits discrimination is a testimony to the power of democracy, the goodness of the American people, and the strength of Christianity as a guide for what is right.

Jamie

I hear a lot of talk by people who don't seem to like America today; some of this comes from black people. When they disparage America, I think they are hanging on to our country's history. They have heard about all the bad things that were a part of slavery, and it still makes a deep impression. I read an article the other day about life on slave ships.[43] It was awful. Something like 6 million black people were put on ships from Africa. What I didn't know was that most of them went to the Caribbean and Brazil. Actually only about 400,000 came to America. But for those who did, it was a brutal 4,000-mile trip across the Atlantic with perhaps 500 other slaves on board that in the early years could take four months.

On board slave ships, slaves were chained together in tight quarters with no toilet facilities. They often died of dysentery, which comes from unsanitary conditions, and if anyone on board had a disease such as smallpox, it spread quickly. When the slave trade started, 1 in 5 slaves died on the journey. As time went along, captains figured out how to keep more alive not because they cared about them but for the sake of profits. Because crew members were afraid of being attacked by the slaves, they were inhumanely treated. Slaves were whipped and subjected to other cruel tortures such as thumbscrews, which inflicted excruciating pain without doing permanent damage. When the slaves got to America, they were treated like property. Families were broken up, and white slave owners fathered children with black slave girls. Even Thomas Jefferson owned slaves and is purported to have had a child by one of them.[44]

I think it's hard for blacks to get those things out of their minds. When President Obama first got elected president, he went overseas and couldn't help but talk about America's failures. Some called it his "apology tour" because they thought he made the country sound like a terrible place as he enumerated its failures. Because white America held black people in slavery for so long, it's hard for some blacks to buy into the American culture. It seems to be a white culture at heart and still racist. They think it was built on the backs of black people, and they resent it for that reason. They also think that if they commit to traditional white values, they are giving up their identity. It's why some blacks resist speaking correct English and scorn black people who do because they say they are "talking white."

But this is part of our problem. There is a mainstream of American life that isn't just white; it's reasonable and good. It is also Christian in its roots. At the core of American culture is the belief that everyone is better off with a good education, a stable family, a commitment to work, and faith in God. I don't think these are white values; I think they are Christian values and ones that black people ought to be able to embrace since so many black people are Christians.

Though this country has its faults, it has a great many wonderful qualities. When I decided to turn my life around, it was America that allowed me to do so. You can't do what I did in every country. You can't do it in China today. Or North Korea. Or Venezuela. But you can make changes to your life and reap the benefits of doing so in America.

When my wife and I first got married, we were living in the projects. That's all we could afford. But we both worked and worked hard. We knew we had to get out of that environment because it wasn't safe. A lady in the apartment next door to us got tied up with duct tape and robbed. When the robber left, she hopped over to our apartment, all duct-taped up, and knocked on the door. My wife and I both kept working and eventually got where we could move into a safer neighborhood. None of this was easy, but we made our lives better by working hard, not doing drugs, and not being involved in crime. We had to decide we wanted to do this, but America allowed us the opportunity.

Bob

What makes America unique is the principles on which it was founded. Many other countries in the world have long histories that help form their national life and governing principles. When the Pilgrims and those who followed them came to America, they had the opportunity to form a nation from scratch, without the baggage that other societies carried. What resulted was a nation founded on reasoned principles that would be better than any other existing country at preserving and protecting the freedoms of its people.

One of this country's founding ideas was that individuals have rights that are not granted by governments but are inalienably derived from God. As obvious as this is to us, it was unheard of to many nations at the time. It was assumed that kings and dictators had rights, but they also had authority to take away the rights of their subjects. The life of the individual belonged to the state. America's founders disagreed. Individuals have rights that come from God. The Declaration of Independence called these "unalienable rights" given to us by our Creator. The founders recognized that government should protect individual rights. They also recognized that government was the greatest danger to abridging those rights.

Among those rights were freedom of one's own person and the right to one's life. No one should take a person's life away except for extraordinary reasons, such as a capital penalty, properly decided by a jury of one's peers. One also had a right to personal property. This is implied in the Eighth Commandment in the Bible, which says, "You shall not steal." The founders understood that a person could not have true liberty if government was allowed to confiscate their property. A person should also be free to speak their mind, worship as they pleased, and write and publish their opinion, even if it displeased someone else. These freedoms are summarized in the statement that we have the right to "life, liberty, and the pursuit of happiness."

From listening to certain groups today, one would think that America is the worst of all possible countries. I disagree. By disagreeing, I am not saying that our country is perfect. The old hymn "America the Beautiful" admits such. In the words of a prayer, it says of this country, "God mend thine every flaw, confirm thy soul in self-control, thy liberty in law." We certainly have flaws as a country, but we also have means for correcting them.

22

DEMOCRACY AND CAPITALISM

Jamie

FOR MOST OF MY LIFE, I never voted. Not many people in my neighborhood voted either. My mom has told me that she voted, but I never knew that. She told me that my grandmother had voted and that she was a Republican, at one point in her life.

When I first got out of jail, I couldn't vote because I was a convicted felon. Different states have different laws about this. At the present time, convicted felons can vote in Georgia when they have completed their sentence, their parole, and any probation time. Some states won't ever let a convicted felon vote, but Georgia does. The Obama administration made a push to have more states allow released felons to vote. Of course, I didn't vote when I was on the streets. If you are a career criminal like I was, you don't think much about politics.

The first time I voted, I didn't really know what to do. My wife and I went downtown. I don't think she had ever voted either. I had heard a lot of people in the black community talking about voting. It didn't used to be talked about, but now it is much more. It's on the radio, and people even come knock on your door encouraging you to vote. I've never seen voting talked about in the black community as much as in this last election. That is part of the reason so many black people voted, some of whom had not ever voted before.

I heard someone say that they didn't vote for candidates anymore but political parties. They said that they used to vote for individual candidates when the political parties were more similar. Now the philosophies of governing are so different that you can't just vote for a candidate. You have to vote for a party because in doing so you are choosing between two very different directions. I thought that an interesting perspective.

Blacks certainly do this; they vote party more than candidate. I have heard that this started during the civil rights movement, when blacks had to band together to win their rights. Blacks almost always vote Democrat, but I think more blacks should question why. Everyone ought to think about why they vote the way they do. If you always vote as a group, it's like letting someone else think for you. I want to vote for whomever I think best and whatever party seems to have my best interests at heart. I'm afraid lots of people vote one way because they think it's the way to get more benefits. We need to remember the old saying, which is that the world's biggest lie is when someone from the government says, "I'm here to help you."

I'm not a Republican or a Democrat. I try to vote for the party and person I think will work for my best interests and the best interests of this nation, including all races. I have heard that more people who self-identify as Christians are registered as Republicans rather than Democrats. But there are slightly more registered Democrats of all races than Republicans, 49% to 44%.[45]

When it came to this last election, most blacks didn't vote for Joe Biden as much as they voted against Donald Trump. Many blacks found President Trump upsetting in his comments and behavior. They voted against him more than for Vice President Biden. I'm just telling how it truly was. For whatever reason, this last election really brought out the black vote. It was the biggest turnout of black voters I've ever seen.

Bob

It seems to me that there is a lot at stake in elections today because the directions of the two parties are very different. Just before the COVID-19 pandemic hit, our family took a vacation to Italy. We knew our oldest son was getting ready to graduate from college. Whatever job he took might not allow him the vacation time he

216

enjoyed as a student. Since it might be our last opportunity to spend a week together as a family, we broke the bank and all went to Italy over the Christmas holiday. It was a marvelous trip, made great by seeing Florence, Venice, and Rome, but more so by the time we spent together as a family.

One of the fun things we did in Rome was take a "Fiat tour" of the city. Two young men had a business where they showed people the sights of the city by driving them around town in small Fiats that were about the size of large washing machines. We crammed in the back of two small Fiats and were driven around town. It was super fun, not only seeing the sights but being in the tiny Fiats.

At one point, making conversation with one of the young men, I asked how the economy was in Italy. From my perspective as a tourist, it seemed to be bustling. Shops were everywhere, and people filled the streets. Vendors sold their wares, and you could get delicious pastries around every corner. His reply surprised me. "It's terrible," he said. When I looked surprised and asked why, he said, "Because the tax rate is 60%. No one can make any money because it all goes to the government. New businesses can't get started because the government takes so much of our money."

European economies have gradually moved toward increasing levels of social programs. They are technically still free market economies but with large government programs that provide free health care, retirement pensions, free higher education, and other government services. It all sounds good except that it is very expensive. The cost of such programs is paid by citizens through high taxes, including individual taxes, corporate taxes passed along to the consumer, and value added taxes on goods purchased. Some countries also have numerous "hidden" taxes to help them procure funding for these programs.

Political scientist Charles Murray notes that economies with large government programs, what he calls "the advanced welfare state" such as you find today in many European countries, are arithmetically unsustainable.[46] The math simply does not work, and

217

insolvency is inevitable. The problem is that the more benefits are offered, the more people there are who need them. With more people needing them, larger government bureaucracies must be created, which require more resources. When more people work in government, there are fewer people in the private sector to fund the government. This reduces income from taxes since "the private sector accounts for either all the production of wealth or all but a trivial proportion" of it.[47] The problem is that the more people receive government benefits, the more they will vote to maintain them and even enlarge them. At some point, the entire system collapses on itself.

It seems to me that the expanding welfare state in America is a tremendous problem that impacts the poor and vulnerable most of all. As nice as the idea of government income sounds, it destroys incentive to work and in the case of the black community has ruined the structure of the family. It is economically unsustainable and also undesirable from a moral point of view.

Jamie

One of the things that black people didn't recognize is how low unemployment was during the Trump administration. There were more black people working during his administration than ever before by a large margin. That is a good thing, but he didn't get much of the credit for it.

Recently a black senator made a speech in which he said that people certainly can be and are racist but that America is not a racist country.[48] He got a lot of grief from some in the black community about that, but I would agree with him. America elected a black president, twice. How can a nation that is racist do that?

I do think racism exists. In fact, everyone can be racist, and it's been that way from the beginning of time. Sure, white people can be racist. They can use stereotypes when they think about blacks. The old saying is "Don't judge a book by its cover," but I think blacks get judged inaccurately sometimes. Of course, if someone is dressed

218

like a thug, he probably isn't the CEO of a large corporation, so not all judgments are incorrect. Maybe one form of racism is when people are just indifferent to the issues other races face.

That being said, I'm not a fan of some of the groups that are prevalent on the racial scene today. Lots of people support Black Lives Matter, but I did some research into them.[49] Their leader has described herself as a "trained Marxist."[50] The leaders of the organization are also heavily into indigenous African spiritual practices. This means invoking the spirits of the dead, which means that they try to call up the dead.

Most people don't realize that this is a part of the Black Lives Matter movement, but it is, and it originates with the movement's founders. When they go on marches, they intentionally try to call up the spirits of people who have been murdered, such as George Floyd and Trayvon Martin. To make this happen, they pour out libations to the dead, which are drink offerings, usually of water, and call out their names. When they call out their names, it isn't just in remembrance but to call up the spirits of those who have been killed by the police. They want the spirits to march with them and work through them because they think it gives their movement power. It does give them power, but it's a dark power. This kind of thing is a type of Voodoo religion that is very prevalent in Africa and which the Black Lives Matter founders have made part of their leadership of the movement.

But when you do that sort of thing, trying to call up the spirits of the dead, you get into dangerous territory. It can be very real, and this is what makes it perilous. The Bible specifically says not to do this, and I don't want any part of it. If you want to be spiritual, why do you need to call up the dead? I'm praying to God and Jesus. I'm not depending on anyone else besides them. So I can't really get past this aspect of the Black Lives Matter organization.

I know that some white supremacist groups exist, like the skinheads. Antifa is supposed to be anti-fascist and anti-racist but they mostly seem to be about making trouble and promoting anarchy. I'm good with just being on the Christian train.

Bob

There is a lot of talk about socialism today, which is basically a plan for the redistribution of wealth. Historically, when wealth gets concentrated in the hands of a few, there are efforts to equalize the distribution. Communist takeovers, such as happened in Russia and Cuba claimed to have this goal; everyone would own property collectively and work together for the common good. The problem is that these systems do not work.

A good illustration comes from the story of the Pilgrims who landed at Plymouth Rock in November 1620. Private investors who wanted to profit from the expedition had funded their trip. In order to safeguard those profits, the investors required all the Pilgrims to work on a collective basis, everyone contributing and everyone receiving equally. This turned out to be a poor way to build the colony however, and the result was that some people were not willing to work, others worked halfheartedly, and, as a result, crop harvests were barely able to sustain community life.

After several years of this experiment, the struggling community took a different approach. It parceled out land to every family and told them to work for their own benefit. What happened was a complete turnaround. People became industrious. More corn was planted than ever, and a new enthusiasm emerged. This new approach made the Plymouth colony one of the most successful in the new land.[51]

There have been successful efforts in America to provide equal opportunities for everyone. The Homestead Acts of the 1860s offered free land, much of it west of the Mississippi, to anyone willing to cultivate it. These acts also allowed blacks in the south to acquire land on which to establish their own farms, though discrimination made this difficult at times.

220

The reality of America today is that wealth is not a "zero-sum game." That is, the rich do not have to become poorer for the poor to become richer. There is wealth available that everyone can acquire through their own labors. In addition, there is a natural redistribution of wealth that takes place in a free market economy. Companies must compete for business; those who do not provide goods and services that others want, lose market share. As one example, only one of the top ten companies in America in 1980, Exxon Mobil, is among the top ten today.[52]

As nice as it might seem to guarantee that everyone will be prosperous, successful, and wealthy, there is no sustainable system of government that can do this. Government cannot guarantee outcome, only opportunity. America was founded to be a place of opportunity. What we make of those opportunities is up to us.

There are several problems with a move toward socialism. One is that larger government means more government control. With government programs come regulations on our businesses, choices, and even our language. Government begins essentially to "own the means of production" through regulation. If we think clearly, this is a bad exchange. America was established so people could be free. It is a terrible bargain to give up our freedoms for government handouts.

The other problem in moving toward socialism is that it reduces the incentive for people to produce. In socialism, a person's energy and attention are focused on what they will receive from the government. The inclination is to relax and let the government take care of you. Capitalism and free market economies place the emphasis on producing something. Capitalism tries to harness every person's self-interest to encourage them to produce something that is needed by someone else, whether in terms of goods or services. In a system that focuses not on producing but receiving, you eventually run out of other people's goods and services and out of "other people's money."

221

Socialism disincentivizes work, creativity, and industry. Free market economies encourage those things. It seems to me that an economy based on producing rather than receiving is far better. In a free market economy, I have to produce something that someone else needs and wants. The words of Jesus appear to support that this is a better way, as he said, "It is better to give than to receive" (Acts 20:35).

23

CONVERSATION ABOUT AMERICA AND POLITICS

Jamie

IF WE ARE GOING TO TALK about America and politics, we have to talk about the riot that took place in Washington, D.C., in January of this year (2021), when a whole lot of white people stormed the United States Capitol building. I'd be interested in your take on this. I have a couple of thoughts. For one thing, I have never seen so many angry white people in my life. My thought was, "This is really unusual; white people don't usually get this upset. I wonder what's going on"?

One of my thoughts is that storming the Capitol was a really brazen thing to do. It's one thing to riot in some city, but to attack the Capitol? Were people really trying to overthrow the government? Another thought I had was that if this had been a group of black people, the police would have not been so gentle. There would have been a lot of bloodshed at the hands of the police. What do you think?

Bob

That was a really ugly moment and an embarrassing one for America. I was embarrassed to see a group of conservative white people breaking into the Capitol building. I do think that the police showed restraint. You don't want to just start shooting people in a crowd. The police may initially have thought they could contain the crowd, but they got overwhelmed. There were just too many people, and they were all coming into the Capitol building. My sense is that they would have shown the same restraint with black rioters too. They didn't want to just start killing people so they tried to contain them, but there were just too many, and it became a mess.

Jamie

I gather that the anger of the crowd was because many of them thought the presidential election was rigged or stolen in some way, but I haven't seen any proof of that. Lots of people have claimed that, but where is the proof? I haven't seen any.

Bob

That is a good question. I think that some white conservatives are very concerned about the integrity of the election. One thing that we do need in this country is fair elections. We don't need suspicious things happening in the middle of the night as votes are being counted or allegations of fraud. Everyone needs the right to vote, but we need to know that there was no cheating going on. If an election is fair and square, then you can accept losing. But neither side trusts the other one today. That's a problem. It seems to me that this is something on which everyone can and should agree. We must work together to insure fair and honest elections.

Jamie

As shocked as I was at the Capitol riot, there have been plenty of riots in the last year, many of them in black inner-city communities. Not all the rioters have been black, but a majority of them have been. The problem has been that blacks have essentially destroyed their own communities and the businesses that they frequent. What sense does that make? The problem is that it will take decades for some of these communities to recover. Property values go down after a riot, businesses leave, and other businesses don't locate in these areas. Why would a business come to one of these areas after seeing other businesses randomly destroyed?

These riots don't reflect well on the black community. It's also true that liberal mayors and administrations run many of these cities. They haven't been very good at keeping law and order. They have been very vocal about defunding the police, but you can see what has happened in their cities when law and order goes out the window.

One of the strengths and weaknesses of the black culture is that we are very passionate people. Just look at how we worship; it is different from white people. Look at how aggressive we can be whether it's when we get into a fight or playing sports. Or even how we react when we are pulled over by a police officer. Black people are just passionate; it's in our DNA. I think maybe it goes all the way back to Africa. I'm not saying white people can't be passionate, but black people take it to another level. Again, I think it is why blacks sometimes vote the way they do. Something gets under their skin, and their passions take over. They just can't get over something that gets under their skin or that belittles them. It's like a dagger into the heart.

Bob

Last summer's inner-city riots caused tremendous property damage, and some people lost their lives. What disturbed so many people was that mayors, city councils, and district attorneys tolerated the behavior of the rioters as somehow justified. Though they were charged with protecting the property of people and businesses in their cities, officials did little to stop the destruction. We have a constitutional right to peaceful assembly but not to damage the property of others.

Some of the cities have not done much to prosecute the rioters, but some have, such as even Portland. I found it interesting that a Washington, D.C., federal judge recently questioned Justice Department prosecutors as to why the January 6 rioters were being prosecuted "significantly harsher" than those accused in the 2020 summertime riots.[53]

Jamie

As we talk about America and politics, I want to come back to the issue of welfare. We've talked about the "dope trap" that traps people in a life of crime and addiction. I think there is another trap; it is the "welfare trap." I would hope that people reading this book would realize that government checks are not the way to a better life. I know it's tempting to think so, especially when you are getting a government check for your food, utilities, and housing. But you are always going to be poor that way.

We see this attachment to welfare here at the Sparrow's Nest. We employ people and pay them far more money than they are bringing in with their disability check. But they get very anxious when they see their check reduced because of their income. They don't want to lose their government check and will sometimes quit in order not to do so even though they make far more money working for us.

All my life I've heard "it's going to get better." A certain political party is going to give you more stuff. A candidate has promised you this or that. But I've been hearing this all my life. People need to ask, "When? When is it going to get better?" If you've been hearing this all your life, but it hasn't gotten any better, maybe it's not going to. Welfare is a trap, and it keeps people dependent. It isn't going to get better if people keep depending on the government. They have to take responsibility for themselves. Go to work. Get all the training and education you can. Then it will get better!

Bob

I understand how people want everyone to be equally successful, happy, and prosperous. That would be nice, but it cannot be engineered by the government. No form of government has been invented that will insure that outcome. One reason is that people are simply different. They have different abilities and energy levels. Some are more creative than others. There is no system that effectively results in equality of outcome, except systems, like the former communist Soviet Union, that make everyone poor except for the oligarchs who manage the system.

The answer to helping people is not an increasing level of government handouts. What we can do is give people freedom and allow them to exercise their God-given abilities. This way every person can rise to the level of his or her ability, energy, creativity, and talent. It is a system of equal opportunity, not equal outcome. This isn't unfair. In fact, it is eminently fair! It gives people equal opportunity; what they make of it depends on them.

The Bible says that God has made us each different. God has given us different gifts, talents, abilities, and energies. We might object that we are not as smart or creative as someone else, but the Bible says that God has given every person sufficient gifts to fulfill their calling and make their way. Every person is important and valuable both in the eyes of God and for his plan in the world.

Obviously, a world in which everyone was alike would be a disaster. How would the world function if every person were a poet, or welder, or truck driver, or professor? The world needs lots of people doing different things. We are each called to put our best effort into the calling God gives us with the talents we have. If we will do this, it will benefit others and us. If we use our gifts and don't envy others, we will be successful, find our way, experience God's blessing, and make the world a better place. The Bible also says that the way to be given more gifts and talents is to use the ones we already have. Use your abilities and God will increase them (Matthew 13:12).

The Bible encourages people to work hard and see their labors as a gift from God. This is a worthy goal: to work so we can support ourselves so no one else has to do so and so we have something to give to those in need. If we will do this, we will live productive and satisfying lives that give more than they receive, which is what Jesus said we ought to do.

Christianity recognizes that there will always be people in need. Jesus said that we will always have the poor with us (Matthew 26:11). It is our duty to care for others, especially the needy. Most would agree that some level of government involvement, in this regard, is a good thing. It is true, however, that Christian organizations are far more efficient than the government and can address issues of the heart, which government programs often neglect. Your organization, the Sparrow's Nest, is a good example of this.

The dream of a socialist utopia is futile. History repeatedly reveals its inadequacy. A story from the past illustrates this. In 1989, Soviet Parliament member Boris Yeltsin was visiting the United States.[54] He had some free time one afternoon and asked to visit an American grocery store. He was interested in seeing how the American people actually lived.

When he arrived at the grocery store, he was amazed. He asked if they had taken him to a store reserved for governmental elites? When he was told that all grocery stores in America were like this, he was stunned. He kept wandering the aisles filled with food of all sorts and shelves overflowing with thousands of cans "He marveled at free cheese samples, fresh fish and produce, and freezers packed full of pudding pops."[55] He commented on how different this was from the food-starved scarcity of the Soviet Union. Even Prime Minister Gorbachev, he commented, did not have that many food choices. In the autobiography of his life, written years later, he said, about seeing all the food in the American grocery store, "For the first time, I felt quite frankly sick with despair for the Soviet people."

On leaving the store that day he said that if the Soviet people saw what he had seen and knew how well the Americans lived, "There would be a revolution." His visit to that Texas grocery store would be instrumental in his determination to dismantle the communist system in favor of something that would bring prosperity to the Soviet people like America experienced.

DISCUSSION QUESTIONS
PART 7 – AMERICA AND POLITICS

1. The nation of Israel makes a point never to forget the Holocaust. Do you think it is hard for blacks to forget the institution of slavery? Why or why not? Is this a good thing or not? What role do you think Christianity had in either the abolition of slavery in America or its perpetuation? Why do you think the theological debate about slavery was so fierce?

2. Do you think of mainstream American culture as white? Explain. Do you think it is hard for a black person to embrace mainstream American culture? Why or why not? Jamie made the point that there is pressure on blacks not to "act white." What do you think of the idea of "acting white"? How would you define this? Is there such a thing as "acting black"? What do you think of the statement that there are racist people but that America is not a racist nation?

3. Bob says that the Civil Rights Act of 1964 and the Voting Rights Act of 1965 were acts of national repentance for the institution of slavery and other acts of discrimination. Do you agree or disagree? Do you think further repentance is appropriate or necessary?

4. In what sense do you think capitalism has advantages over socialism? Socialism over capitalism? Explain. Can you think of biblical references that have a "socialist" tone? A capitalist tone? What do these say about where Christians should fall on the capitalist-socialist spectrum?

5. Were you aware of the prevalence of African religious practices in the Black Lives Matter movement? Or its

connection with Marxist ideology? Do you think that most people who support the BLM organization realize this? Do these philosophical underpinnings matter? Do you think there are radical, white conservative groups active today? Explain.

6. Do you think there was a significant difference between the Capitol riot and other recent riots in major cities? In what way? If it had been mostly blacks who stormed the Capitol, do you think the response of the police would have been different? Explain.

7. What kinds of entitlement programs do you see as problematic? Which do you see as helpful? Explain. What do you think of the phrase "welfare trap"?

8. Why do you think Jesus said that we will always have the poor with us? What does this indicate? What do you think is the most effective remedy for poverty in America today? In what sense are people in America "poor"?

9. Do you think most people tend to vote for a candidate or a political party? Which do you think is the better approach?

10. Do you agree with Bob's assessment that America is unique among the nations of the world because of the principles on which it was founded? How do you think America's founding principles are designed to preserve freedom and individual liberty? Why are these important goals? Do other goals supersede them?

PART 8 – GOD

24

FINDING GOD

Jamie

I DIDN'T GO TO CHURCH growing up. Neither did anyone in my family. The religion I knew most about was African religion, more specifically the Root Doctor.

When my uncle's girlfriend killed him in cold blood, she went to see the Root Doctor. He helped her stay out of prison; that was the word on the street. As far as I know, she never served a day in jail for his murder. People in the projects thought the Root Doctor could conjure up powerful magic and for good reason. Whatever the Root Doctor did, it seemed to work, at least for her.

The Root Doctor is a form of African religion. He or she is a person who knows all sorts of special spells and hexes. For example, a Root Doctor could put a hex on someone. He could give you a mojo bag with some special items in it to protect you. If you were in trouble, he could help you get out. The Root Doctor got that name because they used special roots. They would find a special root from a tree, and it was supposed to have magical powers. You would put it in your pocket and carry it with you. It would help you in your trouble. Or they might give you a mojo bag with some roots in it.

There was a lot of superstition in the projects, and some of it was related to these African religious practices. For example, it was said that you should not eat spaghetti made by your girlfriend. Some girls knew how to make a love potion out of it that would bind you to her. To do that she would put some of her blood in the sauce and

231

put a hex on it. Since the sauce was red, you would never know if she had done it. So people warned you never to eat your girlfriend's spaghetti.

When I was a young teenager, I went to see the Root Doctor because I caught an auto theft charge. It may have been a burglary charge, I can't remember. A friend took me to see a Root Doctor who lived out of town. She was in Rayle, Georgia, over in Wilkes County, and I was only 15 years old. It may have been when my friend and I broke into the elementary school and got caught.

The Root Doctor was an old lady with long silver hair. I remember that her eyes were very mysterious looking. They were a funny color and had rings around them. She asked me what my problem was. Sometimes they would tell you what your problem was even before you said anything, but she didn't do that this time. She did tell me that she knew I was coming.

She said that she was going to fix me up, and it was going to be all right. She told me she had a very special root for me. She had found it in a bed of little snakes. But she wasn't afraid of them. She just shooed them off and reached down her hand to get the special root.

I had heard about the Root Doctor giving people powder to put in the four corners of their house. You put a line of the powder in front of your door, so nothing bad could get in. You also put some in the four corners of your house. She didn't give me powder that day but a root.

Some of the big-time drug dealers are into this and even into ancestor worship. They will have a picture of one of their ancestors in their home. They set up altars and burn candles. Sometimes they put food out. Some of them have a big cooking pot they use. They put some things in the pot that they want protection from. They put a gun in the pot and some handcuffs. They'll also put in some money and dope. Then they drink alcohol and smoke cigars. They spit the alcohol in the pot and blow the smoke over it. That's supposed to protect them from the police and other drug dealers and also help them make money. They also wear special beads and different colors for protection. If they don't get caught for a while, they believe it's their ancestors who are helping them. There is a lot of darkness among those who deal drugs.

All this is a form of witchcraft, and some of it's like they practice in both Africa and Haiti. This all came over with the slaves a long time ago, and some of it is still alive. That the founders of Black Lives Matter use it is evidence it still lives.

People in the projects where I grew up thought there was real power in it. If there is, it's demonic power. When people at a Black Lives Matter march call up the spirits, they wait for them to arrive. Those that know what is going on say they can feel the spirits when they get there and it gives them power.

Of course, the Root Doctor has to be paid. You can't get him or her to conjure for you if you aren't willing to pay. When I went to the Root Doctor, she gave me a root to carry with me. I don't know whether it worked or I was just fortunate, but I didn't get in much trouble. All they gave me for the elementary school break-in was unsupervised, non-reporting probation. Perhaps the devil kept me safe because he was grooming me for more advanced criminal activity.

Bob

I grew up going to church. My parents were not legalistic about it; it was just something we did. We attended a Methodist church when we lived in our first home. When we moved to a new house in the summer after my second-grade year, many of the neighborhood families went to a Presbyterian church in the area. That is where we started attending.

This was an era in which almost everyone went to church. Young men had come back from the Second World War, gotten married, and were starting their families. Part of what that meant was being part of a local church. This was a time in which most

233

churches were full of people, and going to church was one of the things almost everyone did.

There was a family up the street from us who were atheists. I don't remember much about their situation except that they did not have any children, and everyone knew they were atheists. It was an oddity in the neighborhood. Everyone else we knew believed in God, even if they didn't go to church. At least no one else overtly said they didn't believe.

That most people went to church did not mean that church was particularly exciting. The worship service in my Presbyterian church was rather bland, as I remember it. Perhaps this was just my perspective as a child. In that era, however, it didn't need to be very exciting, because people still came. What was exciting was not the sermons, which seemed to be universally dull, but the relationships with others. All the neighbors went, so there were always lots of my friends there on Sunday.

Church was also rather dignified. The men all wore coats and ties, and if you came in late to worship, you could not just walk into the service. The bulletin had an asterisk to indicate times at which visitors could enter, and people had to wait for one of those designated times. In college I served as a deacon and remember, as an usher, standing in the narthex with people, waiting for the specified time, then opening the sanctuary door for them to be seated.

I got more from growing up in church than I might have realized. I learned lots of stories from the Bible for one thing. In the fifth grade, I had two men who taught my Sunday School class for a while, and I remember a set of lessons from the Old Testament that I thought particularly interesting. At one point, I earned my God and Country award in scouting, which was a nice-looking medal to hang on my uniform. As part of that experience, I and two other boys my age recited an entire Bible chapter, I Corinthians 13, from memory in front of the congregation. That chapter has always been special to me, being the first portion of the Bible I ever committed to memory.

Several experiences in church were particularly meaningful growing up. In the seventh grade, I was part of the Confirmation Class program, which was how young people officially became members of a Presbyterian church. It was a series of lessons with the pastor that prepared you to make your own profession of faith and become an adult member. During this time, I remember several weeks in which I felt particularly close to God, even sitting in class in school, thinking about God.

I also remember going to church camp several summers at Camp Calvin. John Calvin was a 16th-century theologian whose theological writings became the basis for Presbyterian beliefs. Not only was he the "father" of Presbyterian theology, but the Atlanta Presbytery named a camp after him. My best friend from the neighborhood, Billy Howard, and I went to camp there for several summers. We swam, canoed, ate in the dining hall, had Bible study, slept in cabins, and generally had a good time.

There is one moment that stands out in my memory from camp. At an outdoor chapel service one day, in about the sixth grade, the young man leading the service challenged us to make a commitment to God. What would we give to God in response to his goodness to us? Being young and naïve, I made a commitment that was impossible to keep. I remember telling God that I would give him a certain amount of my time; it seems like I said 30%. When I got home from camp, I tried to keep my commitment by thinking about God a lot, but this was impossible to do for more than a couple of weeks. I have since wondered, however, if God did not take me up on my offer, eventually calling me into full-time ministry. If, in the end, I will end up truly serving God with 30% of my time, I will feel honored.

By the time I got to be a teenager, I was pretty disinterested in church. Most of my school friends went to other churches. Activities that used to be interesting were less so as a teen. I even remember sitting in church one day, listening to the sermon and thinking that I was not sure what I wanted to do when I grew up.

What I was sure about, however, was that I didn't want to be a preacher. Clearly, God has a sense of humor.

Jamie

I became a Christian at age 17 when I was sitting in jail awaiting my trial for armed robbery and murder. I had not committed the crimes but was looking at two life sentences if convicted. The Fulton County jail on Jefferson Street was my home as I awaited trial. That was the old jail before they built the new one.

One day I was sitting on a bunk in the back of the dormitory playing cards with three other inmates. Someone came down the walkway and said, "Does anyone want a Bible tract?" I had already been reading some psalms because another inmate in the yard had told me I needed God to help me at my trial. My mom had sent me a Bible. She told me, "Look, you're gonna have to give your life to God 'cause I don't have any money to get you out of this mess. You've made your bed hard, and you're gonna have to lie in it." She did end up helping me out with money for an attorney, but what she told me when she first talked to me was that I was on my own. That's why I had to depend on God.

There was a catwalk that went through the middle of the dormitory. This was where the guards patrolled the area, and other visitors could walk safely. They also brought your food trays down this walkway. When I heard that the man was giving out Bible tracts, I went up to the catwalk. He said, "Would you like one, young man?" I said, "Yes, sir" and he gave me one.

It was one of those old tracts with a scary picture on the front. As I recall, it had a picture of a man who was halfway down into hell, where lots of people were hollering and screaming. Up top there were clouds and a cross, but the guy in the picture obviously wasn't going to heaven. It didn't look good for him at all.

I took the tract and was getting ready to turn around when he said, "Excuse me young man. Can I ask you a quick question?" I

236

said, "Sure." He said, "Where do you sleep in here?" I pointed to my bunk and said, "Over there."

I got ready to turn around again, and he said, "Can I ask you another question, young man?" I looked at the man, and he had a big smile on his face, a smile that could light up an entire room. He said, "If you lay down tonight and let's say God came for you tonight to take your soul, where do you think you'll go, young man?" That was a question no one had ever asked me, and I knew in my spirit that it was a true question that I needed to face. When he asked me that question, it was almost like someone hit the "pause" button. Time seemed to stand still.

That was a question I didn't at all know how to answer, and so I just stood there for what seemed like a long time. I guess I was stunned by the seriousness of the matter. I knew that if God came for my soul that night, I wasn't going to make my way to heaven. At that point, I had never heard the Gospel preached or had salvation extended to me.

After what seemed like a long time, he said, "Let me help you, young man. If you have a relationship with the Lord Jesus Christ and you have your life right with God," at this point he looked up at the ceiling, "then you'll go and be with the Father in heaven for eternity. But if you don't have a relationship with the Lord Jesus and don't have your life right with God, then young man, you'll be condemned into the lake of fire and be in hell for eternity." I looked at the man who still had this big smile on his face and said, "What do I need to do?" He said, "Have you been saved before?" I said, "No, sir." He said, "Would you like to be?" I said "yes" and stuck my arms out the bars as fast as anybody could.

The man probably only stood about 5 feet tall, but he had a countenance and wonderful presence about him, and I was very serious about wanting to be saved. He said, "I'm going to pray a prayer and you repeat it after me." He did, and I prayed the prayer after him. He said, "Father God … please forgive me of my sins …

I believe in Jesus ... please save me from my sins ... so I can live in heaven forever."

Then he said to me, "Do you believe Jesus died for your sins?" I said, "I do." Then he said, "The Bible says that if you confess with your lips that Jesus is Lord and believe in your heart that God raised him from the dead, you will be saved. Do you believe that God raised Jesus from the dead?" I said, "Yes." He said, "Then now, my brother, you are saved, and in situations like this the whole heavens rejoice because you have now become a child of the Most High God."

At that point, I didn't know much about Jesus or the Bible. I didn't really know what the Crucifixion or the Resurrection were. I just knew I wanted to believe whatever it took for me to be saved and not go to hell. I suppose that somewhere I had heard about heaven and hell. In my heart I knew that people who did bad things didn't go to heaven, and I was in serious danger of being one of those people. My conscience had obviously been hurting me because of the things I was doing though I didn't recognize what it was. I did know a little about who Jesus was. My grandmother had one of those old paintings of Jesus in her house, the one where Jesus has the long wavy hair. I think it had a gold frame around it, and I knew this was a picture of God.

That experience was very real for me. It was a real conversion experience. I knew I was saved and could feel it. I also made a vow to God that day. I told God that if he would truly save me that I would take the Gospel and preach it around the world.

Bob

I made what I consider my adult commitment to Christ at age 17. By the time I got to be a teenager, my affection for God had mostly worn off. I didn't have a regular practice of reading the Bible, and my prayers were more rote than anything. Other things occupied my attention, and God didn't have much place in my life.

But good things continued to happen to me. I made good grades, played sports, and had lots of friends. The most important endeavor for me was playing football. The high school I attended, Avondale, was a football juggernaut in those days, and playing on the football team was the height of success and recognition. I also loved sports and was reasonably good at them without being one of the true stars. At the end of my junior year, I was scheduled to be starting fullback and defensive back on the team the next year. It was a dream come true and also the result of lots of hard work.

Another good thing had happened to me at the end of my junior year. On a whim, I had run for president of the Student Council and won. This was an unexpected gift and one about which I was tremendously excited. At that point, I knew almost everyone in school and had many friends, enough to put me over the top in the school-wide election. This was an added bonus to my self-esteem and social status. At the end of my junior year, things could hardly have been going better.

Oddly enough, however, I had a strange experience one day during school. I remember exactly where I was and what I was wearing. I was walking down a short hallway by myself at the end of my junior year, when I had an odd feeling of emptiness. Everything good that I had always hoped would happen was coming true, but I felt strangely empty. I remember a fleeting thought that was, "Why doesn't all this feel more meaningful?" It was an "is this all there is?" moment. In that instant, I also knew the answer. It was because I wasn't close to God. I wasn't close to God, and for that reason my life did not have real meaning.

God had things planned just right for me, however. That summer I went on a month-long trip out west with an organization called Young Life that had just started in my high school. We had a great time, and the culmination of the trip was a week at Frontier Ranch in Colorado. During the day we did lots of fun things, but in the evening there were talks about Christianity. The first night the speaker talked about who Jesus was and what he did. The second night was another talk on Jesus. The third night he began to talk about why everybody needed Jesus because no one could be good enough to get to heaven on their own. The talk that evening particularly spoke to me because I assumed I was going to heaven because I was a nice person and generally didn't get into trouble. The speaker said, "No." Not even the best person can be good enough to make up for their sins.

The fourth night was the most important talk of the week. The speaker told how Jesus came for sinful people like we all are. What he did to save us was take our place on the cross. He died for our sins so we would not have to. He died in our place. God raised him from the dead as proof he was truly the Son of God and as evidence we could have eternal life through him.

At this point, I had been in church all my life, and I must have heard these things many times. For some reason, however, that week, it all made sense for the first time. After the Thursday-evening talk, the speaker invited everyone to take 15 minutes to go somewhere by themselves. He said, "If you have never invited Jesus into your life, this is your time to do so." When the meeting broke up, I found a gravel road near the cabin in which we were staying. I leaned against the hood of a car and invited Jesus into my life. I said, "Lord, I know you've been with me, but I've never invited you into my life. I want you to come in and be my Lord and Savior and be with me the rest of my life."

The moment was very real, and I felt God very close. When I got back from the trip, our leader began to disciple the group of guys who had been on the trip. For the first time I began to understand what being a Christian really meant.

25

WHAT IS CHRISTIANITY?

Jamie

AFTER MY CONVERSION, I told my mom what had happened. She was happy for me until I told her I had made a vow to God. She said, "You didn't make no vow to God!" I replied, "I did." That made her very nervous. She said, "Boy, do you know what you have done? This is serious business. You don't go making vows to God. What did you tell God?" I told her I made a vow that I would preach his Gospel around the world. If he would help me get out of the situation I was in, I'd preach his Gospel. I didn't really know much about the Gospel at that point, but I had told God I would preach it.

My mom thought for a moment and said, "Well, I'm gonna tell you something. You've got to keep that vow. If you make a vow to God and don't keep it, he is going to whip you 10 times worse than he would have. You just think you're in trouble now. You go messing with God, and you can really get into trouble." I just stared at her. Finally she said, "Well, you can't do anything about it now because you've already made the vow."

What I knew was that God was powerful. He had reached me in prison. The steel doors and bars hadn't kept him out. He had found me and shown me his grace. I was truly saved, and I could feel it.

Sadly, my conversion didn't take. I have told how T-Bone helped me smoke my first bit of crack cocaine the very day I got out of prison after my acquittal. He was the first person I saw, and it was not a good thing. I just didn't know what to do with my new life as a Christian. I didn't know you had to get connected with a local church. I didn't know how to pray or read the Bible. Christ had found me and I had changed, but nothing else had changed. My friends and family hadn't. The projects hadn't. My old life was waiting for me when I got out of prison, and I fell back into my old habits. I got enveloped back in the darkness I was in before my conversion.

There are a couple of Bible verses I think about to describe what happened to me. One says that our enemy, the devil, "prowls around like a roaring lion, seeking someone to devour" (I Peter 5:8). That is what happened to me: The devil was waiting for me when I got out of prison. I had been doing his work, and he didn't want to lose a good servant. Before I had the chance to really change, he made sure I got addicted to crack cocaine and back into a life of crime.

The other verse has to do with unclean spirits. Jesus said that when an unclean spirit has gone out of a person, it looks to find rest but doesn't find any. So it goes back where it came from. When it gets there, it finds the house swept and clean. Then it brings with it seven other spirits more evil that itself so that the latter state of the person is "worse than the first" (Matthew 12:43-45). That is what happened to me. My house was swept and clean, but I didn't know what to do. The devil came in with a vengeance and took possession again. I got back into darkness and much more deeply than before.

As just one illustration of how bad things got, I almost lost my life because of a crime I committed about three months after I got out of prison. I knew a guy whose uncle owned a car wash off Campbellton Road in Atlanta. One day I was walking by the car wash, and he saw me. It was almost closing time and getting dark. He was the only one working. He motioned me over and said, "Check this out, man. I've been trying to get in contact with you. The boss man left the moneybag in that car over there. Do you know how to get into a car?" I said, "Yeah, that's easy. But where is this money bag?" He told me it was in the back seat.

I said, "Look man, how much money is in this bag? Do you know there's money in it?" He replied, "There's a lot in it because it's the weekend." Then he said, "You get in there and get it real

242

fast, and we'll split it." I said, "OK, where is it?" He pointed to the car and kept doing his job while I went over to the car.

It was locked, but that was no problem. I had a flathead screwdriver with me, so I pried open the back window. Then I reached in my arm and unlocked the door. At first I couldn't find the bag because it was hidden underneath the front seat. When I felt it, I thought it was just checks or something. I went to my friend and said, "Are you trying to set me up?" He said, "No man, there's a lot of money in there." I told him I was going to take it into the woods, and he was to meet me there. We'd split up the money if there was any.

He finished up what he was doing and met me. By then I had cut open the bag with my screwdriver, and he was right — there was a whole lot of money in it. I had already put about a third of it in my pocket. When he got there, he said, "You haven't taken any of it yet, have you?" I said, "Listen man, I've done all the work here. You are going to get what you get and consider yourself lucky." I probably gave him a quarter of the entire amount. All in all, it was about $5,000.

About noon the next day there was a knock on my door. When my mom answered it, there was a very big man standing there. She said, "Can I help you, sir?" He said, "Where's Jamie at?" She said, "What's going on?" He said, "Jamie stole some money from me, and if I don't get it back, I'm going to kill him." My mom got frightened at that point and tried to talk to him, but it didn't do any good. My little brother Ernest was in the house, but the man was coming inside looking for me.

I heard the commotion and came downstairs. I had put my gun in my pocket in case there was trouble. When I saw the man, I said, "What's up boss man?" He came at me and put his hand around my throat. Then he put a gun to my head. It was a big, chrome-plated .357 Magnum, the long-barrel version like Clint Eastwood used in the movies. He said, "Where's my money?"

I didn't have all his money at that point. It was Christmas time, and I'd given some to my mother. She had some things on layaway, and I gave her money to purchase them. I also gave some to my little brother. I had also blessed several people with the proceeds of my theft. For that reason, I didn't have all the money; so before the man could think, I made a break for it. I twisted out of his grip and went for the door. I don't know whether he actually shot at me or not. Several shots went off, but they may have gone into the ceiling. Before he could come after me, however, I was around the corner and into the woods.

When the coast finally cleared, I came back home, and my mother had a suitcase packed for me. She said, "You can't stay here. I've got your little brother to raise, and I can't have this kind of thing happening in my house. Plus, if you stay here, you're gonna get killed. God helped you get out of jail, but now you're back into crime. Get out! Your grandmother is waiting for you in Athens. Go get on the bus and go to Athens."

At that point, I was 18 years old and had made a decision to be a Christian. But I had no roots in the Christian faith and no other Christians to help me out, so I went back to what I knew, which was drugs, alcohol, and a life of crime. I went back into the darkness. It would be a very long time before I came into the light again.

Bob

When I got home from my summer trip with Young Life, in which I had made a commitment to Jesus Christ, I didn't understand much about Christianity. If you had asked me what it meant to be a Christian, I would have said, "Go to church and try to keep the Ten Commandments." I knew that I had experienced an encounter with God at camp, but I didn't know what it meant.

The one thing my counselor told me was that I should start reading the Bible when I got back home. His comment was that it would "come alive and start to make sense." This was a new thought to me. I hadn't ever really read the Bible before, even though I had grown up in church. I certainly did not have the experience of it coming alive.

At the camp where I made my Christian commitment however, they were selling these cool-looking New Testaments that everyone was buying. They had an attractive cover and were in the Phillips translation. I didn't know what a translation of the Bible was, but I purchased one. I would come to learn, later on, that the Bible came in different translations. The Bible was originally written in Hebrew and Greek. For that reason, all English versions were translations. I had seen some newer versions of the Bible; the Good News translation had come out two years earlier, but I had not paid much attention. Most of what I was used to were older versions of the Bible that seemed stilted and difficult to read. It had not dawned on me that it might be interesting, inspiring, or useful to read the Bible. The Phillips translation of the Bible was intended to be a modern, easy-to-read translation. Today it is considered more of a paraphrase than exact translation.

It was easy to read, however, and when I got home, I started reading the Gospel of Mark. What I discovered was that, just as my counselor said, it started to make sense. The story of Jesus made sense, and I understood it, for the first time. What I didn't realize then was that the Holy Spirit was bringing the Bible alive for me. In committing myself to Christ, I had opened myself up to the presence of the Holy Spirit. He was making the words of the Bible "come alive" as I read them. What had been an obscure, impenetrable book to me, suddenly started to make sense.

The other thing that happened was that my Young Life leader, Mal McSwain, started a Bible study with the group of guys who had been on the trip. We met early in the morning before school for breakfast and a Bible study. Over the space of a couple of months, I began to understand Christianity differently. It wasn't primarily a moral code. It wasn't a set of rules; it was a relationship with God through Jesus Christ. It was a religion of grace and wasn't just about being a nice person.

I had assumed that being a Christian was about being nice. That's the message I had heard in church growing up. What I learned in my Bible study was that no person is able to be good enough to make up for their sins. We are all sinful and unable to make up for our sins by our own actions. That was the reason God sent his Son. Jesus Christ was not just a great teacher but God's only Son. He lived a perfect life then gave his life on the cross for the sake of people like me. Because he was the eternal Son of God, his sacrifice was a sufficient payment for the sins of every person, past, present, and future. If I placed my faith in Jesus and believed in what he had done for me, I would be forgiven, and the promise of eternal life would be mine.

Slowly but surely, the light started to come on. Christianity, at its heart, wasn't simply a moral code. It was a relationship with God through Jesus Christ. I was not being invited just to be a good person but to enter into a relationship with God that would give my life meaning and purpose. Walking down the hallway at school that day when I sensed that my life was empty, I knew that purpose was what my life was missing. In my new Christian commitment, I had found it. I had found an overarching purpose for my life that would center it in God. I began to understand that if I would put God at the center, all the other parts of my life would fall into place. I had found what I had always been looking for, something to give my life meaning. I could not have been happier!

Jamie
When I got caught back up in the darkness of street life, my faith in God went out the window. It was actually still there, but it was buried deep beneath a cloud of wrong behavior and bad choices. I had not had anyone to nurture my faith when I got out of jail at 18. A local church fellowship had not become part of my social support system. No one mentored me, and no one had told me I needed someone to do so.

246

So I went back into crime and back to jail. I served a year from 1990 to 1991 for simple assault. I did five years from 1994 to 1999 for the sale of crack cocaine. The third time I went to prison was for auto theft, and that was in 2000. During my third stint in prison, however, something happened. There is a prison ministry called Kairos that is connected to the Walk to Emmaus program. I got invited to that program in prison and went. It would change my life, at least for a while.

The Walk to Emmaus program is a three-day Christian renewal experience that was developed in Spain in the 1940s as a renewal movement for men in the church. It came to be called Cursillo, which means "Short Course" in Christianity. The experience proved to be powerful, and several Protestant versions of the program exist, one of which is called Walk to Emmaus. There is a version that operates in prisons, and it is called Kairos.

I didn't want to go to any religion program in prison. I was 32 at that time and very entrenched in my life of crime. A guy I knew from Atlanta was in prison with me, and he invited me to come to this set of Christian meetings. He had four or five life sentences on him, so he wasn't ever getting out. I said to him, "No, man, I'm good." I was smoking weed every day in prison and doing fine, so I didn't want anything to interfere with that. He said something that piqued my interest, however. He said, "They've got great food there. You'll like it." I said, "What kind of food?" He said, "All kinds of pies and homemade stuff. Things you can't get here in prison." For that reason, I decided to go.

The Kairos program lasted for several days, and I was just there for the food, so I was playing it tough like the other mean guys who were there with me. I wasn't going to let anything touch me. However, there were all these guys there from the outside who had jobs and businesses. I kept wondering why they were helping put on this program; what did they care? I tried not to care; I was just there for the cookies, chips, cakes, and pies. There were a lot of people making speeches about a lot of things, but I wasn't even pretending to listen.

On the second day, we did something new. We started standing around in a circle, singing songs together. I guess it was the singing that started to break through to me because sometime during the singing I felt my heart soften. I felt something I hadn't felt much in my life, the power of love. I felt love in the room, a kind of love I hadn't felt before. In fact, at one point, it was like the power of love dropped on the entire group. When that happened, I started laughing and couldn't stop.

After one of these times, I went back to the table where I was sitting with some of the guys. As part of the program, they had some people write letters to us, telling us that they were praying for us. I started opening these letters, and some of them were from children. I opened a letter from a third grade girl who said, "Mr. Jamie, my name is" such and such. She said that someone helped her write the letter, but she just wanted me to know that she had been praying for me and that she loved me. All the letters kept talking about love, love, love. At one point I broke down crying like the other gangsters at the table were starting to do. They were just like me; they had never experienced authentic love.

That was a very powerful experience for me, but it still wasn't enough. In fact, it didn't take but two days after I got out of prison before all my good intentions went out the window again. God had touched me a second time, but the lure of the streets was too strong. I got back into the dope trap like before. In just a couple of days, once again, I had dope in my veins and a pistol in my pocket.

Bob

When I invited Christ into my life at age 17, I knew something real had happened. Because of the Bible study I was in, I was beginning to understand the meaning of the Christian faith. It was starting to make sense, and I was thrilled, and somewhat surprised, to realize that Christian belief not only made sense in itself but helped me think more clearly about the world and my life. There was only one issue I couldn't get beyond. I didn't really see how the resurrection of Jesus could have happened.

I had heard about the resurrection of Jesus since I was a child. It was what the church celebrated on Easter every year. But I didn't know anything about it except that Christianity believed Jesus rose from the dead. As an 18-year-old who knew some things about the world, I just didn't believe it possible. People don't rise from the dead.

The next summer I got invited to take a course for leadership training through Young Life. It took place on Sunday nights and lasted about eight weeks. I began to memorize my first Bible verses. This was not something I had done before, other than for my God and Country award, and I found it instructive and spiritually nurturing. One evening after the class was over, I happened to walk by the resource table. There on the table was a small booklet called, "Evidence for the Resurrection." I didn't know if there was any real evidence for the Resurrection, but if there were, I was interested in what it was. I bought the book, which cost a dollar, and took it home.

What I read in the booklet surprised me. The author suggested that we ought to look at the resurrection of Jesus like a jury looked at evidence in a trial. The resurrection of Jesus wasn't like a scientific experiment that could be repeated in a laboratory. It was more like an event a jury examined. Juries look at evidence to determine whether certain things are true or not, and whether they actually happened or not. The booklet looked at the resurrection of Jesus from that point of view.

As I began to read, the author looked at one piece of evidence after another that made the Resurrection credible as a historical event. For example, he asked, "Who moved the stone away from the tomb on that Sunday morning?" When the women arrived at the tomb of Jesus at dawn on that Sunday morning, the stone was rolled back from the opening of the grave. That's what all the Gospel accounts say. The women had realized in their walk to the tomb, that they were not strong enough to move it. When they arrived, however, someone else already had. But who? That was the question the booklet asked.

One possibility might have been the disciples, but they were still asleep. In fact they were behind locked doors for fear of the Jewish authorities. So they didn't do it. The soldiers would not have moved the stone because they were charged with keeping the body of Jesus safe. In addition the tomb had been sealed with an official seal. Had the women wanted the soldiers to move it back for them to administer spices, they would probably not have done so, in order not to break the seal. For that reason, they would not even have let the owner of the property break the seal, though he would have had no reason to do so at dawn on that day. So if the disciples or women or owner of the property or soldiers didn't move the stone, who did?

There is, however, said the author, one possibility that perfectly fits with the evidence. It is that, as the Gospels record, an angel came down and moved the stone away from the opening. That is what the Bible says happened. As it turns out, said the author, the angel was the only one with both the interest and the ability to move the stone away from the opening, in spite of the presence of the Roman soldiers. Historically, this is the one possibility that makes sense of the evidence.

As I began to read through this booklet, the author examined one piece of evidence after another like this. As just one more example, he said, if the account of the Resurrection were made up by his disciples or someone else, it would not have been the women who first saw the risen Jesus. For one thing, this made his disciples look bad. After all, the women were up early to attend to Jesus' body, while the disciples were hidden away in fear. That the account is told this way, with the women seeing Jesus first, only makes sense if this is simply the way it happened. It would never have been told this way if the story were contrived.

250

By the time I finished the little booklet, my mind had completely changed, and a great intellectual weight had lifted from my spirit. I had thought I was believing something that wasn't completely true. Now I realized that the resurrection of Jesus was true. It really did happen, and this understanding was a final piece of the puzzle that had not fit together for me. In finding intellectual evidence to support my belief, I was becoming completely convinced, not only that God was real but that Christianity made sense. It was another piece of evidence that made the foundation for my faith secure. I realized that, in believing that Jesus was the Son of God who came to save the world and me, I was standing on solid ground!

Over the years I have learned more about Christianity and Christian belief. To my joy and delight, I have discovered that there is no place where Christianity falls apart. There is no hidden secret that makes parts of it untrue. There is no fatal flaw in its belief system or truthfulness. In fact the more you study Christianity, the more convincing it is, the more it makes sense, and the more reasonable it is. This does not mean that Christian belief no longer requires faith; it only means that faith in God and Jesus is not blind faith. It is consistent with life as we experience it, the world as we know it, and the best aspirations of the human spirit. It makes sense it itself, enables us to make sense of our lives, and helps us makes sense of the world in which we live.

Jamie

Because I was still into crime, I got locked up again in 2005. I was in the county jail in a cell by myself, and I was tired. I had been ripping and running hard for lots of days and was physically exhausted. I was also emotionally and mentally worn down from the kind of life I had been living and the continual stresses it put on my soul. So I slept for three or four days straight. When time came to eat, I'd get up, then I'd lay down and go right back to sleep.

My cell was small, probably 8 feet by 8 feet, and I looked in the mirror. I had lost a lot of weight; my jawbone was showing, and I looked like a wreck. I also knew I was going back to prison. Not only had I violated my probation, but I was facing a charge of armed robbery in possession of crack cocaine. So I knew I was going to do some serious time. Something from deep in my spirit said, "Jamie, aren't you tired of living this way?"

I was. I was very tired of what I was doing and finally wanted a change. I really wanted a change. So as I was looking in the mirror, I said, "God, I see people talking about you on television as if you are real. I just don't know. But if you are as real as people make you out to be, then please help me. If you will, I will give you 100% of my life. I want to submit to you wholeheartedly. Not just 85 or 95 or even 99%. If you will turn my life around, I will serve you all the days of my life."

At that point, I sat down on my bunk to read the Bible. I had asked an officer to bring me one, so there was one in my cell. When I opened the Bible to read it, something happened. The best way I can describe it is to say that the words on the page began to be alive. They were breathing. I didn't have any drugs in my system at this point, so it wasn't that, but something real was happening. The words started actually moving on the page, moving back and forth, as if they were alive to me. They were breathing with God's presence.

When that happened, I turned my head back and forth to see if I was seeing what I thought I was. I even shut the Bible and opened it again. When I did, the same thing happened. It was like there was a wave on the page with the words coming in and out toward me. I thought, "Man, hold on," and shut the Bible two or three more times. I didn't know if I was tripping or if this was God. But every time I opened it, it was the same. The words were alive in front of me. I'd have to say, very simply, that God visited me that day, and I recognized it. Right then and there I knew that God was real.

When I got shipped out to prison for the last time, I continued to read the Bible. In the prison, there was a church, and I started going. One of the women who worked in the prison was a devout Christian. She was the mother of the former University of Georgia football player, now with the Kansas City Chiefs, Mecole Hardman. She began to see my faith and said, "I can see there's something about you." They were starting a library at the prison, and she asked me what kind of books ought to be in the library. We worked on getting some Christian books in the prison library.

She also introduced me to the chaplain, whose name was Stanley Rucker. He began to mentor me as a Christian. At one point, he even wanted me to be an assistant chaplain and work with him. That blew my mind, but I was hungry to know more about God, and he saw that in me. I had never been asked to do something good before, certainly not something that had to do with promoting the Gospel. I said, "Hold on, sir. Are you sure you've got the right person?" He just burst out laughing and said, "Yeah, I'm sure." I said, "Well, why me?" He replied, "Why not you?" So I became the chaplain's assistant.

That started me into working for the Lord in prison. We had a prayer box that people could put prayer requests in. A group of guys and myself formed a little prayer group, and we'd pray over the requests in the prison barbershop. We also formed a prayer group in the yard under the gazebo. I also remember that one day a famous Christian preacher came to visit the prison. His name was Spiros Zodhiates, and he was a very humble man even though he was very renowned. I asked him and his wife to pray for me, and they did.

Not everything went smoothly, however. One day I got into a fight in the prison yard, and they put me into solitary. I was completely embarrassed, but no one was completely surprised. One of the guards came by and opened the flap in the door of my cell. He said, "I've been telling the chaplain you're no good. I've looked up your record. I knew you were playing a game." He just laughed and said, "I knew you weren't going to make it." Then he said, "You know that I'm going to tell the chaplain about this."

I felt so bad and hated to have to face the chaplain. In a couple of days, he came to see me. I tried to pretend I was asleep but eventually got up and faced him. He said, "Everyone makes mistakes, but God's grace is greater than our mistakes. I can get you out of solitary when you are ready. I still want you to come out and be my assistant." I started to cry because I was overwhelmed by his faith in me. He was extending God's love to me, something I had not had happen much in my life. I told him that I had some work to do on my heart, and I'd let him know when I was ready to come out. I was close to getting out of prison at that point and was determined that this time things were going to be different.

26

CONVERSATION ABOUT GOD

Bob

JAMIE, I'VE THOUGHT IT INTERESTING and a little confusing that it took so long for your conversion experience to sink in. You had what felt to you like was a real Christian conversion at age 17, but it wasn't until you were 35 that it finally took hold. That's a long time. Why do you think that was?

Jamie

There were a lot of reasons. One was that I went back into the same environment out of which I had come. It was one full of crime, drugs, and violence. Whatever good intentions I had quickly got swallowed up in the darkness. The power of that environment was too strong for a new Christian who didn't really understand what being a Christian was about.

I also didn't have anyone to mentor me. If I had known to get into a church when I came home and come under the leadership of a godly man, it might have been different. What finally made the difference was that I had a chaplain who took me under his wing and mentored me in prison. He got me into a Bible study and prayer group. For my final two years in prison, I was being discipled as a Christian. When I came out the last time, I had the resources to resist the temptations that met me.

All of this emphasizes how important it is for prisoners not to come out of jail and go right back where they came from. It's just too much for them to handle. This is where the church could do a lot of good, by helping people right when they come out of prison. My story also is a reminder that you shouldn't give up on people. God didn't give up on me, and he finally got through.

Bob

We both had conversion experiences about age 17. There were a couple of things that made my story different from yours. One is that I did have someone to mentor me. I didn't understand Christianity very much after making my commitment of faith. It would take someone teaching me to help me finally understand the meaning of Christianity. It took a while for me to understand that it wasn't just a moral code but a relationship of grace with the living God.

Another thing that helped me was that I already had roots in my faith. I had been in church and Sunday School for most of my life. Vacation Bible and youth group were things I participated in regularly. I had heard many of the stories from the Bible, either in Sunday School or worship. I knew who Jesus was and something of what he did. While all my early church experiences weren't necessarily impactful, they gave me roots. When I invited Christ into my life, it was already a rich soil of Bible stories, Christian knowledge, and beginning faith.

This might not seem important to people, but it is. I knew a guy in high school who ran among a rough crowd. We called him a "hood," and he was a leader among them. Miraculously, he had a Christian conversion at one point and became a very powerful witness for Christ. I went to a rally he held in the school cafeteria after hours one summer, and it was amazing.

But in a couple of years, he had fallen back into his old ways of doing drugs. I was stunned to hear it but think it was because he didn't have deep Christian roots. He hadn't grown up in church and simply didn't have much of a foundation on which to build his life of faith.

This is why it is very important for parents to take their children to church. One of Jesus' famous parables is the Parable of the Sower. In it a farmer throws seed onto the ground. Some lands on rocky soil where it can't send down deep roots. The plant can't grow tall because it can't sink roots. When parents go to church

256

with their children, it gives the entire family spiritual roots and a deep foundation for a lifetime of faith.

I have thought what my life would have been like if I had not become a Christian. The lure of the streets would never have been strong to me; that was not my environment. I would never have become a drug dealer or carried a pistol in my pocket. But I would have still been lost.

What Christianity gave to me was meaning and purpose, which was something my life did not have. Had I not become a Christian, I would have spent my life pursuing happiness but never finding it. I would have tried to fill my life with material things, relationships, hobbies, and successes to try to fill the empty void inside. My soul would have been truly lost, and I can envision many rocks on which it might have become shipwrecked. God saved me from a life of meaninglessness and gave me something for which to live.

One of the things for which I am extremely grateful is having a calling. I think that everyone can have a calling, not just pastors. Many doctors, nurses, and teachers feel a sense of calling. So do many other people. They believe God put them where they are to help others. To have a sense of calling means that I feel like God has given me something to do with my life that makes a difference. The fact that this calling comes from God gives me an even greater sense of purpose as I try to fulfill it.

Jamie

I love how you say that. I heard a pastor named Andy Stanley make a comment I have not forgotten. He said that you ought to look for the one thing that breaks your heart. What is the need or cause or calling that breaks your heart? That's what I've found at the Sparrow's Nest. We have people who come through here who are homeless, who have been caught up in the prison system, and who are going through terrible things. I try to help them with the love of Jesus, and the work has captured my heart. Of course, you've got to have a soft heart to be touched by others, not a heart of stone. I thank God that he took away my heart of stone and gave me a new, soft one. I believe he can do that for others and turn their lives around just like he did mine.

Bob

Roots are important for a life of faith. There is something parents can do to help their children develop their own authentic life of faith. It is to teach them to pray and pray with them as they grow up. Parents can do this with their children at any age, but the perfect window of opportunity is when children are between ages 4 and 12. This is when parents have the most influence on their children's lives, so it makes it easy for them to teach them about God.

I've written a book to help parents do this. It's called, *Pass Your Faith To Your Children –Through The Simple Practice Of Teaching Your Child To Pray*. It teaches parents how to have spiritual conversations with their children and pass their faith along to them in a very practical way that isn't forced or awkward. It gives lots of practical suggestions for how to nurture faith in your children. It also is useful for grandparents and something they can use with their grandchildren.

Jamie

This kind of thing is very important. The proverb says, "Train up a child in the way he should go; even when he is old he will not depart from it." I know that is true. I certainly understand what happens when children don't get trained in the right things, and it doesn't turn out well.

Bob

One of the ways you talk about your relationship with God is to say that you "fell in love with Jesus." What do you mean by that?

Jamie

Turning my life to God has made all the difference. Just look at how my life has changed. I was running drugs on the street, going in and out of prison, and doing all sorts of bad things. All that could have easily cost me my life, either literally or ended me up in jail for life. By the grace of God, it didn't.

One thing having God in my life did for me was help me love myself. I didn't really love myself. I was selfish, that was sure, but I didn't understand how to value myself, treat myself with respect, and do things that made my life better. What coming to love myself helped me do is love others. You can't love someone else if you don't love yourself.

What I experienced was unconditional love; I hadn't ever experienced that. I thought people gave love because they wanted to get something from another person. When I realized that God loved me just like I was, in spite of all my sins, it overwhelmed me.

When I was in prison, I read a lot of religious books. I read the Koran and also some books about eastern religions. The Jehovah's Witness religion was even something I looked at. I wanted to know what was true. That study gave me some head knowledge but nothing that would change my heart. An encounter with Jesus did that, however. It changed my heart. When I fell in love with God, it made everything different. It taught me how to love my wife and other people. This ability isn't perfected in me yet, but it's growing. When I get up in the morning, I try to put on love, just like I put on my clothes.

In the New Testament, Jesus made a comment about someone who had been forgiven many sins. He said that the one who is forgiven little loves little, but the one who is forgiven much loves much (Luke 7:47). I guess I fall into that category. I've been forgiven much. Maybe that's why I love Jesus so much.

Bob

Some people are skeptical about Christianity. They wonder if it's really true or not. There are really smart atheists who say it isn't. But just because a smart person doesn't believe in Christianity, doesn't make it false. It seems to me that many atheists reject God because of a false sense of intellectual superiority, or because they don't like the implications of admitting that there's a God who makes moral demands on them, or simply because they're proud, which is at the heart of sin. I believe most atheists reject God because of heart issues, not intellectual ones. They don't want to believe and find intellectual reasons not to do so.

The reality is, however, that Christianity makes sense, and it makes sense of the world. It gives one a compelling picture of God, a realistic understanding of human nature, and an optimistic hope for the future. In addition, there is no secret inconsistency that makes Christianity untrue. In fact, the more you examine Christianity, the more compelling, attractive, and genuine it is. For more than 40 years, I've been a Christian and studied Christianity. I become more convinced of its truth each year.

If you think about it, what is so difficult about believing in God? Science tells us that the universe came into existence about 14 billion years ago. There are only two possibilities: Either the universe created itself, which would seem to be unlikely, or it had a Creator. Our experience is that houses don't build themselves. Neither do automobiles or airplanes or computers. They all have builders whose intelligence created them. There is no computer so complex as the human mind. It would seem improbable for mindless, random chance to create living, thinking, loving human beings.

The universe also is technically improbable. For example, in the first seconds of the universe's existence, as much as physicists can ascertain, everything had to be perfect to create a universe such as ours. To give just a couple of examples, if the balance of matter to antimatter, in the first moments after the Big Bang, had been different, the universe would not have come into existence. In fact, the balance had to be accurate to 1 part in 10 billion. But it was. In addition, if the rate of expansion one second after the Big Bang had been smaller by one part in a hundred thousand million million, the universe would have collapsed on itself and never formed.

As another example, the earth is perfectly suited for human life. We are just the right distance from the sun, in the solar system's habitable zone. Any closer to the sun and it would be too hot. Any farther away and it would be too cold. The presence of the moon stabilizes our orbit, keeping the planet from having dramatic climate shifts. The earth's rotation also stabilizes its climate, giving the earth night and day every 24 hours. We have an atmosphere and a strong magnetic field that keep cosmic rays from reaching the surface. We are also in the "suburbs" of the Milky Way galaxy, which means we don't have a lot of cosmic activity around us, such as other stars crashing through our solar system. In addition, our sun is a relatively rare type, a yellow dwarf, which is long-lived and stable. This means it does not send out excessive radiation.

There are hundreds of things like this that make the earth a perfect environment for human existence. That it is all accidental strains credulity. As biologist Edwin Conklin said, "The probability of life originating from accident is comparable to the probability of the unabridged dictionary resulting from an explosion in a printing shop."[56] When we see a dictionary, we know it came from a publisher. When we see the faces of the four United States presidents on Mount Rushmore, we know they are not the result of wind, rain, and erosion.

None of these things prove the existence of God, but they are consistent with it. This is just what we would expect if the world were indeed created by God. If there were no God, we would expect that it would be obvious, with our advanced scientific knowledge, but that isn't the case. In fact all the evidence points in the opposite direction, which is what the Bible teaches. It says, very simply, "In the beginning, God created the heavens and the earth" (Genesis 1:1).

Jamie

I would say to a person that, if they don't believe in God, they should. They should believe in God, and they should believe in Jesus Christ. The best way to get to know Jesus is to read about him in the Bible. People should read the Gospel of Matthew, and they will see who Jesus is. They can see for themselves if he is worthy of their love. I found that he is, and I think others will too.

Bob

In addition to all this, Christianity has the ability to break down barriers. There were certainly a lot of prejudices among people in the first century when Christianity started. There were tensions between the Jews and the Gentiles, between Romans and non-Romans, between slaves and those who were free, between people who lived in the cities and people in the countryside, between men and women, and between the rich and the poor. There was great hostility and dysfunction in the cities where people of different cultures and languages were thrust together. Sanitation was terrible, crime was rampant, and the different groups hated each other. The cities of the first century could be awful places to live.

What Christianity brought into that environment was a new way to live. It said that all people were created by God and were valued by him. In Christ, people of different backgrounds became brothers and sisters, with deep bonds of fellowship in God. In the early church, people found a sense of community that nothing else could provide, and that gave them a sense of family, safety, and support. It is no wonder that Christianity caught on in that environment.

Christianity has this same ability today. People who believe in God and call Jesus their Savior have a bond that transcends race, class, and position. People who would never associate with one another become friends, co-workers, and family in Jesus Christ. If there is one thing that has the power to unite people today, it is Christianity and people's love for Jesus Christ.

262

Jamie

This brings us to something I have come to believe. It is that the most important institution in America today is the church. Some people think government is most important. Some in the black community think this. It isn't true. People's trust in government is misplaced. Only God can save us, as individuals and as a culture. God is our only hope. This makes the church very important. The best thing that can happen to us all is start going back to church. Blacks and whites, we need to get back in church and make God our priority. If we will do that, a great many of our other problems will resolve themselves.

DISCUSSION QUESTIONS
PART 8 – GOD

1. Were you aware of the presence of religious practices such as the Root Doctor? Ancestor worship? Calling up the spirits of the dead? Do you believe such practices exist today? Do you think there is actual power in any of these practices?

2. Did you have the experience of growing up in church? If so, what did you gain from it? If not, what do you think you missed? Has the Christian church been a positive experience in your life?

3. What role do you think intellectual understanding, such as evidence for the Resurrection, or evidence for God's existence, plays in people's faith? Do you think Christianity has answers to hard intellectual questions?

4. The authors make the point that Christianity is not simply a moral code or just about being a good person, but a living relationship with God through Jesus Christ. How is this different from the way some people think about Christianity? What questions does this raise for you?

5. What is the importance of religious faith for societal virtues? Is it possible to have societal virtues that are not undergirded by belief in God?

6. Have you ever had the Bible "come alive" for you, in the sense of it speaking to some particular situation in your life? Do you think this is a normal experience for Christians?

7. Have you ever had someone mentor or disciple you? If yes, who have been some of those people? What did they do, and what difference did it make?

8. Do you think going to church gives people roots in their faith? Why is this important? Do you agree that it is important for parents to take their children to church? How often? Explain.

9. Have you ever experienced Christianity breaking down barriers between people, particularly racial barriers? Describe?

10. What do you think of the comment that the church is the most important institution in the country? In what sense is this true for blacks? For whites? Do you think faith in God is important for us as a society and culture? Explain.

PART 9 – WAYS FORWARD

27

FAMILY, WELFARE, AND WORK

FAMILY
"It Is Easier To Build Strong Children Than To Repair Broken Men."

Bob

IN THIS FINAL SECTION, we are going to explore whether there might be ways forward on which we can both agree. We have no illusions that our racial, economic, or social problems are easily solved. We only want to reflect on the stories we have shared to see if there are lessons that might be of benefit to others and helpful in healing our racial divisions. We will examine the various topics we have discussed, beginning with the family.

We have noted that the American family has problems. In the white community, it is the prevalence of divorce. Far too many families are broken by divorce, and this creates difficulties for children. It separates children from their parents, from their church, and often from God. I don't know what the answer is except to say that it is a great crisis. Families would be much better off if they held together. Children would be better off if their parents would figure out how to have a meaningful, satisfying marriage that would provide a stable environment for children throughout their lives.

Families get broken in many ways, and when that happens people have to do the best they can. Nevertheless, we need to affirm the goal for which we strive, which is stable families with both a father and mother in the home. Where that isn't the case, the church especially should rally to provide help and support.

Jamie

The black culture has many social problems. The primary one is the high percentage of births to unwed mothers, over 70% in the black community. No wonder our culture has problems; the black family is in disarray. Is it surprising that many black children start with a variety of disadvantages? No wonder there is social chaos in some of our communities. Without fathers in the home, children are without a crucial element of discipline, guidance, and nurture in their lives.

Bob

I read a story about two famous gay male fashion designers who argued against allowing gay couples to adopt children. This seemed an odd stance for two gay men to take. Their reasoning struck me. They said, if you allow a same-sex couple to adopt, that child will be without either a mother or a father. You are depriving a child of what, by natural design, they ought to have, both a mother and a father. I thought that a fascinating statement. The article I read reported how a group of children raised by gay parents sent a letter supporting them against the backlash they received. They affirmed that being raised by gay parents had deprived them of their "right" to a mom and dad.[57]

Jamie

God has designed the world so that every child ought to have both a mother and a father. In fact, children cannot come into the world in any other way than through that which both a man and woman provide. It requires both to produce a child. That ought to tell us something. It ought to give us an indication of God's design. Women who have children out of marriage automatically deprive

268

their child of an important aspect of life, a father. Every child deserves and ought to have both a father and a mother.

Bob

People have recently asked if America is a racist country. My answer is no, except to say that bad laws can make our problems worse. Jim Crow laws are now illegal, but there can be other laws that damage race relations. Bad laws can make racial issues worse, even though they may be well-intentioned. I think welfare laws have done this by creating monetary incentives for women to have children outside of marriage and thus discouraging marriage. As long as there is a significant number of black families without fathers in the home, there will be significant poverty and disarray in the black culture. This will continue to create disparity between blacks and whites, since white families are less disrupted in this way.

I don't know the answer to the alarming numbers of children born to unwed mothers, and the problem is significant in all major racial groups, including whites. I do believe that sin can get institutionalized into civic structures, such as laws. That is, we can make laws that increase sinful behaviors rather than inhibiting them. When that happens, we need to change the laws so they don't incentivize sin. But I don't think we can count on the government to do the right thing. Some bad laws may not change. For that reason, the remedies may need to come from us and especially from the church.

Jamie

Nineteenth-century abolitionist Frederick Douglass said, "It is easier to build strong children than to repair broken men." I agree. The best way to change our culture is to start with our children. Raise strong children. Teach them to love God and do the right things. Promote virtue and raise them in strong families with both a mother and father in the home. If we would start doing this now, in 25 years

269

the situation of black people in America would be vastly different. We could fix many of our cultural problems in 25 years if we started with our children now. Teach them to value God, work, education, and family. It will change the face of the nation if we can do so.

Bob

From my experience as a father, there is no greater joy in life. There is nothing that has given me greater satisfaction than being a father, raising my two sons, nurturing their lives and faith, and being there for them. When they were growing up, my wife Kim and I tried to tell them regularly that we loved them and were proud of them. We also tried to affirm their gifts and talents, so they could begin to think about what they were good at and what profession they might want to enter. We prayed that God would give them some calling in their lives and lead them to a Christian woman who would make a good wife for them. Every day we continue to pray for God's protection over them and his blessing on them. We will do this until the day we die.

Jamie

My wife and I are raising our granddaughter now and trying to teach her all the lessons we didn't learn growing up. We hope we are doing a good job. One of my great regrets, however, is not having any children of my own. I missed that window of opportunity because I was too busy hustling, committing crimes, and being incarcerated. Oh, how I wish I had understood things differently. I would have had children of my own and built a family around them.

Black men often miss out on this great joy. I'm one of them. If only young black men could see this. The joy of parenthood and family is far greater and more satisfying than being a hustler and a "player." That's a message we need to try to get across to young black men in this country.

Bob

God has designed the family to be the basic unit of society. The family isn't a social construct but part of God's grand design. For most people, the plan of God is for them to get married, have children, and raise them to be good people and good citizens. We depart from God's plan when we don't honor, protect, and promote the family.

Jamie

There is a famous speech given by then-Senator Barack Obama, given in a black church in Chicago on Father's Day, 2008.[58] He affirmed the things we have been saying. I think his words are worth hearing, especially by those in the black community. He said, "If we are honest with ourselves, we'll admit that what too many fathers are is missing – missing from too many lives and too many homes. They have abandoned their responsibilities, acting like boys instead of men. And the foundations of our families are weaker because of it."

He then went on to quote some of the statistics we have already discussed. "You and I know how true this is in the African-American community. We know that more than half of all black children live in single-parent households, a number that has doubled – doubled – since we were children. We know the statistics – that children who grow up without a father are five times more likely to live in poverty and commit crime; nine times more likely to drop out of schools and 20 times more likely to end up in prison. They are more likely to have behavioral problems or run away from home or become teenage parents themselves. And the foundations of our community are weaker because of it. ... We need fathers to realize that responsibility does not end at conception. We need them to realize that what makes you a man is not the ability to have a child – it's the courage to raise one."

I was most impressed with what he said about his own family and his commitment to raising his children. He said, "So I resolved many years ago that it was my obligation to break the cycle – that if I could be anything in life, I would be a good father to my girls; that if I could give them anything, I would give them that rock – that foundation – on which to build their lives. And that would be the greatest gift I could offer." That's it. Black men have to make this same commitment to breaking the cycle of dysfunctional families.

After sharing our stories and all our discussions about the family, here is something on which we both agree. The family is the key. The family is the foundation and heart of our culture. Without stable families that include both mothers and fathers, we cannot have a healthy society and racial healing. For that reason, we all need to do everything we can to preserve and protect the family. Government needs to carefully monitor laws to be sure they promote marriage and the family instead of harming it. Marriage should be highly valued and greatly esteemed by everyone. This is God's plan, and it is a moral issue. It is wrong in the sight of God to have children outside of marriage and children you do not intend to raise.

What are men thinking when they abandon their children? If you are a black man who didn't have a father in the home, aren't you angry at your father for not being there for you? Then don't do the same thing to your son or daughter! Be the man your father was not. Get married and be a good husband. Be faithful to your marriage and create a stable environment for your children. Love your wife and make a good life for yourself and your family. This is a much more enjoyable and meaningful way to live than being a player or hustler or gangster.

We have to talk about his issue, especially in the black community. We cannot be silent any longer. We have to speak out and call black men, black women, and black culture to account. Stop having children outside of marriage! Stop having children you are unwilling to raise! Stop being immoral in the way you live, and start living by God's commandments, which are good for you, good for your family, and good for society.

272

Ways Forward

The family is the key to success for whites, blacks, and people of all races. For that reason, the state of the family, in all segments of society, must be an issue of serious conversation and discussion. In our communities, we need to do everything we can to promote marriage and the family. We must encourage young people to wait to have children until marriage, then stay committed to their family and the children they have brought into the world. It is easier to build strong children than to repair broken men and women. The health and future of our culture depends on the strength of the family, especially in poor and minority communities.

WORK, WELFARE, AND THE PROBLEM OF
ACCUMULATING WEALTH
"Movin' On Up."

Jamie

I REMEMBER WATCHING the television show "The Jeffersons" growing up. It was about a black family living the high life in New York City. The theme song said, "We're movin' on up, to the east side, to a deluxe apartment in the sky. Movin' on up, to the east side, we've finally got a piece of the pie." It was a great show and characteristic of black dreams. Everyone wants their piece of the pie.

One of the realities of America today, however, is that there is a great wealth disparity between blacks and whites. In the chapter on welfare, you talked about how your parents accumulated wealth. You noted how, over their lifetimes, they were able to accumulate significant wealth, some of which they passed on to you and your sister. For a variety of reasons, accumulating wealth has been very hard for the black community. As just one example, according to 2019 data, the median white wealth was $188,200. For blacks that number was $24,100. That is a huge disparity in wealth.[59]

The term median refers to the middle point. It means that there are the same number of blacks who have more than $24,100 in wealth as those who have less. What is striking about that statistic is that white people, in general, have eight times as much wealth as blacks.

Bob

I read that same report. What was interesting about it is that the average white wealth amount showed an even greater disparity. If you average the wealth of all white people, then divide by the number of white people, you get $983,400. For blacks, that number is only $142,500. What that says is that the richest white people have significantly more wealth than the richest blacks. Certainly,

274

people such as Bill Gates (Microsoft), Mark Zuckerberg (Facebook), Jeff Bezos (Amazon), and the Walton family (Walmart) skew the data because they are multibillionaires, but it also makes the point. In 2020, there were 614 billionaires in the United States, but only seven of them were black. Some of the names of black billionaires are familiar, such as Oprah Winfrey, Tyler Perry, Jay-Z, Kanye West, and Michael Jordan.[60] But the richest black man in America, investor Robert Smith, is worth only $5 billion, whereas the richest white person in America, Jeff Bezos, is worth $179 billion.[61]

I recognize the problem of accumulating wealth. My parents started from nothing. In fact, my father came from less than nothing! He could hardly have been poorer. What they had, however, was a good work ethic, some natural intelligence, and Christian values. Their Christian values taught them to be honest, work hard, and do their best. Over their lifetimes, they gradually moved from the lower middle class into the middle of the middle class. By the time of their deaths, they were at the lower edge of the upper middle class. This didn't come easy, however, and it would take their entire lifetimes. My father died three days short of age 95, so it is fair to say that accumulating wealth would take him the better part of 95 years. Most people simply can't get rich quick, but they can accumulate wealth over a lifetime. It seems to me that this lesson has somehow gotten lost on the black community. Am I wrong?

Jamie
Sadly, you aren't. I come out of generational poverty, and it is a miracle I got out. I now have a job, and that has put me into the middle class. If I had stayed in the projects and on welfare, I would still be in poverty. By the grace of God, I got out.

That being said, I'm not among the wealthy. I know a number of white people who are; in fact, they are millionaires. That's not me. I own a home and a car. I almost have a second car paid off. My wife and I both work, so we have some disposable income. We have enough for ourselves and some to give to those in need. We tithe to the church and have our granddaughter living with us.

I don't see myself as ever being rich, but not being in poverty either. We are now in the middle class and intend to stay there. We just refinanced our home so that it will be paid off at my retirement age. That means we will one day own it outright. That will feel like a major accomplishment.

Bob

I can hear the pride in your voice, and that's great. It also highlights a significant disparity between the black and white communities which has to do with home ownership. Many more whites own homes than blacks; 73.3% of whites own their own homes compared with only 42.1% of blacks.[62] What is significant about this is that home ownership is a primary way of accumulating wealth. A person who purchases a home and pays it off over 30 years will own a significant asset that will probably continue to grow in value. Someone who rents or lives in government housing will not acquire wealth in this way. This one factor may be the difference in the wealth gap of $188,200 for whites to $24,100 for blacks.

I know that some have suggested that banks discriminate in making loans, preferring white applicants and discriminating against black ones. The issue, however, is more complicated and often has to do with total wealth. A white person applying for a home loan may have the exact income of a black person applying. The white person, however, will be approved and the black person rejected because of the disparity in wealth. The black applicant may not have sufficient wealth, such as money in the bank, to serve as a safety net in case of difficulty to make the loan company feel comfortable approving the loan. This is an example of how disparities in wealth can perpetuate those disparities.

Jamie

One of the problems of the black community is surviving. When you live on the edge of poverty, you are just scraping by. You aren't thinking about buying a house. That's not even in your dreams. So, if you get a little bit of extra money, you spend it on something that makes you feel good, like some jewelry, or nice clothes, or even a car. These things seem within your reach, so people spend money on them.

I know that blacks who work around a lot of white people in the corporate world feel like they must dress well, even better than their white coworkers. So, they spend more money than they ordinarily would to dress sharp.

I also think there's a subtle dynamic that goes on. When black people begin to move into the middle class, they sometimes want to display the trappings of their achievement. If they have nice things, it shows their black friends that they are successful and are moving up in the world. They want to drive a nice car, wear fashionable clothes, and have some bling, so that's what they spend their money on. But these things tend to decrease in value, so they do not help in accumulating wealth.

Bob

I read an account of a professional black woman who was talking about the problem of accumulating wealth. She worked in a big city, and she and her spouse both made good money, but she still felt like she was behind in wealth accumulation. They both had significant student loans that took a big chunk of their income to pay down. In addition, her mother needed monetary help just to survive. So, in spite of the fact that they both made good salaries, she felt like they still teetered on the edge of calamity. They were spending all their money and not putting any aside in savings.

I can appreciate that problem. I wish there were a magic formula to help raise the black community economically. Some have proposed ideas, but they don't seem workable to me. Some people think the white community ought to pay reparations to compensate the black community for various racial discriminations through the years that have kept blacks poor. Apart from discussing the merits of that argument, reparations are not helpful. There isn't enough money to produce real wealth for the black community. Giving black people a check for $1,500 won't really help. There must be another answer.

I am the beneficiary of my parents' almost 100 years of hard work. They left my sister and me some of their accumulated wealth, but it took them all their lives to do so. They started from nothing in the 1920s, which is 100 years ago. The problem is that someone who is starting from scratch today is 100 years behind. It is also true, however, that our economy today offers many more opportunities than my parents had. My parents grew up in the Depression. Today, people in America live in the greatest economy in the history of the world. There is no reason people can't do, in less than 100 years, what my parents did.

It is also interesting that the period of 2016 – 2019 was one in which the wealth of black families grew significantly. In fact, it grew much faster than white wealth.[63] This was also a period in which black unemployment hit record lows. With a change in administration, we will see if those advances continue.

Jamie

The problem is that many blacks are digging themselves out of a hole. They feel like they don't have anything and don't have many prospects. I don't think there is an easy answer, except education, if possible, and hard work. Not everyone can get an education. People who are 35 years old and supporting a family might not be able to go back to school. But they can get a job and work hard. They can be good employees, not steal from their employers, do their best, and try to rise in the ranks. They may not get rich, but they can have a better life. The other thing they can do is make sure their children get an education and if not their children, their grandchildren.

278

Bob

You've asserted that welfare is a trap. Just like there's a dope trap, there's a welfare trap. Though it seems like a great thing to get a government check, it isn't. It seems to me that the current system perpetuates and even encourages a culture of dependency and poverty. A few years ago, we "celebrated" the 50th anniversary of the Great Society programs that were supposed to end poverty once and for all. What the analysis showed, though, is that while many economic indicators of poverty have improved somewhat, the noneconomic indicators of poverty (crime, drug use, alcoholism, school dropouts, unwed births, suicide, depression, and so on) have all skyrocketed. I wonder if one cause of these increasing problems may be the anti-poverty programs themselves.

I think, like most things we've discussed, the root of this problem is spiritual. God made people to work, to produce things, to pursue accomplishment. Even in the Garden of Eden, there was work for Adam to do! When people don't work to support themselves and their families, it creates a spiritual crisis that affects all aspects of their lives and percolates throughout society.

What is the solution? I sometimes think that persistent problems need radical solutions. For example, imagine a law that stopped welfare payments to future unwed mothers. It would take effect one year from the date it was passed. That would allow any young woman who was pregnant at the time not to be penalized. And you would continue payments to families already receiving them. But this would mark a change for the future. You would spread the word throughout poor communities that welfare payments were no longer going to be made for out-of-marriage births, so don't get pregnant if you are not married. Wait to get pregnant until you are married and can build a family of your own. The government isn't going to be there for you.

Some would object that this penalizes children who are born to unwed mothers, but I think the opposite would happen. People are smart. They would realize that it isn't to their advantage, any longer, to get pregnant without a husband. What would people do if the law created disincentives to having children outside of marriage? They'd stop doing it! I may be naïve, but I think people would absolutely stop. In the long term, this would greatly benefit children, because fewer of them would grow up in single-parent families. If the Great Society laws have made things worse, then they need to be changed.

Jamie
You know that a law like that would never pass both houses of Congress. Not under the present political climate. Perhaps never.

Bob
I do. That's what is so discouraging about our political process today. Few elected leaders seem to have the courage to do the right thing when doing so is difficult, and when they are worried about reelection. Few seem to be able to make the hard choices we need to reform our society.

Admittedly the problems are difficult, and the solutions are not easy to find. Here is another creative solution: The federal government could entirely turn welfare programs over to the states. States today generally manage welfare, but we could let the states administer it without federal restrictions. Give each state an allotted amount of money. Tell them that they can administer it as they see fit and keep any money not used for welfare. Then let the states think about how to get people off welfare. Each state can develop their own programs to promote marriage, encourage honest employment, and keep what is left over. This would allow for a "marketplace of ideas" among states and innovative thinking on their parts.

Jamie
But won't people then just move to states where the welfare programs are more liberal and generous?

Bob

They will, but that will serve as an incentive for states not to be too generous with welfare. If you don't want people moving to your state for free stuff, don't give out free stuff!

Jamie

I grew up in an environment in which everyone hustled. Almost no one had an ordinary job. Everyone had some sort of hustle going on. They woke up in the morning and said to themselves, "How am I going to get some money today?" The answer often involved some sort of criminal activity, selling dope, stealing, or cheating someone out of something. This is a very anxious and dangerous way to live. I know because I lived it for many years. You are always anxious about being caught and put in prison, or about getting into some sort of serious trouble, or even losing your life. In addition, your conscience, while you still have one, always condemns you.

There is a great deal of darkness in some of our inner-city communities. It is a deep spiritual darkness that corrupts hearts, preys on the vulnerable, and ruins lives. The lure of serious money, such as comes from the drug trade, is very enticing. But along with it comes very long prison sentences, and most people eventually get caught. The devil draws people into the excitement of hustling, but the lure is a mirage. He leads people down a dead end that usually ends in tragedy. A life of hustling is no way to live, but it is hard for people who grow up this way to get out of the streets. It often takes a religious conversion and a cleansed heart for people to see the light. That is what finally happened to me and enabled me to understand I needed an honest job.

Bob

Here is something on which we both agree. We both agree that honest work is the key. As you said, "Get up early, work hard, and strike gold." It works for people of all races if they put it into practice. Everyone can better their situation if they work hard. If they work hard over a number of years, they will be able to accumulate wealth, at least more than if they depend on the government or spend their lives in criminal hustles.

Ways Forward

Welfare laws need to be reformed to end a culture of dependence, to encourage work, to encourage marriage, and remove monetary incentives to have children out of wedlock. We should spread the message that, besides the economic benefits of working, you will be happier, more fulfilled, and a more complete person if you do honest work to support yourself and your family.

28

EDUCATION AND SAFE COMMUNITIES

EDUCATION
"Love The Lord With All Your Mind."

Bob

WE HAVE TALKED ABOUT THE PROBLEMS of education in some sectors of the population, especially poor and minority communities. The lack of educational motivation seems particularly acute in the black community. Some have suggested that it is partly a self-esteem issue. A black professor teaching at a major college in California, writing in the early 1990s, noted how his black students seemed to have internalized the message that they could not compete with white students.[64] He said he could be confident that his black students would be at the bottom of the class at the end of the semester and even behind white students of lesser abilities. It wasn't the lack of natural ability, he said, but that black students had gotten the message, somewhere along the way, that they could not compete with white students and therefore performed up to that expectation. They had heard and internalized a message of inferiority. They didn't lack ability but self-confidence and sufficient drive to succeed.

The education gap between whites and blacks has improved slightly over the years but is still significant. To make things worse, some young people from lower economic classes who do graduate from high school still read only at an eighth grade level. One study found that a "kind of norm of minimum effort appeared to exist among Black students."[65] Many black students simply didn't work as hard as they could, either because of peer pressure or for other reasons. It isn't surprising that this would result in futures that do not enjoy a high standard of living and do not acquire high levels of wealth. The question is what to do about the issues at the root of the problem.

Jamie

This is a practical matter and a spiritual one. When Jesus was asked about the most important commandment for human life, he replied that the first great commandment was to love God with our heart, our soul, and our mind (Matthew 22:37). What is surprising is that Jesus included our minds. Are we to love God with our minds? According to Jesus, we are.

Bob

What do you think it means to love God with our minds?

Jamie

I think it means, at the very least, that we ought to think. We ought to be willing to study, learn, and think for ourselves. The old commercial used to say that a mind is a "terrible thing to waste." That's true. To love God with our minds means to use them. Educate them. Learn to think. Don't depend on others to think for us. Be wise and grow in knowledge as our years go along. Education makes you smart, and everyone needs to be smart.

I think this idea is new to some in the black culture, particularly among the poor. We need to change the way people think about things, especially about education.

Bob

I know from talking to teachers that schools are trying to change the narrative about education, particularly among black students. They are trying to get the message out that it isn't "white" to read a book, care about education, and be a good student. It's a hard road, however, and some youth have a number of obstacles in their way.

One obstacle is that other black students sometimes ostracize people of their race, particularly boys, who achieve in school. That makes it hard for good students to fit in with their black peers. One teacher, who has extensive experience in the public school system, said about students in her school, "The cultural identity of black young men seems to fit more with the thugs and gangsters and street hustlers than with dentists and accountants." It's the disrespectful kids who are seen as the "cool kids" in school, not the ones who study and do their homework.

This teacher did observe that black students did better in predominantly white schools because they didn't have negative peer pressure. In the majority black schools however, even middle-class black students got pulled down by the "misbehaving majority." This, in her view, makes it very difficult to change the outcomes of these schools. There needs to be a complete overhaul of the attitude toward education, both in the homes and in the students. This turns out to be incredibly difficult to achieve.

Another obstacle to the educational achievement of black youth seems to be the low expectations of their environment. The teacher I talked to said that many of her black students saw the ultimate goal as getting a welfare check. A welfare check would enable them not to have to work. Then they could hang out and "smoke weed with their friends." What could be better than that?

One possible solution could be the ongoing support and development of charter schools. Charter schools are controversial and sometimes opposed by those in the public school system. What they do, however, is give parents and students choices. If a charter school would be a better learning environment for a student who wants to learn, or who is negatively influenced by school peers, students could attend a charter school. Perhaps a positive step would be to make sure there are enough charter schools that every student who wished to attend one would have one in reasonable proximity.

One more question for you. Some have suggested that the educational system is biased against blacks and other minorities. How would you respond to that?

Jamie

I don't think this is a real problem, at least a significant one. What is white about math? Or science? Or biology? And there is nothing wrong with being able to speak standard English. It is true that some minority students, perhaps many, come into the school system already behind. Even in the first grade, they are behind their white and Asian classmates. However, I honestly think this is a cultural problem more than one of curriculum, teaching methods, or some sort of educational bias. It goes back to the family. We need stable family structures that will support the education of their children and instill worthy goals in them.

Former President Obama made another good point in his 2008 Father's Day speech. He spoke about the need to raise the bar of expectations in the black community. He said, "You know, sometimes I'll go to an eighth grade graduation, and there's all that pomp and circumstance and gowns and flowers. And I think to myself, it's just eighth grade. To really compete, they need to graduate high school, and then they need to graduate college, and they probably need a graduate degree, too. An eighth grade education doesn't cut it today. Let's give them a handshake and tell them to get their butts back in the library!"[66]

He continued and said, "It's up to us to say to our daughters, don't ever let images on TV tell you what you are worth, because I expect you to dream without limit and reach for those goals. It's up to us to tell our sons, those songs on the radio may glorify violence, but in my house we give glory to achievement, self-respect, and hard work. It's up to us to set these high expectations. And that means meeting those expectations ourselves. That means setting examples of excellence in our own lives."

I could not say it better. There has got to be an end to the disdain many in the black community feel toward education. We must teach our children to respect the authority of their teachers and not cause disruption in school. If I could do things over again, I would have a very different educational experience and not be a problem for my teachers. But I came out of an environment that didn't teach me how far a good education could take me. I also didn't have a father in the home to be an authority figure and instill in me respect for the authority of others. As former President Obama said, we need to motivate our children, especially in minority communities, to "dream without limit and reach for those goals."

Ways Forward

We must continue to work to change the narrative about what success means to include educational achievement, particularly for minority and low-income students. We must support teachers and school systems in their efforts to do so. Young people must be inspired to reach for lofty dreams and goals. Educational accomplishment needs to become a family value.

BUILDING SAFE COMMUNITIES – FROM A POLICE OFFICER'S PERSPECTIVE
"Protect and Serve"

A Conversation with Deputy Chief Jerry Saulters of the Athens-Clarke County Police Department

Bob

WRITING THIS BOOK HAS given me the occasion to get acquainted with Officer Jerry Saulters, with whom Jamie had several confrontations as recounted in Part 6. He is still with the Athens-Clarke County Police Department and is now Deputy Chief Saulters. As Jamie and I have listened to him talk about being a police officer, we thought it important that his story and perspectives on policing be heard, especially since many accusations of racism have been made against the police.

Deputy Chief Saulters, as a white police officer, many would assume you grew up in white middle-class America. That's not the case, however.

Deputy Chief Saulters

No, in fact, I grew up in a very poor and dysfunctional home. I was born in Jackson, Mississippi. My mother left our family before I was 2 years old, and I've never really had contact with her since. My father was a truck driver, which meant he was on the road a lot, so my grandmother took custody of us. My father got addicted to methamphetamine, speed, so he was not much of a parent even when he was home. He remarried at one point, and my stepmother turned out to be very abusive, both physically and emotionally. Needless to say, this was not a good environment for a child to grow up in. At age 14, I essentially had no parental supervision.

At that point, a family court judge placed me into foster care. I was placed into a group home called Southern Christian Services in Jackson, Mississippi. I didn't want to go there, but the judge told me that he thought God had a plan for my life, and I needed a more stable environment in which to grow up. At that point, I was living in a trailer park. My family would live in a trailer until the rent got so far behind that they made us move. Then we'd move to another trailer park, and the cycle would repeat. I was moving from trailer park to trailer park before being placed into the group home. I was the only white child in the group home.

In spite of my terrible upbringing, I did have a vision for my life at that point. My stepmother made us go to church every Sunday. It wasn't because she was religious but because we got donations from the church at Christmas and other times. She made us go to church to keep the donations coming. That turned out to be a gift from God, however, because I gave my heart to Jesus Christ at one point and made a vow that I would break free of the cycle of dysfunction in which I had grown up.

I also began to feel a calling to be a police officer. I knew that some people had normal lives and healthy families. I knew that life could be different than the one I had. I suppose what I wanted to do was help people do the right things and live good lives. Since I didn't have that growing up, I wanted to devote my life to helping others live decent lives. Being a police officer seemed like a way to do that.

One day I had a conversation with a police officer and asked him what I should do to get into law enforcement. At that point, I was behind in high school, so I went to Jackson State University to finish the coursework for my GED. Oddly enough, I went to that historically black college on a minority scholarship. Since I couldn't afford college, the police officer suggested I go into the military as a way to qualify as a police officer. That's what I did.

I would spend seven years in the U.S. Army. In the service, I got married to my best friend, and we had two children. I was stationed at Fort Stewart, Georgia, and was preparing to leave the Army to start my career in law enforcement. There was a job fair at the military base, and I applied to as many police departments as I could to see if one might give me an opportunity.

Jamie
The way you say that makes it sound like you thought it would be hard to get on as a police officer. Today it seems like departments are begging for applicants. Was that the case then?

Deputy Chief Saulters
No, it wasn't. It was very hard to get hired as a police officer because so many people wanted to be one. I ended up getting the opportunity to come to Athens, Georgia, and join the police force here and felt very fortunate. They had numerous applicants for only three positions, and I got one of the offers. When I came to visit Athens, I liked the diversity of the community, so I took the job. I had been used to diversity both in the group home and the military, so that was the kind of environment in which I thought I could relate to people and do some good. I also thought Athens would be a great place to raise my kids. That was 23 years ago, and I could not be more grateful for the opportunity I was given.

Bob
Can you talk about the experience of being a police officer?

Deputy Chief Saulters
I'm not on the streets any longer, but my first assignment was. I got assigned to work the streets in what we called Zone 5. That was a section that was full of projects, like Rock Springs, Broad Acres, and Pauldoe. I'd get calls about all sorts of things, whether thefts or fights or shootings. My job, as I saw it, was like being a sheepdog. I was keeping the sheep safe from the wolves. For example, we might get a complaint that a group of people were hanging out drinking and shooting dice, so we'd go there to clean it up. That may sound

harmless, but gambling is illegal, and that sort of thing typically led to trouble, such as drug sales. So we'd go in and break it up.

Policing is about improving the quality of life in the community. People who live in neighborhoods and communities don't want bad activities going on around them. They depend on the police to keep their communities safe. All neighborhoods want this. People in the projects would say to us, "You don't allow this kind of activity in the rich neighborhoods of town; why do you let it go on here?"

As police officers, we try to get to know people. One of the things about me, I guess because of my background, is that I was never scared to go up and talk to people. When I came up on a group of guys, I wanted to get to know them. Eventually I would know all their names. When someone told me what a certain person who committed a crime was wearing, I would often know who it was by what he wore.

I always tried to keep down crime in my area. If I suspected someone of something, I wanted to catch them and keep them from doing whatever bad thing they were planning. If I thought they had a gun, I was going to pat them down. I would treat them fairly, of course, but I wanted to know who they were and why they were standing on that street corner.

Jamie, you and I had lots of conversations when you were selling drugs. When you didn't have any drugs on you, we could have a friendly conversation and even talk and laugh. But when you were "stepping," trying to get away from me, I knew you were doing something that was illegal. I believed you were a good person inside, but you were also an addict. I knew that one of the reasons you were selling drugs was to feed your habit.

One of the difficulties is that lower-income neighborhoods are often riddled with drugs, and the drug trade is very dangerous. If you are dealing in drugs, you automatically have two things other people want. You have money and drugs, and there are people who want them both. They will try to get both your money and drugs, through violence if need be. So lots of people get hurt and killed in the drug trade. As a police officer, when I see someone just standing around on the street corner, I know there's a good chance he's dealing drugs. That's when I make a move.

The drug trade is a major problem. In certain communities in Athens, drugs were rampant and still are. There is a lot of crime that goes with that and a lot of people coming in from the outside to buy dope. So I felt it was my responsibility, my job, to protect the people who just wanted to live in the neighborhood and be safe. I wanted kids to be able to throw a football in the streets of their neighborhood and not be in danger of getting shot and not have to watch criminal activity.

The vast majority of the people in these neighborhoods were glad you were there. Of course the criminals don't want you there. They'd go behind the houses and throw rocks at your police car. I've had all my tires flattened. It eventually got where we had to park down the street and walk into some of the neighborhoods.

In doing all this, you have to do it according to the law. You can't go rogue, or you'll get your case thrown out in court. So you have to treat people fairly and obey the laws. But you see the effects of drugs on people and want to stop the drug trade. After you've done CPR on people a few times, trying to keep them from dying, you understand how many people the drug trade hurts.

The sad reality is that addiction does not discriminate. It knows no color or socioeconomic class. Many middle- and upper-class white people are addicted to drugs too. While the drug trade in lower-class neighborhoods gets most of the press coverage, there's plenty of crime in more affluent neighborhoods. You just don't see it as readily. Surprisingly, the majority of the criminal activity today revolves around marijuana. That's where people are getting killed because there are so many customers and so much money involved.

Jamie

Let me ask you about policing today. How does it feel to be a police officer today in our cultural climate when every move you make, as a police officer, is under a microscope?

Deputy Chief Saulters

It's pretty discouraging to be a police officer today. Being a police officer doesn't pay very well. Most of our officers have bachelor's or master's degrees. They could be doing a lot of other things, but they have a heart to help their community and make a difference. But when you have public officials bashing you, whether it's locally, nationally, or on the state level, it's disheartening, and it's causing people to leave this career. I worry about what policing is going to look like in the future.

Let me be clear that a bad cop needs to be in jail. We have to follow the law just like anyone else, and I think there are lots of ways we can do better. But everyone can make a mistake, and police sometimes do. The difficulty of what officers face in trying to enforce the law needs to be taken into consideration. When cops do the wrong things intentionally or carelessly, they need to be held accountable. But the vast majority of police I know want to go out every day and make a difference in the community. They want to find the lost child, get the bad guys off the streets, and make the community safer. But when the police are disempowered, it emboldens the bad guys because they don't believe the police are going to do anything. When I was on the streets, I didn't put up with criminal activity, but it's getting harder for the police to do their job.

As an example of how policing is harder, it used to be that you would walk up to a crowd of young guys on the street corner and have a conversation with them. Now when you walk up you face a barrage of curses, and everyone pulls out their cell phone and starts taking a video. Being on camera all the time makes policing very difficult today because everyone makes mistakes at times. In addition, cops of all colors get called racist just for trying to do their jobs.

I wish people could understand what police officers have to do to keep the community safe. For example, it's not natural to get into a fistfight. Police officers are often in violent confrontations, and though we have training, we aren't supermen and women. When there is a violent confrontation, we are vulnerable just like anyone else.

If you intend to arrest someone, you may grab them by the arm and tell them to turn around and put their hands behind their back. But if they don't want to get arrested, they are going to fight you. They may know they are going to jail for a long time if they get arrested, so they resist. They will swing an elbow at your face or do something else to try to get away. When that happens, the fight is on, and as the police officer, you have to try to win. You can only use certain measures, however, and you have to play within the rules, even though the other person doesn't.

The problem is that every violent confrontation with a police officer involves a gun because the police officer has one. Every fight can turn deadly because if the offender overpowers the officer, he or she can take the gun and kill the officer. So as a police officer, you have to fight with everything you've got and try to end the confrontation quickly so you can get the person into custody. And then, you have to treat the person who just punched you in the mouth with courtesy. They just spat on you, cursed you out, and punched you in the mouth, but you have to treat them with dignity. That's why police officers have each other's backs and help someone calm down when they need to back off. We are trained to help each other in that regard.

The other thing people don't understand is that we have to make split-second decisions, some of which are life and death. No police officer wakes up in the morning and says, "Today I'm going to take another person's life." I've been a police officer for 23 years, and by the grace of God, I've never taken another person's life. I hope I never will.

Bob

The reality is that police officers are humans. You have emotions and feelings just like everyone else. You can make mistakes just like everyone else. But you find yourselves in situations that most of us never dream of.

Deputy Chief Saulters

There are certainly a lot of swings of emotion that officers have to deal with. I may be in a situation in which I've just had to give CPR to a baby until the EMS got there to take the child to the hospital. Or I may have gotten into a fight with someone selling dope before I finally subdued him. In the back of the police car on the way to jail, he may have been cussing at me and talking about how racist I am. I drop him off at the jail, and then my next call is to the house of someone who had their bicycle stolen. Or who lost their dog. Or had their mailbox damaged. And the people are mad because you didn't get there sooner.

If people wonder why police seem stoic at times, this is why. They may have just come off a call where they had to deal with something very difficult, and their emotions are still all over the place. Then you go to a call that requires you to be calm and pleasant. The next call you get might be a bank robbery that is underway, and you end up driving your car 100 miles per hour, with lights flashing and siren blaring, trying to catch the robbers while not having a wreck or endangering someone else.

What people don't realize is that police officers get scared in these encounters. You get into a fight with someone, and it's very real. Or you are walking around looking for someone whom you know has a gun. Sometimes at the end of one of these encounters, your hands are shaking from the adrenaline and sheer stress of the experience. But often you don't have much time to cool off and get things together before the next call.

Jamie
I have heard you talk about sitting on the porch talking to people in the community. Why do you do this?

Deputy Chief Saulters
When I was working the streets, I would often see someone sitting on the porch in their rocking chair in one of the communities to which I was assigned. I'd go up and speak. If they offered me a glass of iced tea, I'd take it. Then we'd have a conversation about what was going on in the neighborhood. Eventually they'd tell me what was really going on, like where the crack houses were, and ask me to clean it up if I could. Sometimes I'd hide in the bushes till I knew what was going on and could catch the people selling their dope.

If I knew drug activity was taking place, I'd park my police car right in the middle of it. I'd tell people that I was going to stay right there until they moved on. I'd get a sandwich and eat it while sitting on the hood of my car. I wanted to send the message that they weren't going to sell drugs in that neighborhood, at least not on that day. My job as a police officer was to help build a decent community with a good quality of life, and that meant keeping the drug trade out, as much as possible.

One time I parked my car in a neighborhood where a crime had taken place. A 15-year-old boy walking home at night had gotten beaten up for his cellphone and his shoes. I was working homicide and wanted to know who had done it. People kept coming out and asking what I was doing. They said, "Why aren't you leaving?" I said that I wasn't leaving until I found out who had committed the crime. After about two days, a lady told me where the guy lived who did it. She didn't know his name, but he stayed with his girlfriend, and she knew what kind of car he drove. I said "thank you" and told her I'd be gone as soon as I caught him.

About five minutes later, he came out of the apartment and got into the car. Since someone had identified him, I could arrest him. This was a big dude, so it wasn't easy, but I took him into custody. When we searched the apartment, we found the boy's property. I was able to go to the young man's family and tell them we had found the guy who had beaten up their son, and he was going to jail.

One of the things I can do, even when I can't bring back someone who has gotten killed, is solve the case and tell their family that we have locked up the person who did it. It gives them some closure and relief. I had one mother of a murder victim come hug me in tears the day they issued the guilty verdict for her son's murderer. As the detective who solved the case, I was the first person she came to thank.

As another example, there was a horrific murder that took place in Athens a few years ago. I knew that a young lady had been present, but she wouldn't talk. So I sat down with her and said, "I don't want you to say anything to me right now because I don't want you to lie to me. I want you to go home and pray about this. I know you have a good heart. Here's my cellphone number. When you get ready to talk, give me a call." The next morning, she called and said "I'm ready." We went over to the crime scene, and I recorded her walking me through exactly what happened. Her account corroborated what we already knew, and we put the murderer behind bars. I was able to tell the family that we had solved their son's murder.

The other thing that is tremendously rewarding is seeing people who turn their lives around, like you have done, Jamie. You are now doing great things in the community, and that is tremendous. As police officers, it makes us feel like we are doing some good when we see people like you.

Jamie

We were at the opposite end of things at one point, and I'm glad not to be in that place anymore. I can't tell you how grateful I am for your service in this community and that of the other police officers in this city. I mean this wholeheartedly, in my heart of hearts. Thank you. From the bottom of my heart, thank you.

One thing that is very clear listening to you talk about being a police officer is that this really is a calling from God for you. God is using you and many like you to do good and make our community a better place. Thank you.

Bob

I completely agree. We are grateful to you and to all those who are committed to protecting and serving our community. One more question. What do you say to the charge that police are racist?

Deputy Chief Saulters

I'd say that for the vast majority of police officers and departments it simply isn't true. We don't see color. We work to keep the peace and help people live in safe communities. To those who are nervous about the police, I say, do the right thing and you won't have any trouble with the police.

Ways Forward

We cannot have a healthy, safe society without an effective police force. We should always strive to reform police practices where needed and insist that police departments do so. The police must be supported and protected, however, so we can all live in safe neighborhoods and communities.

29

GOD AND THE PROBLEM OF RACISM

RACISM
"Red, Brown, Yellow, Black, and White, They Are Precious In His Sight."

Bob

I S THERE RACISM IN AMERICA? Of course. People of all races can have prejudices, treat others disparagingly, and look down on people who are not like them. I also recognize that it is more difficult to be black in America than white.

I read an interesting book by author Cassi Pittman Claytor called *Black Privilege*. It is about the black middle class, and in it she chronicles how middle-class blacks living in New York City, making between $50,000 and $100,000, continue to experience forms of racism. She says, for example, that when shopping at retail stores, blacks are often stereotyped as "poor, criminal, poorly educated, and financially irresponsible."[67] They face various forms of discrimination, such as poor service and the assumption that they cannot afford the more expensive items in the stores. While these might seem small things, she notes that they are the real experience of many blacks.

She discovered that being educated doesn't remove all racial issues. Educated middle-class blacks, for example, must find ways of coping with various racial rebuffs by doing things such as shopping in black-owned establishments and dressing better than their white co-workers at the office. Many middle-class blacks, in her words, must "maneuver white spaces," meaning work and shop in mostly white places. This means conforming to white "cultural tastes, traditions, ideologies, and styles."[68] She chronicles both the privileges that middle-class blacks enjoy and the ongoing struggle to maintain their black identity when living and working in what feels like a white world.

As another example, she details the housing choices middle-class blacks must make between living in a white neighborhood or a black one. Mostly white neighborhoods may be safer and located closer to preferred shops and restaurants, but black people often feel disconnected from their roots in them. On the other hand, one black professional woman reported enjoying the connection she felt with other blacks by living in Harlem, even though she had to put up with occasional catcalls when walking on the street: "Hey, baby, let me walk with you. How you doin'? Hey sexy, can I talk with you for a moment?"[69]

She also discusses a phenomenon that was the central thesis of a classic book published in 1957 by black author E. Franklin Frazier, titled *Black Bourgeoisie*. He detailed what he called black "conspicuous consumption," the practice of purchasing goods designed to enhance outward status. It was his thesis that middle-class black consumption is often driven by a desire to "prove themselves worthy" of esteem and respect in the eyes of others, both blacks and whites. This is an often-mentioned practice in some segments of black culture, and today even poor blacks spend what some consider "inordinate amounts of money" on symbols of status, such as $100 sneakers, sports jackets, and gold chains.[70] You have already mentioned this phenomenon.

All this is to acknowledge that, as it appears to me, the black struggle with racism, stereotypes, and self-esteem is real. The black CEO of a major corporation has noted how whites in the workplace often have low expectations of blacks because they see them with various stereotypes.[71] Supreme Court Justice Clarence Thomas has said that when he graduated from law school, employers "assumed that he had benefitted from preferential treatment and couldn't do the work, notwithstanding his good grades" and impressive degree.[72]

One black person who grew up being hassled by police found the experience frustrating. His comment, however, was that this was, in part, because of the past behavior of other blacks. He expressed his frustration that high levels of criminality by black youth made him, as someone not engaged in crime, more likely to be profiled by the police. His frustration was not primarily with the police, whose profiling was based of probability, but the practices of some in his culture.[73]

I can understand how black culture is caught in a tension that is difficult to navigate, which is how to continue to appreciate and enjoy black culture while gaining a comfort level with the American mainstream, which is dominated by white people.

Jamie

As I have moved into the middle class, I haven't lost touch with my black roots, but much of that still has to do with poor black culture. At the Sparrow's Nest, I deal with a lot of people from the projects and who are homeless, both black and white. But now that I think about it, many of my middle-class and upper middle-class associates are white. Perhaps we need to develop a new idea of middle-class black culture that is uniquely black but isn't focused on gangster life or exactly like white culture. I think that would be a great project for the black community. And like you said, simply seeing ourselves as Americans isn't a bad thing. Our nation is the envy of millions of people around the world who would love to be Americans and have the opportunities we have.

Bob

One of the questions that pervades our discussions about race today is, "Are all white people racist?" As it turns out, there is a political philosophy today that asserts that they are. If people have heard the phrase "Critical Race Theory," it is this philosophy. This is important because some want it taught to students in school. Many parents are adamantly against doing so.

Critical Race Theory is a complex philosophy and set of ideas about the nature of human interactions. Though it has been around in academic circles since the 1970s, it has become a topic of conversation beyond academia. What makes it appealing to some is that it provides a worldview different from the traditional Western cultural narrative. In general, Critical Race Theory sees the world as divided into two basic classes of people, the oppressors and the oppressed. If we ask from where this framework comes, the answer is complicated, but it certainly has many connections with Marxism, which sees the basic nature of human society as the struggle between classes.

Critical Race Theory says that a fundamental reality of America, perhaps the basic reality, is that racism is part of the fabric of our culture. In fact, racism is embedded in many, if not most of our laws and social structures. This is the nature of society. Those in power organize society to their benefit and to disenfranchise others. This is what white people have done in America for hundreds of years. Because they have controlled the structures of society, they have used them to oppress blacks and other minority groups, though sometimes unconsciously. They have "rigged the game" in their favor, whether they have realized it or not. They still do so today, though the oppression is often hidden and subtle. According to Critical Race Theory, all other assessments of American society are false, and denials of this are, in fact, ways for the oppressing whites to continue to keep minorities under their power.

According to Critical Race Theory, people don't always see this racism, because it has become part of the warp and woof of our culture. But it's there. In fact, those who are the oppressors, in our case whites, can't see it as well as the oppressed and don't want to see it because it benefits them. The oppressed, however, see it and experience it in daily life. They also have the job of pointing out these truths to the oppressors. In this sense, the oppressed have a unique perspective from which to see what is really going on. They

302

see reality more clearly than the oppressors, and therefore their viewpoints are authoritative on this subject.

In addition, according to Critical Race Theory, evil is not primarily what is done by individuals, but structural power used to perpetuate the interests of one group over others. For that reason, only those in power can be racist, and they are. Those out of power cannot be racist because racism has to do with power. Racism doesn't just have to do with skin color, attitude, or individual actions but the ability to exercise power.

From this perspective, some view all white actions as a ruse, even those that appear to seek to improve race relations. They are ultimately ways to continue to maintain power and oppress the minority. White people, as those in power, are driven by self-interest and never truly work to share power with the oppressed. For that reason, the only productive outcome is an overthrow of the system in order to establish a new order.

Jamie

I can see a lot of things that I disagree with in this viewpoint. For one thing, it does not seem biblical in most respects. One problem is its definition of social justice. Biblical justice means doing the right thing to and for all people irrespective of class, economic position, or power. A person in a position of power can act unjustly, but so can a poor person living on the street. You are just as likely to be cheated by a homeless person as a CEO. In addition, biblical justice does not mean raising the oppressed to rule over the oppressors, but living justly, honestly, and compassionately with other human beings.

Bob

I also think that the Bible does not view human motives in the same way as Critical Race Theory. It is true in human societies that people in power make laws and support institutions that are good for themselves. But Critical Race Theory is wrong when it teaches that

303

only those in power act unjustly. The Bible teaches that all people can act corruptly. On the other hand, all people can do justice. It is possible for people, even people in power, to do good to others, even though every person is ultimately flawed by sin. Most people would agree that President Abraham Lincoln's Emancipation Proclamation was an act of justice, and that it is absurd to consider it an act of oppression.

One flaw in Critical Race Theory is its definition of the problem. The primary human problem, from a Christian point of view, is not racism or oppression or structural injustice, but sin. Sin is at the root of humanity's problems, and every person is infected by it. For that reason, no one can understand reality clearly. The oppressed have no greater access to the truth than the oppressors. Everyone is able to speak about their own experience, but no one avoids the blindness that sin brings. For that reason, all people need illumination and help. Christianity believes that the Bible brings clarity to the human situation. It calls all people to repent, rich and poor, powerful and weak, oppressed and oppressor. Critical Race Theory obscures the matter of individual moral responsibility because of its focus on human structures and institutions.

Jamie

The other problem with Critical Race Theory, as I see it, is that it misinterprets and misrepresents both society and the path toward utopia. Christianity sees a future in which everyone prospers when people and groups cooperate together. This was, in fact, the vision of the American founders. They envisioned a society in which people would cooperate for the greater good, agree to live by shared values, and order their lives by the rule of law. This, they thought, was the best and happiest way to live, both for individuals and as a society.

What Critical Race Theory gets right is that societal structures can be sinful. Because laws are made by sinful people, they can advantage some and disadvantage others. When this happens, great

304

harm can be done to large numbers of people. I believe that bad welfare laws fall into the category of bad societal structures.

Critical Race Theory sees the path to a better world as primarily happening through rebellion and revolt. It believes the system is completely broken and needs to be rebuilt from the ground up. That is why some of its proponents did not disparage our recent racial riots. In contrast, our American system has avenues for reform but provides for those through orderly processes rather than radical means. The stability of our political system has been one of its hallmarks and one of the things that has made it different from many other countries. I can understand, however, why some are not confident about the possibility of meaningful reform from within.

Critical Race Theory is also naïve in its hope for equality of outcome. There simply isn't a way for everyone to achieve the same outcome. Systems, such as socialism, that have attempted this have succeeded only in making everyone poor and unhappy.

Bob

The idea of equality is appealing and noble. In the New Testament, the Apostle Paul encouraged people to be generous with those in need, so that everyone would flourish. "For I do not mean that others should be eased and you burdened, but that as a matter of fairness, your abundance at the present time should supply their need, so that their abundance may supply your need, that there may be fairness" (II Corinthians 8:13, 14). The difference is that Paul encouraged a voluntary generosity. Various forms of socialism seek to impose fairness through redistribution of wealth dictated by government.

Historians Will and Ariel Durant, in their classic work *The Lessons of History*, note that freedom and equality are incompatible with one another. In their words, "Freedom and equality are sworn and everlasting enemies, and when one prevails the other dies."[74] They note that nature loves differences. We see this in the vast variations in nature and in people. Not only is the natural world inundated with diversity, but every person is different in a multitude of ways. All attempts to blunt this diversity are doomed to failure.

We would not want to live in a world in which everyone was alike. It is variety that makes the world interesting. Nor would a civilization in which there was forced equality be one that would advance and flourish. Successful civilizations affirm and applaud differences. It is the highly gifted people among us who seize opportunities, make discoveries, and move science, technology, and medicine forward. It isn't a good tradeoff to squelch the freedom of people to discover, create, and innovate for the sake of those who achieve less than others.

The Durants observe that freedom works against equality. Free people are free not only to expend energy on their endeavors, but also be lazy. They are free to do the wrong things, to fail as well as succeed, and to make wrong choices. They are free not to work or to labor diligently. Our nation's founders thought freedom a greater gift to people than an artificially forced equality. In fact, they thought freedom a God-given right that belonged to every person. Because of the innate human yearning for freedom, the quest for equality of outcome is futile. As the Durants conclude, after their decades of studying history, "Utopias of equality are biologically doomed."[75] In fact, they say that the best we can hope for is "an approximate equality of legal justice and educational opportunity."

Jamie

There is one system that does create an important and critical kind of equality. It is Christianity. This is not an equality of wealth, intelligence, giftedness, or other earthly measures but of status before God. Christianity affirms that everyone is equal in the sight of God. One thing this means is that there is no class distinction in the Christian church. While there are different roles and functions, no one stands as lord over another. This is a central tenet of Christianity. Jesus put it this way, "Whoever will be great among you must be the servant of all." He also said that the "first will be

306

last and the last will be first." Whatever roles people play in the church, the words of Jesus make it clear that God's evaluation of every person is what matters. God knows who does right and will reward them appropriately. Those who do evil will face God's judgment, and there is no partiality with God.

The Apostle Paul says the same thing in encouraging people in the church to live and work together in love. He reminds them that the church is like a body. It has many parts, and those that are most visible are not necessarily the most important. While we see the color of a person's skin, their heart is more important to God. In the church, the widow quietly saying her prayers at home may be the most important person. The poor person may be more esteemed in the eyes of God than the one with great wealth. In fact, wealth is often a detriment to a life of humble obedience to God.

There is a song that children sing called, "Jesus loves the little children." It says, "Jesus loves the little children, all the children of the world, red, brown, yellow, black, and white; they are precious in his sight. Jesus loves the little children of the world." This is true, and for this reason, there should be no racism in the church. Jesus loves children and adults of every color. This is why the solution to racism in our country is a greater embrace of Christianity, not a distancing from it, because there is no class or racial distinction in the church.

Bob

I've heard you talk about the story of Jesus and the woman at the well, in the Gospel of John, Chapter 4. How do you think that story relates to racism?

Jamie

It tells us how we ought to act. One day Jesus met a woman at a well in the region of Samaria (John 4:1-42). The Jews considered Samaritans outcasts and spiritually unclean. They had a strong racial prejudice against them. But Jesus didn't treat the woman that way.

He got into a conversation with her and treated her as a person of worth.

She wasn't the most moral person, but Jesus treated her with respect anyway. He saw behind any prejudices others may have had and treated her as an individual. This gives us a pattern to follow. Jesus looked beyond prejudice, and so should we. Jesus saw her as an individual and someone of value. What would happen if we acted like Jesus and didn't see race but people?

Bob

It seems to me that this is important. We often find our identity in our culture, as black, or white, or part of some profession or social group. But if we have faith in God, our identity, first of all, is found in God. God made every person in his image and likeness. Every person is unique. Every person is gifted in some way. Every person is of value to God and in God's plan. It seems to me that we can celebrate our various cultures, races, and backgrounds without defining ourselves or others solely by them. We are each, first of all, children of God. We need to find our primary identity in this. In our relations with others, we need to see people not just as a person of a certain race or group but as individuals. That is what Jesus did. He saw people as individuals and dealt with them as such. We need to try to have eyes like Jesus that see beyond stereotypes.

Jamie

In a recent interview, Kenneth Frazier, the black CEO of the multinational pharmaceutical company Merck, said that his father gave him some psychological armor with which to live in the world, which turned out to be the single most important piece of advice he ever received. His father told him, "Kenny, what other people think of you is none of your damn business, and the sooner you realize that, the better off you'll be." Frazier said that his father meant that he shouldn't spend his time thinking about what white people think about him. He was also saying "don't spend your time thinking about what black people think" about you. If you want to be a good student, but it isn't "cool," be a good student anyway.

Frazier says that he grew up in an environment in which his father gave the family the strong values of dress, behavior, speech, school, and going to church on Sunday. This gave him an advantage that other young people did not have. It was the advantage of being able to be his own person, choose his own path, and not have to fit in with the crowd. Frazier encourages young people today to believe in themselves, realize that they have potential, and know that God has a purpose for their lives. These beliefs, says Frazier, can help young people defend themselves against both racism and peer pressure, both of which can hold them back.

Bob
Throughout this conversation, I have come to recognize that your experience of life is vastly different than mine. I think I better understand that the black experience is not like the white experience. This has given me, I hope, more empathy for those in minority cultures, particularly blacks. I also hope I will be less indifferent to injustices done to minorities and social obstacles placed in their way. This is something white people can do and should do to bridge the divide that so often separates us from our black brothers and sisters.

Ways Forward

We should treat others as individuals, not simply members of a race or group. Jesus saw people as individuals who were valuable in God's sight and treated them with respect, kindness, and goodwill. We should too. Since God created us, we should understand that God has a purpose for our lives and not let our paths be determined by others, either through racism or peer pressure. We should also recognize that Christianity has great

resources to unify us as a culture. In fact, Christianity is the only force with the power to do so. The ultimate answer to our racial division lies in religious faith.

GOD
"In God We Trust"

Jamie

WE HAVE TALKED ABOUT MANY THINGS in this book, especially poverty and wealth. We've encouraged hard work as a way to "get ahead." I want to make sure that people don't think we are saying that Christianity is all about having a high standard of living, being materially prosperous, and attaining wealth. Nothing could be further from the truth.

Bob

That's exactly right. The goal of life, according to Christianity, is not material things. As the Bible says, "We came naked into the world and naked we will depart from it" (Job 1:21). We won't take anything with us when we die, only our faith, or lack thereof, and our good works. In fact, Jesus said that riches often hinder people from coming to God. We get comfortable in our standard of living and think we don't need God.

I wonder if this is not our problem in America today. We are so materially comfortable that we think we can get along without God. Even poor people in America today have televisions and cellphones. Because we have so many things, we depend on ourselves and don't look to God.

Jamie

There are certainly greater purposes in life than having material things. Some of the great stories of history are about people who left everything to serve others. In the New Testament, the Apostle Paul did this. He lived a life of dedication and service to God, not focused on wealth but on spreading the Gospel. Jesus lived this way and so did the Twelve Apostles. Most stories of great people are about the sacrifices they made for the sake of others.

Bob

We have been blessed in America. This is a land rich in resources that has given us the chance to be very prosperous. There is nothing wrong with having things, according to Christian belief, if they don't become idols. Because we, as Americans, have so much, we can help others. It would be great if every nation around the world were prosperous like we are. Jesus also said that to whom much is given, much will be required. We have an obligation to use our resources not just for ourselves but for others.

Your conversion story is more dramatic than mine. What your story makes clear is how great an impact faith in God can make. It made all the difference for you and completely changed the direction of your life.

Jamie

It made all the difference for me, and it can make a difference for others too. The church is strong in the black community, but has lots of work to do. Many black people have a vague notion of God but don't really understand the Christian way of life. They need to conform their lives to God's way. This means first of all to believe. Believe in God and his Son Jesus. This is the first thing God asks us to do, simply believe in Jesus, place our faith in him, trust him for our salvation, and give him our heart. When we place our faith in Jesus, he forgives our sins and gives us a new heart from God. Because we get a new heart, we can begin to live honestly, turn away from evil, treat others as we would like to be treated, and put God first. This is the secret to living successfully, but it's really no secret. Everyone knows this, but few do it. As the author G.K. Chesterton said, "Christianity has not been tried and found wanting; it's been found difficult and not tried."

Bob

We are reaping the disastrous fruits today in our country of a turn away from God. We have let ourselves drift from God, and it's creating all sorts of problems in our society. The fabric of our culture is beginning to unravel, and nothing seems to be stopping the process. I believe that the only solution is a return to God. We need a return to God in our country, a return to faith, a return to Christian belief, and a return to Christian good works.

There are a lot of forces that are working against that, however. Christianity believes the devil works behind the scenes to oppose God and the church. We don't see the devil, but he is hard at work, convincing people that they don't need God and that, in fact, God is hindering their lives. We are beginning to see, however, what life without God is like. It has no center, no purpose, no direction, and no hope.

The official motto of the United States is "In God We Trust." Even though this statement was adopted only in 1956, it expresses a fundamental truth that goes all the way back to the founding of our country, which is that God is and should be at the heart of our culture. Most people agree with this sentiment. In America today, 65% of people identify themselves as Christians.[76] Even though this percentage was higher in previous years, Christians are still a majority in the United States. We should not let detractors rob our nation of its faith.

Jamie

It seems to me that we have lost some of our core principles as a nation. One of those is God. People came to this land because they wanted freedom to worship God as they saw fit. In this new land, they saw great hope for a new day of freedom in a land of great opportunity. They didn't come here because they wanted freedom *from* religion but freedom *for* religion.

Bob

The reality is that this nation was founded on great principles, many of which come from Christian beliefs. These basic understandings were the groundwork out of which this nation and its freedoms emerged. When the framers developed the Constitution, laying out the foundational principles of this nation, it was with these core beliefs in their minds.

We have mentioned some of our founding principles before, but they are worth repeating. At the top of the list is a belief in the value of the individual. Why do individuals matter? The Bible has a clear and definite answer; they matter because they are important to God. God values every person; for that reason, no government or monarch should devalue or abuse anyone. This idea was in stark contrast to the view of European monarchs that the individual belonged to the state. The value of the individual is enshrined in the words of the Declaration of Independence, which says, "We hold these truths to be self-evident, that all men are created equal, that they are endowed by their Creator with certain unalienable Rights, that among these are Life, Liberty, and the pursuit of Happiness."

This great sentence in the Declaration of Independence asserts several immutable rights. A right is a foundational principle that is true, right, and good for people in all times, circumstances, and places. Why is this? Because these rights are given to humans by God! They are not social inventions that can be changed according to circumstance. They are rights established by God and therefore ones that neither monarch nor government should take from people. The first of these, according to the Declaration, is Life. This asserts that no one has the right to take the life of another person. This comes from the Bible and is enshrined in the Sixth Commandment, which says "You shall not kill" (Exodus 20:13).

The second right is Liberty. This also comes from the Bible. The great story of the Old Testament is the Exodus of the children of Israel from their bondage in Egypt. God set them free to live as his free people. The story of the New Testament is that Christ came to set all people free from their bondage to sin and death. As we have said, it took the Christian world much too long to recognize that this meant freedom for people of all races, but it did eventually come to this realization.

314

For this nation's early Pilgrims and other settlers, freedom was paramount. Had the British dealt more gently with the new land's people and allowed them to determine more of their own fate, the American Revolution might not have happened so quickly. The hard thumb of the English king made the colonists recognize that freedom was a right so precious that they were willing to fight and even die for it. Patrick Henry immortalized their passion when he said, "I know not what course others may take; but for me, give me liberty or give me death!"[77]

The importance of this right was the reason the founders set up so many safeguards against various threats, one of which was the tyranny of government. They understood that governments could be an abuser of human rights because governments tended to accumulate power, and power corrupted. For that reason, they instituted limited government, particularly the federal government, in order to protect the rights of citizens and the states. They divided the responsibilities of the various branches of government, separating the powers so that no branch could misuse its power. They also instituted a system of checks and balances, whereby each branch can restrain the actions of the other branches. It also established a federal system of government that would allow for state and local control over most issues.

The third right listed in the Declaration of Independence is the pursuit of Happiness. This was also about freedom – freedom to worship, speak one's mind, own property, peacefully assemble, publish one's opinion, bear arms, not be unjustly imprisoned, and have a speedy trial. It was also understood that one of the places where this happiness was found was in the family. This idea also had a Christian origin. From a Christian viewpoint, the family is sacred. It is the place God has ordained for the training, nurture, and protection of children. For that reason, our founders thought, government ought to protect the family, stay out of its business, and promote the kind of morality that made for healthy families and good citizens.

315

It is hard to overstate the importance of Christianity and the Bible in the formation of this country. The character of the people of the United States was formed, particularly in its early years, by one important book, the Bible. From the Bible, people were encouraged to have true compassion for others, be honest in their dealings, work hard in their professions, consider the needs of the poor, and care for the sick. From these basic virtues came hospitals, orphanages, and ministries to the poor. It was Christians who led the push to end slavery and allow all people to vote, no matter their color or gender. It was the Bible that built a nation of hardworking, practical, and inventive people who, given the freedom to pursue their dreams, became a great and prosperous nation.

Jamie

The reality is that, for many blacks, the American dream has seemed out of reach. It has been a dream for others, not for them. This has created resentment and anger among blacks. Some have refused to participate in what seemed to be a white system. Others have purposely tried to cheat the system by getting something for nothing or by stealing from those who have more. For a variety of reasons, black America has found the American dream hard to achieve.

There have certainly been obstacles placed in the way of black people, but I'm afraid the real reason we haven't achieved has been a lack of the basic virtues required to excel in a free society. Those are honesty, integrity, hard work, determination, and respect for others and their property. As I said, everyone I knew growing up hustled. They tried to "game" the system rather than working within it. It's time for my people to realize that freedom has both opportunity and responsibility. You don't get something for nothing, but if you work hard and do right, you can live a happy, responsible, and meaningful life.

Bob

As a white person, I must confess that our nation has not always been good at opening the dream of a better life to everyone. A great many impediments have been placed in front of minorities, particularly blacks, as they have attempted to make their way to a better life. The American dream, however, isn't intended just to be a white dream but a dream for every person. It is the dream of living in freedom, prospering through the work of our own hands, and enjoying the fruits of our labors.

To live in freedom is a great gift, but we must guard it. Our founders understood this. The inscription around the Jefferson Memorial rotunda in Washington, D.C., is a quotation from Thomas Jefferson. It says, "I have sworn upon the altar of God eternal hostility against every form of tyranny over the mind of man." He was right in recognizing that we must be strong in order to hold fast to the principles that have made this country a place where everyone can seek their dreams. It is a bad exchange to give our freedoms away for the sake of lesser values. Someone always stands ready to gather power for themselves at the expense of our liberties. We must not let that happen.

It is clearly in our nation's best interest if everyone, no matter their color or gender, succeeds. It is in everyone's best interest not to have one group of people who cannot find a way up. Achievement and prosperity are goals toward which we must work together. In trying to achieve this, Christianity's view of life and the world is a help, not a hindrance. We will do well not to forget the Christian foundations on which our nation rests, but it also calls us to certain responsibilities that go with our freedom.

I believe that many of the issues we have discussed are what author Erwin Lutzer calls "within culture issues." That is, they are problems that are not going to be solved by others, especially those outside particular cultures, and certainly not by government. Whites have to deal with their own apathy toward the plight of others and work to live with open hearts toward those whose way is more difficult than theirs. I hope this conversation will soften the hearts of many people like myself.

Jamie

I don't think it is the responsibility of whites to solve the inner-culture problems of the black community. Nor can government programs solve them. The solutions have to come from within the black community and particularly from the black church. Each of our cultures has work to do, and it seems to me that the church has to be at the heart of it. The church has to raise awareness, encourage Christian virtues, and be bold to talk about problems we face. The church has a great opportunity to bridge the divides that separate and help us cooperate, blacks and whites, to discover a new day in our country.

This is to reaffirm what we have said before, that God is our ultimate answer. While laws exist to compel compliance through the threat of punishment, no set of laws is able to govern an immoral people. It is morality that makes us virtuous as a nation, and real moral behavior comes only from faith in God. We need to renew and reclaim our faith in God as individuals and a nation. If we will renew our faith in God, I believe he will help us. He will help us as a country, and he will help us as individuals. That is my story. God has helped me tremendously. I fell in love with Jesus. He entered my mind, heart, and soul. It changed me from a person who robbed and conned people to feed his addiction to a person who is healthy enough inside to think about others, not just myself. God is the one who can help us see beyond color and stereotypes to become a nation of people who are known, as Dr. Martin Luther King Jr., said, not by the color of their skin but by the content of their character.

Bob

We have discovered, in writing this book, that many aspects of our lives could not have been more different. As I think about my life, it has often been like a long-distance race, without great sprints, excesses, or victories along the way, more characterized by steadiness than brilliance, persistence than genius, and determination than virtuosity.

Jamie

Your life has been full of many experiences of family, parents, education, and encouragement that my life lacked, particularly until recently. It may seem exciting to live on the edge of danger, as I have often done, but such a life runs the risk of ending in a tangled mess of wrong beliefs, ruined relationships, terrible choices, and unalterable consequences. Only by the grace of God did my life avoid the many disasters it deserved; I hope God spared me in order to tell my story so others can avoid what would have been, except for my own call of faith from Jesus Christ, a ruined life, wasted and thrown away, like so many of those with whom I grew up.

Bob

I think we ought to close this conversation together with prayer. I've enjoyed having discussion with you about these things. We have both tried to be honest. We have both shared our stories. I hope this has shed some light on our racial issues as a country. I know it has opened my eyes and understanding. I also think it has opened my heart. My goal is to be a better person, fight against any prejudices I find in myself, and try to see people of all races as individuals and people of value. Writing this book, I believe, has helped me do so.

Jamie

I have also found this to be stimulating and enlightening. You have become a friend to me in this process, and I value that. I also think we should close this discussion with prayer. I'm going to say a prayer for individuals and invite people to join me in this prayer. Then maybe you can say a prayer for our nation. I'm going to ask people the same question the man asked me in prison that day. If

God required your soul tonight, how well prepared would you be to stand before him? If people are like I was and can't answer that question, then this is an opportunity for them to get things right. Let's pray.

> "Dear God, O how we need you as people. You know all the ways we wander from you. You know all the ways we resist you. Help us. Help me as a person to put my life in your hands. God, I commit my way to you. I give you my heart, not just a part of it, but 100%. If you will save me and help me, I will be your disciple. I will serve you. I will follow you. I will go to church and get around other Christian people who can help me. Please save me and help me. I need you so I can find my way, keep in your path, be the person you want me to be, and have eternal life in heaven. Thank you, Jesus, for hearing this prayer. Thank you for coming into my heart and life."

Bob

Now let's pray for our nation.

> "Dear God, we need your help as a nation, people, and culture. Our racial divisions pit us against one another when we ought to work together. We ought to cooperate with each other, but we don't. We ought to obey the rule of law, but we don't. We ought to want the best for each other, but we disparage and reject one another. Help us, O God. Help us find ways of peace, ways of justice, and ways forward. Most of all, O God, help us find you. Help us as a nation return to you, renew our faith, reclaim our Christian heritage, and restore our commitment to all things that are good. Lord Jesus, be in our midst, so we might see the true light of your mercy, grace, and peace. Be our Prince of Peace that we might find healing for our national wounds

and be a light set on a hill for others to see. Hear these our prayers, we ask. In Jesus' name, Amen."

Ways Forward

There is no real, lasting solution to cultural disorder and racial disparity other than a return to God. We need national repentance for our sins, a new turning to faith, and the humility to admit that we have turned away from God. The Bible promises that if we will turn ourselves to God, as a people, God will bless us with his grace and make us a nation in which we can safely raise our children in freedom and be a beacon to the world in which we live. Now is the time to reclaim and renew our faith as a country!

DISCUSSION QUESTIONS
WAYS FORWARD

1. The problem of broken families, whether because of out-of-wedlock births, divorce, or absent fathers, has been discussed. From your point of view, are there any practical things that might be done to support and encourage healthy families? What role do you think the following organizations and/or groups should play? The government. The church. Nonprofit organizations. Individuals.

2. Can you think of practical ways to increase the attractiveness of education among young people? Among minority groups? Among the poor?

3. What problems do you think need fixing in the welfare system today?

4. For a young person willing to work, how would you counsel them about accumulating wealth?

5. How familiar are you with Critical Race Theory? How would you describe its important elements? What things about it do you disagree with? Are there things with which you agree?

6. What did you think about the statement that Christianity is a great "equalizer"? In what sense do you believe this to be true? Not true?

7. Do you think that seeing other people as unique individuals, rather than members of a certain race or group, is helpful? Is it possible? In what ways would this help racial problems?

8. Were you surprised by any aspect of policing as discussed by Deputy Chief Saulters? Is there any place you would push back against something he said?

9. What "within culture issues" do you think the white culture should address? The black culture? Other minority cultures? Do you agree that some issues can be effectively addressed only by people within their own culture?

10. In what ways might God be an answer to racial problems in America? In what ways might God be an answer to other problems, such as crime, human trafficking, domestic violence, poverty, violence, etc.?

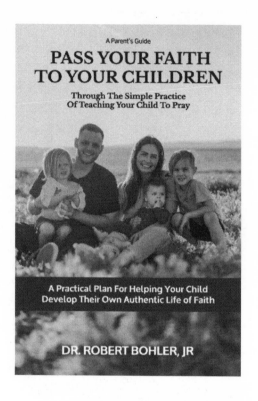

ANOTHER GREAT BOOK BY BOB BOHLER

What is the most important job you have as a Christian parent? It is to pass your faith along to your children. But how to do so effectively? In this book, Bob Bohler helps parents develop a deep and authentic faith in their children through the simple practice of teaching them to pray. This is something every parent can do, with a little instruction AND IT IS THE MOST IMPORTANT JOB A PARENT HAS!

Available on Amazon

[1] Helmuth, Laura. "The Never-Ending Battle Between Doctors and Midwives. Which Are More Dangerous?" *Slate Magazine*, Slate, 10 Sept. 2013, slate.com/technology/2013/09/death-in-childbirth-doctors-increased-maternal-mortality-in-the-20th-century-are-midwives-better.html.

[2] Stritof, Sheri. "Median Age of First Marriages From 1890 to 2018." *The Spruce*, 1 Dec. 2019, www.thespruce.com/estimated-median-age-marriage-2303878.

[3] "Unwed+Births+by+Race - - Image Search Results." *Yahoo!*, Yahoo!, images.search.yahoo.com/yhs/search;_ylt=AwrCmmQMDRxgJ3oAMiwP xQt.;_ylu=Y29sbwNiZjEEcG9zAzIEdnRpZAMEc2VjA3Nj?p=unwed%2 Bbirths%2Bby%2Brace&fr=yhs-iba-syn3&hspart=iba&hsimp=yhs-syn3#id=3&iurl=http%3A%2F%2Fwww.personal.psu.edu%2Fglm7%2Fm 827_files%2Fimage050.gif&action=click.

[4] Kalahar, Dean. "The Decline of the African-American Family." *American Thinker*, 29 Mar. 2014, www.americanthinker.com/articles/2014/03/the_decline_of_the_africanam erican_family.html. Also see - Hymowitz, Kay S. "The Black Family: 40 Years of Lies." *City Journal*, Manhattan Institute For Policy Research, 15 June 2019, www.city-journal.org/html/black-family-40-years-lies-12872.html.

[5] Rector, Robert. "How Welfare Undermines Marriage and What to Do About It." *The Heritage Foundation*, 17 Nov. 2014, www.heritage.org/welfare/report/how-welfare-undermines-marriage-and-what-do-about-it.

[6] "The Consequences of Fatherlessness." *National Center for Fathering*, 9 Apr. 2021, fathers.com/statistics-and-research/the-consequences-of-fatherlessness/. "Effects of Fatherless Families on Crime Rates." *Effects of Fatherless Families on Crime Rates [Marripedia]*, marripedia.org/effects_of_fatherless_families_on_crime_rates.

[7] Staff, Politico. "Text of Obama's Fatherhood Speech." *POLITICO*, 15 June 2008, https://www.politico.com/story/2008/06/text-of-obamas-fatherhood-speech-011094.

[8] Coastline Staff. "Why College Grads Earn A Million More Than Those Who Don't Go." *Coastline College Blog*, 26 Sept. 2019, 7:41:05 AM, blog.coastline.edu/why-college-grads-earn-a-million-more-than-those-who-dont-go-2.

[9] Ibid. The following statistics come from this article. The calculations about how this is true are our own.

[10] "Thinking of Skipping College? Here Are 6 Stats to Change Your Mind." *Lifelong Learning Matters*, Cornerstone University, 10 Jan. 2017, www.cornerstone.edu/blog-post/thinking-of-skipping-college-here-are-6-stats-to-change-your-mind/.

[11] White, Deborah. "Obama's Inspiring 2004 Democratic National Convention Speech." *ThoughtCo*, www.thoughtco.com/obama-speech-2004-democratic-convention-3325333.

[12] "2021 Poverty Guidelines." *ASPE*, Office of the Assistant Secretary for Planning and Evaluation, 29 Mar. 2021, aspe.hhs.gov/2021-poverty-guidelines.

[13] "Effects of Out-of-Wedlock Births on Poverty." *Effects of Out-of-Wedlock Births on Poverty [Marripedia]*, Marripedia.org, marripedia.org/effects_of_out-of-wedlock_births_on_poverty.

[14] "Study: Poverty Not Main Cause of out of Wedlock Births." *Whole Reason*, Thoughtful Christianity, 7 July 2017, www.wholereason.com/2017/07/study-poverty-not-main-cause-of-out-of-wedlock-births.html.

[15] "Conservatism and Race: A Positive Path Forward | Christ Chapel Drummond Lecture Series." Lecture by Robert Woodson, *YouTube*, YouTube, 30 Apr. 2021, www.youtube.com/watch?v=fCZWZCV3LRk. Black entrepreneur Robert Woodson makes this comment in a speech delivered at Hillsdale College as part of the Christ Chapel Drummond Lecture Series.

[16] Bureau, US Census. "Income and Poverty in the United States: 2020." *The United States Census Bureau*, 14 Sept. 2021, https://www.census.gov/library/publications/2021/demo/p60-273.html.

[17] Jeffrey, Terry. "The Enduring Path to Financial Health: Graduate, Work, Marry and Have Children." *Townhall*, Townhall.com, 15 Sept. 2021, https://townhall.com/columnists/terryjeffrey/2021/09/15/the-enduring-path-to-financial-health-graduate-work-marry-and-have-children-n2595908.

[18] *Making Whiteness: the Culture of Segregation in the South, 1890-1940,* by Grace Elizabeth Hale, W. Ross MacDonald School, Resource Services Library, 2004, p. 21.

[19] *Return Flight: Community Development through Reneighboring Our Cities,* by Robert D. Lupton, FCS Urban Ministries, 1997, pp. 13–16. Robert Lupton documents the problems of the inner city and talks about the possibility of reinvigorating them through community development and re-neighboring. His is a marvelous and challenging book about bringing new life to troubled inner city areas.

[20] McCausland, Phil, and Kalhan Rosenblatt. "Georgia Tech Student-Activist Shot Dead by Campus Police." *NBCNews.com,* NBCUniversal News Group, 18 Sept. 2017, www.nbcnews.com/news/us-news/georgia-tech-student-activist-shot-dead-campus-police-n802146.

[21] Chan, Melissa. "Georgia Tech Police Shooting: Student Armed With Knife Dies." *Time,* Time, 18 Sept. 2017, time.com/4946024/georgia-tech-police-shooting/.

[22] *ABC News,* ABC News Network, abcnews.go.com/US/man-dead-shot-atlanta-police-gbi-investigating/story?id=71232363.

[23] Moreno, J Edward. *Atlanta Wendy's Where Rayshard Brooks Was Fatally Shot by Police Burned Down,* www.msn.com/en-us/news/us/atlanta-wendys-where-rayshard-brooks-was-fatally-shot-by-police-burned-down/ar-BB15s1Fm.

[24] Pariona, Amber. "US Prison Population By Race." *WorldAtlas,* WorldAtlas, 18 July 2019, www.worldatlas.com/articles/incarceration-rates-by-race-ethnicity-and-gender-in-the-u-s.html.

[25] Admin. "AMERICAN POPULATION BY RACE 2020[UPDATED STATISTICS]- ALL YOU NEED TO KNOW." *KenyaPrime,* 27 Mar. 2021, kenyaprime.com/american-population-by-race-2020-updated-statistics-all-you-need-to-know/. An article on the American population, by race.

[26] Carson, Ann. "Prisoners in 2019." *U.S. Department of Justice,* Office of Justice Programs, Bureau of Justice Statistics, Oct. 2020, www.bjs.gov/content/pub/pdf/p19.pdf.

[27] "Crime in the United States, 2019." *U.S. Department of Justice*, Federal Bureau Of Investigation, Criminal Justice Information Services Division, 22 Sept. 2019, ucr.fbi.gov/crime-in-the-u.s/2019/crime-in-the-u.s.-2019/topic-pages/tables/table-43. Table 43

[28] Judge, Monique. "Study Shows Black Cops Just as Likely to Kill Black Suspects as White Cops." *The Root, The Blacker the Content the Sweeter the Truth*, The Root, 18 Aug. 2018, www.theroot.com/you-don-t-say-study-shows-black-cops-just-as-likely-to-1828436093.

[29] Ibid.

[30] Tate, Julie, et al. "Fatal Force: 2019 Police Shootings Database." *The Washington Post*, WP Company, 10 Aug. 2020, www.washingtonpost.com/graphics/2019/national/police-shootings-2019/.

[31] Rizzo, Patrizia. "Black Americans Are Three Times More Likely to Be Killed by Cops than Whites." *The US Sun*, The US Sun, 3 Sept. 2020, www.the-sun.com/entertainment/1417426/unarmed-black-people-killed-police-blm/.

[32] Department, Published by Statista Research, and Mar 31. "People Shot to Death by U.S. Police, by Race 2021." *Statista*, 31 Mar. 2021, www.statista.com/statistics/585152/people-shot-to-death-by-us-police-by-race/.

[33] "Crime in the United States, 2019." *U.S. Department of Justice*, Federal Bureau Of Investigation, Criminal Justice Information Services Division, 22 Sept. 2019, ucr.fbi.gov/crime-in-the-u.s/2019/crime-in-the-u.s.-2019/topic-pages/tables/table-43. Table 29

[34] Harrell, Erika, and Elizabeth Davis. "Contacts Between Police and the Public, 2018 - Statistical Tables." *U.S. Department of Justice*, Bureau of Justice Statistics, Dec. 2020, www.bjs.gov/content/pub/pdf/cbpp18st.pdf.

[35] Reuters Staff. "Fact Check: False Data on U.S. Racial Murder Rates." *Reuters*, Thomson Reuters, 17 July 2020, www.reuters.com/article/uk-factcheck-data-racial-murder-idUSKCN24I2A9. The exact number for 2018 was 88.9%

[36] "Officer Deaths by Year." *National Law Enforcement Officers Memorial Fund*, 23 Mar. 2021, nleomf.org/facts-figures/officer-deaths-by-year.

[37] Berger, Russell, and Sean Demars. "Defend and Confirm Podcast." Season Episode 55, episode Critique of Critical Race Theory, Part 2. Berger and Demars make the point in this episode that people who are not armed can still be very dangerous, especially a large man in relation to a smaller female police officer.

[38] Saxena, Vivek. "The Real Number of Unarmed Black People Killed by Police You Can Share with Your Liberal Friends." *BPC - Business and Politics Review*, 23 Apr. 2021, www.bizpacreview.com/2021/04/23/the-real-number-of-unarmed-black-people-killed-by-police-you-can-share-with-your-liberal-friends-1063902/.

[39] Ibid.

[40] Russell, Jeffrey B. "Christianity and Black Slavery." *Christian Research Institute*, 26 Feb. 2015, www.equip.org/article/christianity-black-slavery/. Several ideas in this section come from this article.

[41] Ibid.

[42] "The Civil War as a Theological Crisis." *The Civil War as a Theological Crisis*, by Mark A. Noll, University of North Carolina Press, 2006, p. 50.

[43] Hewitt, D.G. "10 Miserable Things a Slave Experience During Life on a Slave Ship." *HistoryCollection.com*, 11 July 2018, historycollection.com/10-miserable-things-a-slave-experience-during-life-on-a-slave-ship/9/. The information in this section about slave ships comes from this article.

[44] "Monticello Affirms Thomas Jefferson Fathered Children with Sally Hemings." *The Jefferson Monticello*, A Statement by the Thomas Jefferson Foundation, www.monticello.org/thomas-jefferson/jefferson-slavery/thomas-jefferson-and-sally-hemings-a-brief-account/monticello-affirms-thomas-jefferson-fathered-children-with-sally-hemings/.

[45] Gramlich, John. "What the 2020 Electorate Looks like by Party, Race and Ethnicity, Age, Education and Religion." *Pew Research Center*, Pew Research Center, 26 Oct. 2020, www.pewresearch.org/fact-tank/2020/10/26/what-the-2020-electorate-looks-like-by-party-race-and-ethnicity-age-education-and-religion/.

[46] *Coming Apart: the State of White America, 1960-2010*, by Charles Murray, Crown Publishing Group, 2013, p. 300. The ideas in this

paragraph are explained by Murray as part of his prediction about the inevitable implosion of the European welfare economies.

[47] Ibid. Footnote 19, page 394.

[48] "Sen. Tim Scott Delivers Republican Rebuttal to Biden's Address to Congress." *Fox News*, FOX News Network, 29 Apr. 2021, video.foxnews.com/v/6250975846001#sp=show-clips.
[49] Watson, Alexander. "BLM Leaders Discuss 'Resurrecting a Spirit So That It Can Work Through Us'." *CNSNews.com*, 22 Sept. 2020, www.cnsnews.com/article/national/alexander-watson/blm-leaders-discuss-resurrecting-spirit-so-it-can-work-through-us. Foley, Ryan. "BLM Leaders Practice 'Witchcraft' and Summon Dead Spirits, Black Activist Claims." *The Christian Post*, 1 Sept. 2020, www.christianpost.com/news/blm-leaders-practice-witchcraft-and-summon-dead-spirits-black-activist-warns.html. BLM Discuss Groups Occult Practices of 'Invoking Spirits' & African 'Ancestral Worship.' *Blm+Leaders+Discuss+Resurrecting+a+Spirit at DuckDuckGo*, 30 Aug. 2020, duckduckgo.com/?q=blm%2Bleaders%2Bdiscuss%2Bresurrecting%2Ba%2Bspirit&iax=videos&ia=videos&iai=https%3A%2F%2Fwww.youtube.com%2Fwatch%3Fv%3D4hWOhX3g2pU. Nefernitty. *Black Lives Matter and Ancestor Worship??* *YouTube*, YouTube, 10 Oct. 2020, www.youtube.com/watch?v=8qBEquuVnXA&t=4s.

[50] Steinbuch, Yaron. "Black Lives Matter Co-Founder Describes Herself as 'Trained Marxist'." *New York Post*, New York Post, 25 June 2020, nypost.com/2020/06/25/blm-co-founder-describes-herself-as-trained-marxist/.

[51] Raleigh, Helen. "Socialism Failed Miserably For The Pilgrims, Just Like It Does Everywhere." *The Federalist*, 24 Nov. 2020, thefederalist.com/2020/11/24/socialism-failed-miserably-for-the-american-pilgrims-just-like-it-does-everywhere/.

[52] Hornberger, Jacob G. "Redistributing Wealth." *The Future of Freedom Foundation*, 31 Mar. 2021, https://www.fff.org/2021/03/31/redistributing-wealth/.

[53] Ngo, Andy. "More than Two Dozen Antifa Rioters Charged for Portland Mayhem." *New York Post*, New York Post, 6 June 2021, https://nypost.com/2021/06/06/more-than-two-dozen-antifa-rioters-charged-for-portland-mayhem/. "Judge Asks Prosecutors Why Jan 6

Protesters Are Being Treated Worse than BLM Rioters." *Business and Politics Review*, 3 Oct. 2021, https://www.bizpacreview.com/2021/10/02/judge-asks-prosecutors-why-jan-6-protesters-are-being-treated-worse-than-blm-rioters-1143057/.

[54] Miltimore, John. "How a Russian's Grocery Store Trip in 1989 Exposed the Lie of Socialism." *The Federalist*, 13 Nov. 2019, https://thefederalist.com/2019/11/13/how-a-russians-grocery-store-trip-in-1989-exposed-the-lie-of-socialism/.

[55] Ibid.

[56] Conklin, Edwin. "The Probability of Life Originating from Accident Is Comparable to the Probability of the Unabridged Dictionary Resulting from an Explosion in a Printing Shop.", https://www.quotes.net/quote/12135.

[57] Martin, Sami K. "Children Raised by Gay Parents Pen Letter of Support to Dolce and Gabbana." *The Christian Post*, 25 Mar. 2015, www.christianpost.com/news/children-raised-by-gay-parents-pen-letter-of-support-to-dolce-and-gabbana.html.

[58] Staff, Politico. "Text of Obama's Fatherhood Speech." *POLITICO*, 15 June 2008, https://www.politico.com/story/2008/06/text-of-obamas-fatherhood-speech-011094.

[59] Bhutta, Neil, et al. "Disparities in Wealth by Race and Ethnicity in the 2019 Survey of Consumer Finances." *The Fed - Disparities in Wealth by Race and Ethnicity in the 2019 Survey of Consumer Finances*, Board of Governors of the Federal Reserve System, 28 Sept. 2020, www.federalreserve.gov/econres/notes/feds-notes/disparities-in-wealth-by-race-and-ethnicity-in-the-2019-survey-of-consumer-finances-20200928.htm.

[60] Rogers, Taylor Nicole. "There Are 614 Billionaires in the United States, and Only 7 of Them Are Black." *Business Insider*, Business Insider, 4 Sept. 2020, www.businessinsider.com/black-billionaires-in-the-united-states-2020-2?op=1#4-michael-jordan-used-his-success-as-a-basketball-player-to-build-a-best-selling-footwear-brand-4.

[61] Dolan, Kerry A. "The Forbes 400 2020: The Richest People in America." *Forbes*, Forbes Magazine, www.forbes.com/forbes-400/.

[62] "U.S. Home Ownership Rate, by Race 2019." *Statista*, 20 Jan. 2021, www.statista.com/statistics/639685/us-home-ownership-rate-by-race/.

[63] Bhutta, Neil, et al. "Disparities in Wealth by Race and Ethnicity in the 2019 Survey of Consumer Finances." *The Fed - Disparities in Wealth by Race and Ethnicity in the 2019 Survey of Consumer Finances*, Board of Governors of the Federal Reserve System, 28 Sept. 2020, www.federalreserve.gov/econres/notes/feds-notes/disparities-in-wealth-by-race-and-ethnicity-in-the-2019-survey-of-consumer-finances-20200928.htm.

[64] Steele, Shelby. *The Content of Our Character: a New Vision of Race in America*. HarperPerennial, 1998, page 27.

[65] *Please Stop Helping Us: How Liberals Make It Harder for Blacks to Succeed*, by Jason L. Riley, Encounter Books, 2016, p. 44.

[66] Staff, Politico. "Text of Obama's Fatherhood Speech." *POLITICO*, 15 June 2008, https://www.politico.com/story/2008/06/text-of-obamas-fatherhood-speech-011094.

[67] *Black Privilege: Modern Middle-Class Blacks with Credentials and Cash to Spend*, by Cassi Pittman Claytor, Stanford University Press, 2020, p. 170.

[68] Ibid. p. 31

[69] Ibid. p. 76

[70] Ibid. p. 152-153

[71] "8th Grade Reporters Interview Merck CEO Kenneth Frazier." *YouTube*, YouTube, 1 June 2021, www.youtube.com/watch?v=mvbh1r3-v8A. Merck CEO Kenneth Frazier makes this comment in a YouTube interview.

[72] *Please Stop Helping Us: How Liberals Make It Harder for Blacks to Succeed*, by Jason L. Riley, Encounter Books, 2016, p. 166.

[73] Ibid. p. 64.

[74] Durant, Will, and Ariel Durant. *Lessons of History*, Simon & Schuster Paperbacks, New York, 2010, p.20.

[75] Ibid. p. 20

[76] "In U.S., Decline of Christianity Continues at Rapid Pace." *Pew Research Center's Religion & Public Life Project*, 9 June 2020, www.pewforum.org/2019/10/17/in-u-s-decline-of-christianity-continues-at-rapid-pace/.

[77] Henry, Patrick. "The Speech." *Historic St. John's Church, 1741*, https://www.historicstjohnschurch.org/the-speech/.

Made in the USA
Columbia, SC
09 December 2021

50811251R00205